INSIDE IMPROVISATION

*The Science Behind Theatrical Improvisation
and How To Get Better*

Richard Bennett

First published July 2018
Academy of Improvisation Press, Sydney, Australia

30

Cover and internal artwork by Louise McManus
Cover and Easter eggs designed by Richard Bennett

© 2019, Richard Bennett

All rights reserved. No part of this book may be reproduced in any form or by any electronic or mechanical means, including information storage and retrieval systems, without permission in writing from the author, except by a reviewer, who may quote brief passages in a review.

Please send corrections to:
corrections@insideimprovisation.com

For all other contact please write to *Academy of Improvisation* via the contact form at www.academyimprov.com/contact, or the postal address:

PO Box 732
Gordon
NSW 2072
Australia

Academy of Improvisation publishes an emailed newsletter which includes new and updated research and information as a digital addendum to this book.

www.academyimprov.com/news-blog/newsletter

ISBN 978-0-6483698-2-0 (hardcover)
ISBN 978-0-6483698-0-6 (paperback)
ISBN 978-0-6483698-1-3 (Kindle eBook)

For Mum and Dad, who saved me.

For Molly and Louise, who fixed me.

For Jason Chin, who confirmed my path.

And for everyone gracious enough to listen and consider.

Contents

Preface vii
Improv isn't just improv 1
The modern era 9
The improvised mind 25
What is improvisation? 47
1600s to 1920s 75
Spontaneity science 89
1930s to 1940s 103
Approaching scenes 109
1950s to 1960s 125
Scene progression 133
1960s to 1970s 171
Theatre, acting and empathy 179
1970s 201
How scenes work 205
General topics 227
Becoming a better improvisor 275
Conclusions 305
Acknowledgements 309
Bibliography 313
Extended Table of Contents 331

Preface

This book came about through a personal struggle I had with learning how to be a better improvisor. What started as an interest in learning more about the confusing contradictions between teachers and their theories on how to improvise, turned into an analysis of what improvisation is, what happens inside us when we improvise, and led to the discovery of a lot of new information on how to become a better improvisor. More than ten years in the making, the resulting book is very different to what I'd originally planned.

Like most improvisors, I don't live in Chicago or Calgary where the main improvisation "gurus" have traditionally resided, and so I went through the impro training system that's here in Sydney, Australia, learning improvisation according to the rules of my teachers and their system. Like most improvisation communities outside the main U.S. and Canadian hubs, we have our own unique style of play[1] — a style of play that originated back in the mid–1980s, and which has been taught and performed pretty much the same for the last 30 years. If you live in such a city, I suspect you also

---

[1] Lyn Pierse's book *Improvisation: The Guide* — previously *Theatresports Down Under* — details the rise of *Theatresports* in Sydney and the unique style of play that has developed here.

have your own style of play, possibly handed down since the first local improvisors figured it out, and you may not even know that you do.

Your more experienced local players probably just thought all improvisation works the same way. That's not their fault, it's just the nature of their time, their backgrounds, and the limits of what was then known about improvisation. And while in Sydney there were changes in style and other discoveries made over the last 30 years, the basis of what is taught has remained pretty much unchanged from when the ten commandments of impro were handed down to us by Keith Johnstone in the early 1980s.

As time went on, books about improvisation began to appear which explained the technical aspects of improvisation as understood by particular authors. In Sydney, Keith Johnstone's *Impro: Improvisation and the Theatre* was the bible, followed by the odd dabbling with Viola Spolin's *Improvisation for the Theater* and later Johnstone's *Impro for Storytellers*. In Chicago though, Spolin's work was the bible of improv, along with Jeffrey Sweet's *Something Wonderful Right Away: An Oral History of the Second City and The Compass Players*, which was, as the title states, more of a history through interviews than a technical manual. And then there was the landmark *Truth in Comedy* by Del Close, Charna Halpern and Kim Johnson. None of these Chicago long-form related books were very well known in Sydney until the mid-2000s.

Thanks to the Internet however, it became much easier to see what other improvisation groups around the world were doing, and it didn't take too much digging to figure out that Sydney's impro rules and techniques, and our "guru" of improvisation — Keith Johnstone — wasn't the same as in other cities around the world. Reading newsgroups, listening to podcasts, watching videos, and then suddenly realising that there were differences between cities, in many cases large ones, was startling.

And then the international guest teachers started arriving. Some would teach the same core principles that we'd learned in class, but others would teach the opposite, often quite strongly stating that what we'd learned was completely wrong.

For decades, our Sydney community assumed that improvisation was the same the world over, and any idea which challenged the standard approach to what was taught in Sydney, was often seen as just plain wrong. And when someone did travel and experience new ways of improvising, once they returned they would often become detached from the impro community, and it wasn't unusual for them to then stop improvising altogether.

Unfortunately, or fortunately as it turned out, the Sydney style of impro conflicts a lot with other styles, and this led me to question what improvisation is, and in turn to question everything I'd ever been taught. I threw everything out and started again, even going back and building myself up from the core principles that we all take for granted.

I discovered that what I was taught the first time around was simply one way to improvise, out of the many that exist around the world. Different "gurus" have discovered different approaches and techniques, often through random events or experimentation based on what other domains they were experts in, which have since been refined over time as they and their disciples have explored and advanced their ideas. These different approaches are not just extensions to general improvisation skills, but completely different and incompatible models of how theatrical improvisation works.

The idea that there are different styles is still fairly new. Recent books such as *The Improv Handbook: The Ultimate Guide to Improvising in Comedy, Theatre, and Beyond*, by Tom Salinsky and Deborah Frances-White, do mention that there are differences between styles, and if not directly then at least implicitly in books such as *Keith Johnstone, A Critical Biography* by Theresa Robbins Dudeck. However, these tend to assume the differences are at the show structure level, and that the core principles and rules are the same across all styles.

Other books, such as *Theatrical Improvisation, Short Form, Long Form and Sketch-Based Improv*, by Jeanne Leep, are even clearer in their declaring that all improvisation is the same, give or take a few little differences. And because these authors are experienced practitioners or theatre academics, students don't think to question them, and the idea then perpetuates.

In Sydney specifically, the introduction of *Theatresports* in 1985 brought Keith Johnstone's method to prominence and this is still the primary improvisation method taught around the country. Australian high school drama programs all teach his method as if it is the only way to improvise, and truly competitive *Theatresports* — not Johnstone's original intention — has become an increasing phenomenon in many Australian schools and universities. Even adult drama schools, including the country's top institutions NIDA (National Institute of Dramatic Art) and WAAPA (Western Australian Academy of Performing Arts) don't teach or even reference that there are other methods let alone a Chicago method[2]. Although more recently a few smaller acting schools have begun to adapt and look to Chicago method teachers for input.

When I began writing this book, it was assumed that theatrical improvisation techniques were all the same, regardless of whether you called it improv, impro or just improvisation. Over time, the world suddenly woke up and began to realise that all improvisation is not the same. Many discussions and arguments then happened online, and that finally lead to the view that once again all improvisation is really the same after all.

They're wrong, and it's about time we brought all these different methods together under the same banner of improvisation, celebrated their differences, and gave them equal respect and a voice through which they may be heard by the next generation of improvisors.

Using this book

Firstly, I'm Australian, and in Australia we use mostly British English. So, when discussing theatre, colour, centre, improvisor, internalise and more, I use the British spelling. Americans often find British quaint anyway, so there's that. In quotations however, the original spelling is always used.

The word "improvisation" is a generic term, and it can be used in many disciplines, including sport, business, the performing arts — including music, dance, acting, comedy — cooking[3], and life in general. This book is about theatrical improvisation — acting in the moment to produce theatre from scratch, with varying degrees of preparation. Most of our focus will be on comedic theatrical improvisation — commonly known as improv or impro depending on where in the world you are — but is not limited to it.

While the information in this book is in some cases relevant to other types of improvisation, especially in the performing arts, it has not been generalised in any way to make it more relevant for other uses. So whenever the term

---

[2] This was true as I was writing this, but with the recent increase in popularity of improvisation, I would hope that this is changing.
[3] For example, *The Improvisational Cookbook* by Sally Schneider.

improvisation is used, it is always in reference to theatrical improvisation unless specifically stated.

I've used the Latin derived and British influenced spelling of "improvisor" instead of "improviser". There are many arguments why each is better than the other, even though these days "improviser" is the most common spelling. My reasoning is that the agent suffix "–or" is more often used for professions and words with Latin origins, whereas the "–er" suffix is more for actions and activities. So, actor, professor, doctor, improvisor for example, arguably puts us in grander company than say builder, printer, butcher, baker, candlestick maker, except of course when in the company of grand builders, printers, butchers, bakers and candlestick makers.

There are differing opinions on whether players should be called "improvisors" or "actors", even though not all improvisors can act, and not all actors can improvise. I think both are fine, so for the sake of variation in this book they mean the same thing unless specified otherwise. The term "character" on the other hand refers directly to the character that the improvisor/actor is presenting to the audience, as distinct from the improvisor/actor. The improvisor/actor and the character are different people. The improvisor/actor portrays a character in a scene, and the character contributes — directly or indirectly — to creating empathy in the audience.

The target audience for this book is fellow improvisors. That's you and me. We know what it is like to improvise to varying degrees and with varying levels of experience, from beginner to expert. Non–improvisors are of course also welcome, and the lack of performance experience shouldn't detract in any way from understanding what is written. This book alone won't teach you how to improvise — you also need class time, teachers and practical experience — but it will improve the skills of those who can, and enlighten those who can't.

Improvisation can't be explained linearly — from the initial moment of being present, up through scene work, and through to the final detail on show forms — as there are too many first principles to explain and understand that are also dependent upon other first principles. Likewise, we can't look at the history of improvisation in a useful way, without first understanding some of the science and theory, and vice versa. The history, science and theory run in parallel, meaning that they must also be explained in parallel. For example, we need to know some of the differences between Keith Johnstone's and Del Close's ideas, and some of the science, to understand why the *Harold* long-form works better using Del Close's methods. Yet we'll find it difficult to understand the differences between their teachings if we've not learned some detail on how and why a *Harold* works, which in turn requires some knowledge of Del Close's ideas and some of the science and theory, and so on and so forth.

A full history followed by all the science and theory would seem a better narrative choice — and that's what many other books do — but it's not the best choice for understanding the material. As such, this book may seem as though it jumps around somewhat, but that is by design, to give you the very best description of how theatrical improvisation actually works.

Enjoy.

Improv isn't just improv

In 1979 I was in my first year of high school in Sydney, Australia. We had two periods of sport each week, and in winter we learned how to play rugby league — originally a British variation of football that's like soccer, but where you can pick up the ball in your hands. Rugby league is the most popular winter sport in our state, and is even more popular in our state than anywhere else in the world, including Britain.

Over the first few weeks we learned how to run and pass and then how to tackle, which was a bit scary as I wasn't sporty or beefy by any means. It was fun learning how it felt to actually play the game that I'd watched on TV when I was younger. I started thinking about the game more, and applying my new found knowledge of it to watching the games on TV. I had a new appreciation for rugby league that I hadn't had before, and I was now part of a special club: players, not just watchers.

Then eventually we moved on to scrums, which for the uninitiated is where three rows of players from each side push against one another and try to kick the ball, which has been thrown into the middle, backwards into their own team's possession. I had a few issues with scrums, mostly related to physical contact with certain body parts, but more importantly I was a little confused at how much attention they were given. You see scrums are used mostly for penalties and possession changeovers, or at least they were until more recent changes in rules reduced it to just penalties. I figured it was just the way the game was taught, you had to understand all the core principles of play in order for it to become second nature. But still, there was something about it that seemed odd.

That soon passed, because we then learned how to pass the ball and score tries. This was the core of the game in my opinion, passing the ball from player to player, and then putting it down behind the opposing teams goal line, similar to a touchdown in American football — gridiron. It was exciting, because now I was not just playing but also scoring points. I felt I could now play a full game of rugby league, if the teacher would let us.

Then a few weeks later we learned lineouts.

Lineouts are where two rows of players line up facing the sideline of the field, but perpendicular to it. One player throws the ball over the other players' heads, and they all try to jump up and flick it into their team's possession. I spent the whole session wondering what on earth this was, because they don't use lineouts in rugby league, and in fact I'd never even seen a lineout before.

It took a school friend later that day to explain to me — after embarrassing myself by loudly expressing my thoughts on lineouts — that for the last two months I'd not been learning rugby league, but rugby union. Rugby union wasn't particularly popular outside of private — non-government — schools, universities and the upper middle class. Or as I'd just learned, my public — government run — school.

If we'd never seen union or league before, we might be forgiven for thinking they were the same game. While there are obvious differences, there are many more similarities. You see league and union were once the same game called rugby football[4], before there was a split in 1895 over whether the sport should be professional or amateur. Over time the rules of league changed to improve creative play and excitement, and one of these changes was dropping the lineout.

In the era I was at school, union was the faster running game, and league was much more stop and start. Union also tends to have more kicking of the ball,

---

[4] Rugby football was also the precursor for American gridiron football, and over the years some gridiron rules have also been adapted back into rugby league.

and more contention for kicks, whereas in league kicking tends to be more for specific tactical use. Tackling in union is all about body position, because once stopped, the ball is still in play as other players come in to ruck — take — the ball. Whereas in league it's not that important, because once tackled, play stops, and a wider focus is required for a more tactical restart of play. It can take a while to learn all the different play methods in union, whereas league is a simpler and thus more TV friendly game, hence much of its popularity.

So the skills required for each game are different, the rules are different, and the tactics are different, and subsequently the training is also different. But to the untrained eye, they can still look very similar to the point we just can't put our finger on what's odd about it, and at times they can even look the same.

It is the same with improvisation. There are many different ways to improvise, but as beginners we don't yet know enough to ask if there are other methods or styles, and if so which method we'll be learning. We assume there is just one way to improvise.

Improvisation training outside the main hubs is also as different in quality as in distance. It's even common to find two different methods taught in the same city, and there are very often differences between cities which are supposedly using the same methods.

Even later on, many advanced improvisors don't think to ask if there is any other method aside from the one they've been taught. And before they know it, ten years have passed, they are very set in their core techniques, and very few of them finally figure out "I learned rugby union specifically, and not just football". By then however, the ability to switch methods becomes much more difficult.

After learning that there were not two but several different types of rugby football, and that the differences came down to decisions often no longer relevant, or lost in the history of the sport, I gave up any remaining interest I had in either rugby league or rugby union. Sometimes we learn a game that doesn't work for us, and we quit, which is a shame, because often it's not football that is the problem, it may well be just rugby union. Ironically the same thing happened to me again later when I learned improvisation — it wasn't improvisation, it was the method I'd been taught.

Method conflict and context

Most popular books on improvisation focus on a particular style, method, school, or whatever approach the author found works for them. There are some great books out there, by great improvisors, but they're usually written based on the author's experience, and of use only if we follow their specific path to greatness. In fact, we can almost pick two books at random and very often find clearly contradicting advice. As we'll see later, contradicting views are usually both correct, it's just that the reader often doesn't know how to put the conflicting information to use. They don't understand the context.

For example, the UCB *Comedy Improvisation Manual* states that "The sooner you establish the Who, What, and Where at the top of the scene, the better." Much of this harks back to Viola Spolin's work and the origins of the Chicago method of improvisation. But then Mick Napier in his book *Improvise: Scene from the Inside Out*, says that establishing the who, what, where in the first three lines of a scene "reads really stale to an audience, and puts an unneeded burden on the scene." Keith Johnstone on the other hand makes no reference to Who, What and Where, or whether we should or shouldn't initiate a scene with it, in either of his two books, *Impro: Improvisation for the Theatre* or *Impro for Storytellers*. This is interesting when we consider that many of his devotees apply much weight to the CROW principle of Character, Relationship, Objective, and Where, and their interpretation of Johnstone's method of building a platform for a scene.

It would be great if all these authors' experiences and instructions were the same, and if we as people all learned the same way. They aren't, and we don't. So, newer improvisors cherry pick from teachers and books, finding what works best for just them. In much the same way that we can't cherry pick rugby union tackle techniques from rugby league, we can't cherry pick improvisation techniques from different books or teachers. Cherry picking techniques from different sources and then integrating them into our own method for improvising, especially if we're unaware of the background and context of the techniques, is a bad idea.

You probably disagree right now, and have probably already cherry picked ideas that seem to work for you from several different books. Certainly, many experienced teachers give this exact advice, to steal what works for you, so it couldn't possibly be a bad thing could it? As we'll see later, doing so often gets improvisors stuck in a loop, learning contradictory skills thinking they're learning new things, when in fact they're really going around in circles. For example, they may get sick of focusing on story as recommended by Keith Johnstone, and instead start looking specifically at the relationship between characters. After a while they may begin to wonder why their scenes aren't going anywhere, so they start adding back in a focus on active story advances. And around they go over and over again, when their real problem may well be specificity and making more active choices.

What if instead of there being lots of different ways to *learn* improvisation, there were instead lots of different ways to actually improvise? And what if each book on improvisation, instead of teaching a different approach to the same craft, actually taught a variation of an approach to a whole different way of improvising? Wouldn't it make learning how to improvise pretty difficult if we were not just cherry picking from different approaches, but were actually cherry picking from different ways to improvise? This would be like picking up a book called "How to play football", assuming that it was specifically about rugby league, when in fact it was about rugby union, gridiron or soccer.

This is what happens in our first improvisation class. We're taught the basics according to the teacher's or school's beliefs, and it is never made clear that this is just one of many different methods[5]. There are techniques and first principles that improvisors just take for granted because that's what they were taught, there are skills and techniques that only work together in certain combinations, and there are many different ways to improvise, not all of which are compatible.

Impro or improv?

The terms and phrases used in improvisation theory have many sources, and most were coined when they were discovered in different parts of the world. There are varying terms for things which are the same between the different methods and styles, and even similar names for things that seem the same at face value, but often aren't. This causes improvisors to vary how they play to fit a term which they think is something that it is not.

---

[5] As a teacher, I usually discuss the different main methods as part of early improvisation training, and I find it makes learning faster because they're no longer confused about all the contradictory improv books they're reading or what they learned on the Internet.

Communities of improvisors have built up around the people who discovered and named many of these ideas, and their techniques have been handed down from student to student as the years went on. With the rise of global communications in the late 1990s however, these communities began to come into contact with each other. And as improvisation became more popular, improvisation theory became more available through more avenues than ever before. These days there are more than enough books, blogs, discussion forums, videos and podcasts for a student of any particular school or style of improvisation, than at any time in history. And the awareness that there are other schools is now becoming a normal part of learning the craft[6].

Improvising on stage is usually referred to as either impro or improv, depending on where we live in the world. Other terms such as spontaneity — which we'll cover later — and impromptu, have also been used over the years to name improvisation, but for various reasons are no longer used.

The term impro is used in Europe, the Asia Pacific and parts of Canada, whereas the U.S. and other parts of Canada mainly use the term improv. The word improv is also spreading worldwide as a generic term for theatrical improvisation and as a replacement for the term impro.

Initially you might think they're just different terms for the same thing, as that's the word that was used by that group at the time. And you'd be right. But the difference in spelling is also useful because the core techniques are also different. The term impro comes mainly from Keith Johnstone's first book[7], *Impro: Improvisation and the Theatre* and is usually used by groups following Johnstone's techniques, or as Theresa Robbins Dudeck calls it in her book *Keith Johnstone: A Critical Biography*[8], "Keith Johnstone's Impro System®".

The term improv on the other hand originates in the U.S., with most of the key developments coming from the cities of Chicago, St Louis and New York, and which is often called the Chicago style. Keith Johnstone's impro and

---

[6] Although still rarely in lower levels of training.
[7] There are however earlier references, but Johnstone's book was the main influence.
[8] Ironically enough, Dudeck's book isn't so much a critical biography as it is a glowing history and analysis of Keith Johnstone's impro by a self-confessed fan. But it is required reading for those wanting a better grounding on the development of Johnstone's system.

Chicago style improv are different methods used for improvisation and for the most part are incompatible with each other.

Having a single word for improvisation might sound like a good thing, but this just confuses people. We should instead take advantage of the different terms, and use them to classify either Keith Johnstone's techniques or the Chicago style. And while we're at it, the Chicago style isn't a style, so let's call it what it is: the Chicago method.

Impro is not improv, and improv is not impro. They may look the same or similar in performance to the untrained eye, but to the experienced improvisor they are different systems, they are different methods. And while it would have been better to leave this clarification until later once we've looked at each of these methods in detail, for now you'll have to just trust me on this. They're different, and it's important to name them correctly.[9]

From here on, this book uses the term impro when referring to Keith Johnstone's impro system, and improv when referring to the Chicago method, including when referring to other methods and styles which have branched off from them and which use them as initial influences. When speaking generically, the term improvisation or theatrical improvisation is used. Where organisations or groups have used the terms differently — such as the *Canadian Improv Games* which is now based on many of Johnstone's teachings — the group's chosen name is used.

This book is about impro, improv, theatrical improvisation, how it works and how to get better.

---

[9] The term "impro" had been used universally in Australia for over 20 years, until Peter Lead and I, each coming from different groups within our improvisation community, agreed in 2005 to start using and spreading the term "improv". This began to spread over the next few years to the point where these days most Sydney players now call it improv. This is particularly true with new and intermediate players, much to the chagrin of many of the older players. I now regret doing this, because it confuses newer players about the differences between Johnstone's impro and Chicago method improv. Not all progress is good progress, and I apologise profusely.

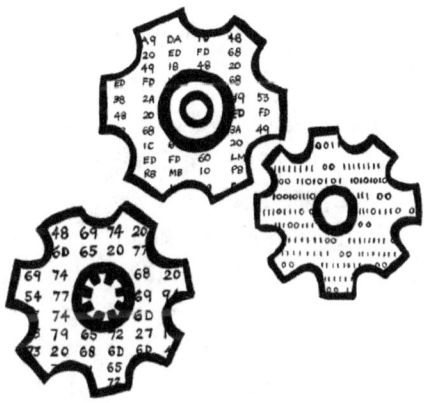

The modern era

In 2014, Peter Mortimer and Nick Rosen released their film *Valley Uprising*, a hugely successful and multiple award winning documentary about the 50 year history of rock climbing in California's Yosemite National Park, and the counter-culture which built up around it. It covers the early competitiveness of climbers Royal Robbins and Warren Harding in the late 1950s and 1960s, through to the two groups who continued to later dominate climbing in Yosemite: the Stonemasters in the 1970s, and the more recent Stone Monkeys. I don't know much about climbing, but I can see how terrifying climbing can be, and how talented and crazy these guys all were. But that's the problem. I wasn't there, so I don't know any better.

You see *Valley Uprising* has received some flak from climbers, for the history they chose to ignore, as well as the history they decided to include. Like most populist histories or documentaries, the documentarians' interests often dictate their focus on specific people and events, when the truth is usually far more complex and varied. There are hundreds of routes up El Capitan — the main granite rock formation in Yosemite — along with all the world records that go with them, and the hundreds of climbers who took part in those records. Yet *Valley Uprising* only focuses on a few. For every Royal

Robbins and Warren Harding, there are hundreds, possibly thousands, of unknown climbers who also advanced climbing, step by step, in Yosemite. *Valley Uprising* is an exciting, compelling and factually correct story, but it is apparently not the one we would have experienced if we were there at the time.

It is the same with theatrical improvisation. For example, most improvisors would be forgiven for thinking that the only improvisation that existed between 1955 and 1964, was: *The Compass Players*; Keith Johnstone's early explorations in improvisation at the Royal Court Theatre; the founding of *Second City* in 1959; and the short time that the original *The Committee* existed in 1964. But while these are big names in the history of improvisation, they are by no means the only groups that were exploring theatrical improvisation around that time. The late 1950s and early 1960s was a golden era for improvisation, with groups forming, exploring and disbanding all the time, all over the U.S. [10] Which groups are now well known, often has a lot more to do with their members who later became "gurus", than the groups themselves. For every well-known group that Del Close, Nichols and May, and Keith Johnstone worked with[11], there are dozens, perhaps hundreds that were just as or even more experimental or innovative, but their members later moved on to other things outside improvised theatre.

Most books about theatrical improvisation include a history, or at least a version of history according to the author's understanding of improvisation. Some books have no mention of the history of other methods or "gurus", because the author never encountered their work. And some books do mention different methods, but treat them as mostly the same method, either because the author is not an improvisor, or because they're not familiar with the detail of one of the methods[12]. Very few histories cover the history of

---

[10] For a more detailed coverage of Chicago method improvisation in the U.S. from 1955 to 1968, see Lee Gallup Feldman's 1969 University of Denver dissertation *A Critical Analysis of Improvisational Theatre in the United States from 1955-1968*.

[11] Del Close up until 1957 was an actor and comedian, with no particular experience with improvisation, and certainly no improvisational theories. And Keith Johnstone was still a writer with the Royal Court Theatre and in 1964 was still 15 years away from publishing his first book.

[12] There are books on Keith Johnstone's methods, that you can tell have had references to the Chicago method added almost as an afterthought, as if an editor mentioned it after the manuscript had been delivered. There are also references to Johnstone in Chicago method books, where the author almost dismisses his work as either "useful work on status" or "was doing similar things in England at the same time". Such references are a useful way to tell how

each method, the differences, and their cross pollination by the various transient and fringe theatrical improvisation groups that existed over the last 100 years.

History also isn't as linear or chronological as often written. No guru is an island, developing every technique alone and in sequence — even gurus are influenced by the gurus who came before them or who were active at the same time. For example, Keith Johnstone did not invent spontaneity, story or mask — three of the four key chapters in his first book *Impro: Improvisation and the Theatre*. He developed his theories over many years in various roles, using these — in most cases already known — techniques, along with input from other practitioners. What makes Johnstone unique, is the way he brought these techniques together, along with his application of status transactions, to completely change the way improvised scenes worked in Europe at the time, and his philosophy on theatre which lead to the development of *Theatresports*.

We won't look at a comprehensive history of everything, as there are numerous books which do that for different branches of improvisation and acting and performance studies in general. But we will look at some of the key developments in improvisation which are required to understand the different methods and what may have led to their success. To give some context, we'll start with the modern era and how improvisation is used today, then we'll go back to where it all began and follow the history all the way through the key developments.

The Chicago method

Starting with the modern and most well-known era, the late 1970s and early 1980s began with several key accidents which lead to the development of modern theatrical improvisation. As with many of these developments over the years, in the U.S. it started with a man named David Shepherd. Shepherd had a history of starting new theatre and improvisation groups across the U.S., and in 1981 came back to Chicago to audition players for a show he was working on called *The Jonah Complex*.[13] While there, improvisor Charna Halpern convinced him to help her produce a Chicago version of *Improv*

---

much the author knows about improvisation in general, as opposed to their specific area of expertise.

[13] Shepherd had spent many years in Chicago prior to this, including with the founding of *The Playrights Theater Club* in 1953 and *The Compass Players* in 1955.

Olympics, a competitive team–based show format for short–form theatre games. Shepherd and Howard Jerome had been producing versions of the show throughout the U.S. and Canada since 1972, where it rapidly expanded over the next 10 years as the *Canadian Improv Games*. By 1981 Shepherd had moved on to other projects, but was convinced by Halpern to help develop her own version of the show. *Improvised Olympics* — later shortened back to *Improv Olympics* and then *ImprovOlympic* — ended up as a resident show at a Chicago cabaret bar called Crosscurrents.

In 1982, Del Close was at the end of a roughly 10 year stint — the second of two — directing at *Second City*. He was an actor and director who had been performing improvised theatre since the late 1950s, and was a key cast member and director of groups we'll cover later. A number of reasons have been cited for him leaving *Second City*, including not being able to use the "Invocation" exercise — which is now often used as a *Harold* show format opening — and arguments with then owner Bernie Sahlins over whether improvisation, and *Harold* in particular, could be used as a performance form and not just as a rehearsal or sketch generation technique. For whatever reason, Close was fired by *Second City*, and this became one of the more significant events for the future of improvisation.

Most improvisation at that time was used either for the development of scripted material, as a rehearsal technique, or had pre-set rules such as theatre games or scenarios — rough script outlines of a play in which actors improvise the action and dialogue. Close believed that public theatre could be completely improvised from start to finish, without any preparation. Amongst other endeavours post-*Second City*, Close was performing in a sketch trio called the *Post-Rational Players*, which also ended up with a residency at Crosscurrents, the same venue as *ImprovOlympic*.

Del Close had worked for David Shepherd in the late 1950s at *The Compass Players* in St Louis, but didn't think much of his style or theories on improvisation. By the time Halpern and Close bumped into each other at Crosscurrents[14] however, Shepherd had again left Chicago — mostly due to creative differences with Halpern. With Shepherd gone, Halpern was free to direct *ImprovOlympic* how she saw fit. First, she engaged Close to run a

---

[14] Halpern and Close had already met at a Halloween event in 1982, and much more detail of this and their subsequent partnership may be found in Kim Johnson's book *The Funniest One in the Room*.

workshop for her players, and then at Close's suggestion they ended the short-form theatre games and began to work solely on the *Harold* improv format — a free form exploration of themes through a connected montage of improvised scenes.

At that time, *Harold* was a long meandering improvised piece of just under an hour. It was originally developed in 1967 by *The Committee* in San Francisco as a rehearsal technique, although they'd been using a similar exploratory and thematic form since 1965. While the original development was a group effort — one particular story states that 3 different people each came up with it on their own while teaching classes — it was Close that saw the full potential of *Harold* as a new form of improvised theatre that could stand on its own in front of an audience, instead of improvisation just being used as an offstage writing and rehearsal technique. At *ImprovOlympic*, Close refined the free form *Harold* into a more structured version — later referred to as the "training wheels *Harold*".

Whether Close would have been as revered as he is today had he not met Halpern is unclear, however he would mostly likely not have succeeded at developing *Harold* without a strong-willed partner to guide and support him. Without Halpern, *ImprovOlympic* would not have become *iO* — which in the early 2000s was arguably the world's largest improv school — and Chicago may not have been the main hub of that method of improvisation. Close also had problems with substance abuse throughout the 1960s and 1970s — he was also an alcoholic but had given up alcohol in 1978 through aversion therapy — which probably contributed to why he was without work and still in Chicago. Considering that most talented improvisors end up moving on to greater things, if Close had been clean, he may never have continued developing *Harold*, and *iO* may possibly have never existed. Halpern set Close up with accommodation and administration, and helped him off hard drugs — although much of this was Close's doing and as a response to the death of friend and ex-student John Belushi — so that all he had to do was turn up, teach and experiment with improv. And without David Shepherd and his *Improv Olympics* format, or his visiting Chicago for *The Jonah Complex* auditions, Halpern would most likely not have developed *iO* or formed a working relationship with Del Close.

Keith Johnstone's impro system

Born in 1933, Keith Johnstone is a theatre director based in Calgary. Originally from England, Johnstone started out as a school teacher, and went on to be a play reader, writer and director at The Royal Court Theatre starting in 1956. For several months from 1958 to 1959, a group of writers mostly from the Royal Court Theatre would meet each week to discuss their work. Eventually the group — at Johnstone's suggestion — began to include improvisation to show instead of explain their work, and this then developed into improvisation workshops, exploring their own plays as well as improvisation techniques handed down from practitioners such as Jacques Copeau, his nephew Michel Saint-Denis and the Russian director Konstantin Stanislavsky. In 1972 Johnstone moved to Canada to become a professor of acting at the University of Calgary, where he stayed until he retired in 1995.

In the late 1970s he co-developed *Theatresports*, an improvised show format where teams compete against each other playing scenes and sometimes theatre games, to judges and an enthusiastic audience, just like a sporting contest. *Theatresports* is faux competitive, in the sense that it is not a real competition where the point is to win.

Johnstone formed *The Loose Moose Theatre Company* in 1977 and shortly after the company produced the first public *Theatresports* performances. After using a few different venues, it ended up at Calgary's Pumphouse Theatre, until in 1982 when it moved into its own theatre — previously a cattle auction house — which Johnstone titled The Simplex, as opposed to the big complexes being built downtown. Johnstone went on to develop a number of different improvised show formats which often addressed problems he saw with improvisors and *Theatresports*, as well as continuing to write and direct plays.

Johnstone isn't an improvisor. While he would have improvised in the writers' group of 1958–1959, and has been seen on stage from time to time, most of his work has been as a director and teacher.

Improvising in practice

Experimenting with improvisation techniques only goes so far with simple exercises and games. Exploring an entire improvisation method requires a more complex piece of work, presented to an audience and in an actual theatre. Both Del Close and Keith Johnstone used specific show formats to fine tune their work, which at the same time improved their show formats symbiotically in line with their methods.

For Keith Johnstone, that initial format was *Theatresports*, and while many of his initial ideas on improvisation were formulated in the 1960s, it was *Theatresports* that caused his method to take off and which eventually lead to a number of his later techniques such as platform/tilt and "not advancing", that are now key parts of his method.

In Del Close's case, it was *Harold*.

Harold

Harold is a performance format developed over several decades by Del Close, and is the most well known performance form for Chicago method improvisors. And while it is the bread and butter of long–form improvisors in Chicago, L.A. and New York, it is greatly misunderstood and often held in distain by improvisors elsewhere, particularly those who are trained in Keith Johnstone's methods.

While the original *Harold* was developed in the late 1960s by *The Committee*, it really began to develop once Del Close was at *ImprovOlympic* in the 1980s. There he refined it into what was referred to as a "training wheels *Harold*", with semi-fixed beats and rules. In later years *Harold* has generally stuck with this semi-fixed form, even though Close's intention was still that it should be freeform and without structure. These days the term *Harold* usually refers to the more structured training wheels *Harold*.

The training wheels *Harold* is roughly nine scenes connected in rows and columns of three scenes — called beats — each, like in a naughts and crosses game. Patterns are then formed across and between beats and with three additional all–in group scenes — called "group games" — between each row of 3 beats.

The entire structure begins with an "opening" scene or theatre game with all the players, which generates ideas and themes for the rest of the form. Then 3 unique scenes are performed which each draw upon a different idea from the opening scene. This is called the first beat, and the scenes are often labelled 1A, 1B and 1C. Then another scene with all the players —a "group game" — is performed, which draws upon another idea from the opening.

This is followed by 3 more scenes, each of which further plays with the ideas in the corresponding first 3 scenes. These scenes are labelled 2A, 2B and 2C, with 2A linked back to 1A and so on and so forth. Then another all–in group game scene is used to explore one more additional idea from the opening, before heading into the final third beat of scenes. These are labelled 3A through 3C, and serve to pull together and resolve all the ideas explored in the earlier beats and group games into a conclusion. Unlike the earlier beats, the third beat can have between 1 and 3 scenes, depending on how the players wish to resolve the work.

One unique attribute of the training wheels *Harold* is the number of embedded references to the rule of three. *Harold* is seven to nine scenes, with roughly three sets of three scenes or beats, where the three beats in each set are pattern connected, as are the three sets of three, and as are the three influencing group games which are interspersed between each series of beats. With patterns within patterns and patterns across patterns, the form can be fairly complex when analysed in this way retrospectively, so much so that it is arguably not possible to even perform a perfect *Harold*, although teams who have trained together for years and years may come close.

Because *Harold* is the primary form used by most of the Chicago method schools, it has become incredibly popular, because it is typically the only way for students to initially get stage time. And once you buy into *Harold*'s complexity, the challenge to perform it correctly becomes a primary focus for many improvisors, along with the credibility and respect that hopefully comes from being cast in the upper echelons of in–house *Harold* teams.

And because perfecting *Harold* is so multi–faceted, improvisors spend a lot of time also watching other *Harold* teams, which increases the audience for *Harold* performances, which popularises the want to be in a *Harold* team, and round and round it goes. But whether a *Harold* would really sustain a regular theatre going audience who do not have an understanding of improvisation or the *Harold* structure, is unclear, because as improvisors we're not in a good position to know. So, the question still remains: is *Harold* really the embodiment of Del Close's dream of creating a high quality and popular and standalone improvised theatre for a non–improvising audience?

Harold was devised and fine–tuned over several decades using the Chicago method of improvisation. This means that it does not include many of the techniques which are unique to Keith Johnstone, such as intentional story and status transactions — both of which we'll look at in detail later. This gives rise to more thematic, character and relationship-based patterns in *Harold*, than if it were narrative or advancing action based, and is what makes *Harold* the way it is. Performing *Harold* in Johnstone's impro just isn't *Harold*, and most groups attempting this usually end up dismissing the form as silly instead of learning the form in the correct method.

Theatresports

Keith Johnstone had been using theatre games and team–on–team exercises in acting classes for many years before moving to Canada, and during the mid–70s this developed into *Theatresports*. The format originally developed out of players competing for stage time in Johnstone's workshops, first with challenges using status transaction exercises, and then later extending to other types of challenges such as "no blocking"[15]. Johnstone had the idea for theatre as sport, like pro wrestling, where the show is presented as a competition even though the point is not to try and win. But unlike in wrestling where the winners, losers and show arc are all pre–set, in *Theatresports* the outcome is improvised.

Teams compete against each other playing scenes and to a lesser degree theatre games, to judges and an enthusiastic audience, just like a sporting contest. Throughout the show, the cast are improvising on two different levels. They are improvising scenes as part of the presented competition, but are also performing "on their benches" as team players, as they are waiting to compete against other teams.

Theatresports was developed by both Johnstone and many of his students in 1977. On hearing of his interest in improvisation, his students asked him to give improvisation workshops, which led to them competing for stage time with status transaction challenges — an exercise Johnstone had used with students back in the U.K. This quickly developed into other challenges and open scenes, and began to include actors not in Johnstone's classes or even at his university. Pretty soon they were entertaining themselves with a format which seemed destined for the stage.

In the early 1990s, controversy developed over who invented *Theatresports*. Many of the early players felt that Johnstone was taking credit for its

---

[15] To "block" in Johnstonian terms, is to stop the advancing action.

invention when many of the developments were made together as a group. Johnstone himself addressed many of what he thought were incorrect claims about the origins of *Theatresports*, in an essay in the April 1993 edition of his *Theatresports and Life–game Newsletter*. One of his main arguments is that much of its development was done by him outside of classes or rehearsals, both in the U.K. and later in Calgary, and that he often presented them to the players as having just come up with them on the spot. Eventually the players had their say when the book *Something Like A Drug: An Unauthorized History Theatresports* by Kathleen Foreman and Clem Martini was published in 1995, containing the story of the development of *Theatresports* in the words of many of the players who were there at the time. Unfortunately for Johnstone, we may never know the real story, however the evidence seems to suggest that it is somewhere in the middle. Johnstone may well have thought he was developing *Theatresports* by himself, and the players may well have assumed that they were assisting or even co–devising. Either way, it would seem extremely unlikely that all the players who contributed to *Something Like A Drug* could have conspired to rewrite history.

Theatresports as Johnstone sees it now, isn't supposed to be a real competition. It is faux competitive in the sense that there is a competition presented to the audience, but the players aren't actually competing to win. For example, a team might embrace constantly losing a challenge, then play up and tease the audience and the judges, and then embrace being the bad guys for the rest of the show. The winners in *Theatresports* are the entire cast of players, working together to present the most fun and entertaining show they possibly can, and often the team with the lowest score can even be the audience's heroes.

Some theatre companies however do see *Theatresports* as a true competition, which then tends to bring in selfish play and less respect for the show as a whole. Players will often choose challenges or scenes that they know work to their advantage, or that they've better rehearsed. Or they might not be playful outside of scenes in case this affects the way the audience or often inexperienced judges treat them in the competition.[16]

---

[16] This isn't to say that such shows are bad — I've seen some fantastic scenes in such shows — but they just aren't as Keith Johnstone sees *Theatresports*.

Viola Spolin & Paul Sills

Viola Spolin is often considered the mother of improvisation. She was born in Chicago in 1906, and went on to develop acting and directing exercises which contributed heavily to the development of improvisation in the U.S. Her 1963 book *Improvisation For The Theater*, along with its numerous adaptations, has become a classic text for improvisors, containing over 200 different acting and improvisation exercises.

Her son Paul Sills, continued some of her work and co-founded *The Playrights Theatre Club*, *The Compass Players* and *Second City* — a succession of theatre groups which together developed improvisation into a method for generating new comedy sketches.

Viola Spolin died in 1994, and Paul Sills in 2008.

Jacob Levy Moreno

Jacob Levy Moreno — often called J. L. Moreno or just J. L. — was born in Romania in 1889, and in 1925 moved to the U.S. and developed psychodrama, a clinical method where a group of clients[17] may act out events from their own lives or from others within the group. His institute in Beacon, New York State went on to influence the development of Jonathan Fox's *Playback Theatre* in 1975.

Moreno was also the first person to explore and write about theatrical improvisation. His spontaneity theatre in Vienna in the 1920s, and his subsequent 1947 book *The Theatre of Spontaneity*, foretells the later development of scenario plays, audience interaction, social commentary and game of the scene, as well as highlighting production and directorial problems and solutions which improvisors still deal with today.

Moreno and Viola Spolin were acquainted with each other's work, with Spolin's early work sometimes referred to as "sociodrama" — a Moreno term used for acting out plays as part of group therapy. While Spolin's work wasn't for therapy, she did consider her work therapeutic, even though it ended up being appropriated by improvised theatre. Moreno's work on the other hand, originated with improvised drama and went on to be used for therapy.

---

[17] Patients.

Moreno died in 1974 at the age of 84, and the epitaph on his headstone is roughly translated from the German as "The man who brought joy and laughter to psychiatry". He should be considered as the father of improvisation, to Viola Spolin's mother of improvisation.

ComedySportz

ComedySportz was founded in 1984 by Dick Chudnow, as a family friendly sporting version of *Theatresports*, focusing more on the comedy side of improvisation than acting out scenes. Like *Theatresports*, *ComedySportz* has become a franchise with licensing fees and strict production rules, and also uses many of Keith Johnstone's techniques. *ComedySportz* is now better known than *Theatresports* in the U.S., and is often used as a blanket term in the U.S. for short–form improvisation, much like *Theatresports* is throughout the rest of the world.

Playback Theatre

Playback Theatre was originally developed in Beacon, New York state, around November 1975 by Jonathan Fox, with his wife Jo Salas intimately involved with the company and as music director.

In 1973 Fox and Salas were living in Connecticut, with Fox having begun training in psychodrama at the Moreno Institute — also in Beacon — while running his theatre company *It's All Grace* with Salas. In 1974 the idea for *Playback Theatre* began to form in Fox's mind, and by 1975 he'd begun trying to convince the rest of his company of its merits. Fox imagined a theatre where personal stories were told on stage under a spotlight, followed by the actors acting out the story. It was improvisation for and involving an audience, but with a therapeutic focus.

It's All Grace put on a test performance of the new format in August 1975, which wasn't received as well as expected by either the audience or the cast. So Fox and Salas decided instead to move from Connecticut to Beacon and form a new theatre company called *Playback Theatre*, specially dedicated to the new form. The first shows began in early 1976, and from 1980 onwards — after a successful tour of Australia and New Zealand — *Playback Theatre* companies started popping up all over the world.

But the links with Moreno don't end there. Moreno's wife Zerka, also an expert in psychodrama, took over the Moreno Institute for several years after

Jacob Moreno died, and by 1975 Fox was officially working for the institute. To confuse matters further, Fox's stepfather had recently left his mother and had also begun training at the institute, where he and Zerka ended up in a relationship after Jacob died. The links between *Playback Theatre* and psychodrama are deep.

The Upright Citizens Brigade (UCB)

In the early 1990s, Del Close was working with an *Improv Olympic* house team called *The Family* — formerly named *The Victim's Family*, but which was changed when team member Rick Roman died when he accidentally drove his taxi into the Chicago river. The name *The Victim's Family* was copied from a punk band of the same name, who are still together as *The Victim's Family*.

The Family was a vehicle for Close to once again experiment, developing *The Movie*, *Deconstruction* and *Living Room* improvised show forms, as well as the shows *Three Mad Rituals* and *Dynamite Fun Nest* amongst others. The main cast of Matt Besser, Ian Roberts, Adam McKay, Neil Flynn, Miles Stroth and Ali Farahnakian, went on to become significant people in the Chicago method improv world, as well as successful actors and writers.

While *The Family* was active, another group appeared called *The Upright Citizens Brigade* — shortened to UCB — which would put on sketch and improv shows, as well as experimental work such as street improv and using video in their shows. UCB had a large revolving cast of Chicago improvisors, including many from *The Family*. Eventually settling on a cast of four in Amy Poehler, Matt Besser, Matt Walsh and Ian Roberts, UCB moved to New York City in 1994 and began performing shows and running workshops.

In 1997, UCB scored a sketch TV show with Comedy Central where each episode was structured as a *Harold* performance. First broadcast in August 1998, it went to air just in time for Del Close to see how far *Harold* had come, before passing away six months later on 4 March 1999.

UCB's workshops continued into a fully blown system of class levels, and today they have two theatres in L.A. and two in New York, with thousands of students going through classes every year. They took Del Close's idea of having a game within a scene, into a formal method for improvising scenes by finding a single game that is the scene and heightening it. We'll look into game of the scene in much more detail in a later chapter.

The Internet

Like most ideas, the Internet has contributed enormously to the popularity of theatrical improvisation, and the state of improvisation would not be what it is today without it.

Before the web became mainstream, improvisation was mostly an acting skill, taught in acting schools. Improvisation only schools did exist, such as *Improv Olympic*, *Second City*, and *Players Workshop* in Chicago, and *The Loose Moose Theatre Company* in Calgary, but their influence wasn't well known. Students from these schools who did go on to careers in the performing arts, weren't known publicly as having trained in improvisation — partly because the public didn't care, and partly because they didn't think it anything more than an acting skill.

Mick Napier — author of the 2004 book *Improvise: Scene from the Inside Out* and co-founder of another Chicago school *The Annoyance Theatre* — embraced the web early on, and wrote a series of journal entries in 1996 while directing the *Second City* mainstage show *Paradigm Lost*.[18] While not the first to write about improvisation on the web, he was certainly the first to write publicly from inside a *Second City* production process.

Another early adopter is Kevin Mullaney, who set up the *Improv Resource Center* website, wiki and community forums. Along with similar websites appearing later, centralised and globally available information and user discussion began to bring together views from different schools, different cities and ultimately different countries.

As improvisation became more popular, more books were written, which were now available from online stores like Amazon, from anywhere in the world. And with the rise of Wikipedia, online news and publicly available industry news, people became more aware of how many people in the performing arts had learned improvisation.

Without the Internet and global communications, a majority of improvisors in the world today probably wouldn't have discovered it. And if they had, improvisation would not be as developed as it is today, and finding a class nearby would be impossible outside of a few key cities.

---

[18] This kind of journal is now known as a blog, and in Napier's case his journal is now included as a chapter in the second edition of his book *Improvise: Scene from the Inside Out*.

The other side to this however, is that the coming together of improvisors the world over also brings together a misunderstanding of techniques. Most improvisors still don't realise there are other ways to improvise than what they've been taught, and so they integrate what they've read, take classes with people who play differently, and end up with a mix of styles that doesn't work as well. And so, we begin to lose the great diversity that we currently have in theory and technique.

Movies and television

These days the majority of film and TV fans are well aware of what improvisation is, and how it is used to generate scripts and shoot scenes, and this has only happened in the last ten to fifteen years. Before that, improvisation was already being used, but the public wasn't very aware of it outside the use of ad–libs.

The first television show to really popularise improvisation, is *Curb Your Enthusiasm*, which uses a simple episode outline — often called a "scenario play" — through which the actors are free to improvise. More recent shows such as the U.S. version of Ricky Gervais' *The Office* and *Parks and Recreation* for example, also use improvisation as part of their standard production process, either running improvised versions of scenes after shooting the original scripted ones, or by using improvisation entirely. Many of these shows now also prefer to hire actors who've trained at the major improvisation schools.

But the use of improvisation in film and TV goes back much further. Mike Leigh uses improvisation to develop characters and stories for his films and plays, and John Cassavetes used improvisation and his own spontaneity inducing techniques to create more realistic delivery of scripted dialogue in his films. Most of the dialogue in Rob Reiner's film 1984 *This Is Spinal Tap* is also improvised, as are the later films of Christopher Guest.

The future

Methods and techniques are already fragmenting and there are more unique methods for how to improvise than ever before. Methods for how to make an improvised scene work have become almost scientific, with countless approaches and processes to choose from. Will improvisation theory in the future fragment further, or will it coalesce around a number of clearly defined methods as it has in the past? With the popularity of theatrical improvisation currently exploding, it remains to be seen.

The improvised mind

Improvisation was developed mostly by trial and error. As early practitioners in different parts of the world stumbled across techniques and exercises that seemed to work, these almost magical incantations would be added one by one to their model of how improvisation works. At the same time, science has been busy working out how our minds and bodies work, and a lot of this research now explains why various improvisation methods work the way they do, and why those early explorers found the solutions they did. This also explains why certain exercises are better than others, and what improvisors can to do to become better improvisors.

With the increased use of applied improvisation — improvisation used as a tool for life, business or other creative endeavours — the way improvisation is taught is changing. Eventually, teaching the first principles won't begin with being in the moment, being fearless, and playing classic theatre games and exercises while facing out behind the fourth wall. The first principles will soon be what happens in our brains, and how that leads to and supports spontaneity and improvisation.

So, what does happen in our brain when we improvise? To answer that question, we need to know how our brains works, which is something scientists have been trying to figure out as far back as the early Greek philosophers. However, in the last 50 years scientists have made a lot of headway, and while we still don't know everything, we do now have some pretty strong theories to explain what is a very complex system of processes.

Sigmund Freud

In the late 1800s and early 1900s, Sigmund Freud, the father of psychoanalysis, theorised that our minds are partitioned into two main areas, which he called the conscious and the unconscious. The conscious is where we do our thinking, so any thoughts you have right now are in your conscious. You may be thinking about what this text is saying, but you might also be thinking about how you're holding this book or the device containing it. You might also be thinking of when you should put the book down and have a break or have dinner. This is all our conscious thinking.

On the other hand, the unconscious is where we have any additional thoughts that we don't realise we're having. Freud reasoned that the unconscious is an area of our brain into which information is stored and hidden by our controlling conscious, and is thus not available to our conscious thoughts. Freud's idea was that certain conscious thoughts can be pushed into the unconscious in certain circumstances, such as with emotional or physical stress, or as undealt with desires. The terms "repression" and "repressed memory" are often used to explain this, but conceptually it's more like suppression, in that the controlling conscious suppresses certain desires and concepts into the unconscious.

What this means for improvisation is that there is potentially information available to us of which we're not consciously aware, and that this can unconsciously change our behaviour, particularly while improvising. Freud identified the split between the conscious and the unconscious, but it took a later psychoanalyst — a friend and collaborator of Freud's — to determine where the real control of our mind is located.

Carl Jung

In the early to mid-1900s Carl Jung took the unconscious a step further, surmising that while the conscious does repress information into a personal unconscious, there is also a "collective unconscious" which collects and organises our experiences and knowledge of the world. This collective store of knowledge only allows information into the conscious as and when it is needed, meaning that the conscious is subservient to the unconscious and not the other way around.

For improvisors, this means that the unconscious is the main source of information and processing in our mind. And because our conscious only has access to what the unconscious allows, improvisors are better in a state where the unconscious can take over most of our actions. This opens up a whole new understanding of how the unconscious can work for improvisors without very much conscious thought.

The Cartesian Theatre

For the conscious however, it wasn't all bad news. Until the early 1990s, it was assumed that there was still a central part of the brain which co-ordinates everything coming from all the other areas of the body and brain, and that ultimately the conscious still decides what our bodies should do next.

Our brains are made up of various areas which perform certain functions, both conscious and unconscious, sensory and otherwise, including smell, taste, feeling, hearing, vision, and other higher level areas such as comprehension, mathematics, emotion, short and long term memory, justice, empathy, time etc. Each of these it was thought, sends information to a central conscious decision making area — mostly the pre-frontal cortex of the brain — which decides what to do next, and then takes the appropriate action.

Called the "Cartesian theatre" of consciousness, this centralised model has been challenged since the early 1990s, and there are now much more likely models of how consciousness works, ones which make much more sense in relation to improvisation.

Fame in the Brain

The "Multiple Draft Brain Model" is a theory originally proposed by Daniel Dennett, an American philosopher and cognitive scientist, in his 1991 book *Consciousness Explained*, and which has been refined and renamed in subsequent books as "Fame in the Brain"[19]. His theory includes the idea that

---

[19] Clayton D. Drinko explains Dennett's "Multiple Draft Brain Model" in much more detail in his 2013 book *Theatrical Improvisation, Consciousness and Cognition*, and uses this to explain some of Viola Spolin's and Del Close's work. Drinko earned his PhD in Drama and Theatre Studies from Tufts University, where Dennett has his professorship.

there is no clear delineation between the conscious and the unconscious, and that the conscious is simply a blurred attention to information that carries more significance than other information at the time.

Information is constantly flowing in from sensory inputs, and together this builds "mental spaces" or "mental models" of concepts and understandings, such as "how to pick up an object", "understanding written language" and "how to enter my house". This information isn't always detailed, and when memory stores models away, typically the information loses resolution and only the main concepts required for comprehending the model are filed away. Our brains then have the ability to extrapolate detail from these low resolution models when they are restored from memory.

All these mental models are continually writing draft versions of reality as they currently see it, based on the core concepts within each model. So if I look at my young daughter, my unconscious detects her emotional state over and over again, constantly updating what that model assumes is the truth, using inputs from my various senses, especially sight and sound, along with information from other models which may or may not be going through the same process. I perceive her emotional state until something contradicts this mental model of it, but until that moment, the model keeps updating itself based on the information it has at hand.

Dennett theorises that consciousness is thus the attention given to any particular models, collections of models, or parts of models at any particular time, and the draft versions of reality that our mind has at that moment. Consciousness isn't a compartment where information resides, it is the awareness of these mental models in the unconscious, much like moving a magnifying glass around from model to model.

So what makes certain models important enough that they become conscious? It is not known exactly, but certain events and effects contribute more or less to whether this happens. Motor skills for example are particularly important — how we grasp something, how we walk, whether we will fall over, whether we need to eat, or whether we need to sleep — and emotion also plays a big role, with strong emotions giving much more weight to whether affected models become conscious.

What this means for improvisation is that the unconscious mind is continually analysing the world, and that only some of this becomes conscious. Some information stays in the unconscious and is integrated into various models for later use, and some is deleted because it doesn't fit with a specific model. Gut feeling, unconscious reading of body language, problem solving overnight while you're asleep, etc., mostly all happen in the unconscious, updating mental models without becoming conscious, and only becoming conscious later when the conscious for some reason needs to draw upon the model.

One of the more interesting ideas to come from this is that if the conscious is simply parts of the unconscious which are given more attention, then the unconscious must always know things before the conscious does. That's an astounding realisation for improvisation, and something we'll look at in more detail later when we look at *memory of the future*.

Global Workspace Theory

Originally proposed in 1988 by Bernard Baars, "Global Workspace Theory" is another popular theory of how the unconscious might work. Proposed before Dennett's "Multiple Draft" model, more recent experiments on physical brain function give it even more scientific support than it had in the past, to the point where more GWT research is currently going on than ever before. Like the Cartesian Theatre, Baars also uses a theatre metaphor to explain his model, however it has more in common with Dennett's "Fame in the Brain" than Cartesian Theatre.

GWT states that the conscious is like a theatre play, with a spot light shining down onto the centre of a stage within the brain. The various brain systems and mental models are the actors, and they move in and out of the focus of the spot light as they shift in and out of consciousness. Activity in these systems trigger whether they move into the spot light, and when they do, activity messages are broadcast to other systems within the brain telling them what to do or influencing their behaviour.

The point is that there is no single controlling viewer — us — observing the play on stage, which makes it different to the Cartesian theatre.

We still know so little about consciousness, that there are still a lot of different models of how it may work, with GWT alone having been adapted into a number of new and different models of consciousness. Ultimately though what most of them share is that we have no real control over what happens in our brains, and we are at the mercy of the unconscious and the very little it allows us to see as consciousness. The unconscious is where most of the useful work happens, and drawing upon that in improvisation is going to give us better quality work.

The inner game of everything

We've looked at consciousness, and some of the theories for what it is and how it works, so let's now look at the effects of harnessing the unconscious to work for us.

The term "thin-slicing" was coined in 1992 by Nalini Ambady and Robert Rosenthal, in their 1992 paper *Thin Slices of Expressive Behaviour as Predictors of Interpersonal Consequences: A Meta-Analysis*. Thin slicing is the theory that from very short observations of expressive behaviour, our unconscious can predict objective outcomes over the long term. What this means is that the unconscious can predict things based on limited experience.

The classic example of this is their later 1993 paper *Half a Minute: Predicting Teacher Evaluations From Thin Slices of Nonverbal Behaviour and Physical Attractiveness*. They found that showing a short — under 30 seconds — silent video clip of a new teacher to new students, would yield similar judgements of the teacher as those given by the same students at the end of a semester. The same was the case in the judgement of school teachers by school principals. In each case the participants only needed to see 30 seconds to know what the teachers were really like.

Thin slicing is the ability of our brains to make fast objective judgements based on previously understood behaviours. Theoretically the unconscious looks for recognisable patterns in sensual input, and this allows it to make decisions quickly based on comparing these patterns to ones the unconscious already knows. The unconscious then begins to take action if necessary, before the conscious is even aware of it.

Malcolm Gladwell's 2005 book *Blink* popularised *thin-slicing*, but a much earlier book marked the practical use of techniques such as thin slicing, muscle memory and the unconscious.

In 1974 Timothy Gallwey wrote his book *The Inner Game of Tennis*, the first in a long line of sports psychology books which highlighted the ability of the unconscious to do much of the mental processing required to play sport at a high level, or in this case tennis. He reasoned that by making the conscious non-judgemental, the unconscious could then make decisions on both motor skills and tactics, without being infected by incorrect conscious reasoning.

When an experienced player receives a serve for example, the unconscious very quickly processes the trajectory of the ball, based on: the server's movement; the ball's movement; the state of the court; the weather; the history of both the server and the receiver's previous shots; and the physics of the flight of a tennis ball. Very quickly the unconscious predicts how best to return the ball and which motor movements will be required. These are built up as various unconscious mental models, and this happens well before the conscious is aware of it. And obviously so, because as we know mental models exist in the unconscious before the conscious can start noticing them and making its own subjective decisions.

So if the information is already in our unconscious, then why not let the unconscious also return the ball, bypassing the conscious which tends to make emotionally charged, slow to respond, and often irrational or illogically reasoned decisions about how to act?

This was subsequently proven with Benjamin Libet's experiments in the early 1980s, which showed that the unconscious initiates action responses up to half a second before the conscious is aware of them. For example, when we physically move a part of our body, the brain usually decides to move it up to a half second before it actually moves. Only part way through this period does the conscious become aware that we even want it to move.

Libet also found the while the conscious does have a filtering and veto effect on actions, the unconscious has already typically made its own decision on what responses or actions should be taken before we are aware of them. Once our conscious is aware of the decision, we are fooled into believing that it was consciously thought of to begin with.

The key thing here is that the unconscious has already been trained in tennis techniques. It can't make informed decisions without already having the expert knowledge required to do so. What seems like a random decision in the moment, has actually been expertly made by the unconscious, based on experience.

Muscle memory

Common returns in tennis are usually committed to muscle memory, where — through repetitive practice — the muscles physically change to better repeat certain motor activities. The unconscious then memorises the movements required to perform them. This prevents the need for the conscious to be involved, and thus prevents "attention switching" — consciously thinking one thing, and then switching and thinking about something else.

Studies show that muscle memory is a mostly permanent process, and that once you learn a motor task through repetition, the brain's memory changes and permanently records the movement. Coming back to a movement many years later becomes a simple process of reactivating those memories. This is why we can remember how to ride a bike for example, or perform specific sports at a high level, because we remember them even if it's been many decades since we last performed those actions. Hence the saying "just like riding a bike", meaning that once we learn, we never forget.

When returning to an activity after a long break, we also see an initial peak in performance, followed by a drop off in performance. This is due to us remembering how good we were, or how much we enjoyed the activity, thus removing self doubt and conscious thinking. After returning to the activity, we then suffer a drop in performance because our conscious begins to analyse our performance which brings into play our conscious thinking processes. Our muscle memory reminds us how to perform the activity, but our conscious then becomes involved and we suffer a drop in performance.

By retaining muscle memory of various tennis motor tasks, not only is the unconscious doing the analytical work for the return shot, but once it has decided which action to take, it can often also provide that action quickly and accurately through previously learned muscle memory, all before the conscious is aware of any of it. Preventing conscious attention switching allows the conscious to be more focused on higher level analysis of the game and tactics, and for the unconscious to play out the motor skills for a game of tennis.

Have you ever driven home after a long day at work, only to find that when you arrived home you didn't remember driving home? Or have you ever driven somewhere that takes most of the same route you take every day to work, but changes half way through the journey, and you then ended up continuing toward work instead of taking the correct change in route? That's your unconscious pulling up the model of driving your regular route, and if you're not paying conscious attention, such as when you're talking to a passenger or thinking about something unrelated, then there's a good chance your unconscious is driving the car and using the model it thinks is correct. These are examples of the unconscious working for us in ways that we don't consciously realise, and how it has much more information available to it than does our conscious.

Priming

In the 1970s it was discovered that when a person is exposed to a certain stimulus, such as a word, an image, or a thought, the time it takes to recognise similar stimuli is decreased, and the ability to consciously acknowledge them is enhanced. This is called priming.

For example, if you were to see the word "door", then you would recognise the word "house" faster than you would "donkey", because mental models which contain these associations have been consciously acknowledged, ready for use. Basically if you think about something, then your brain prepares related mental models of things which are most likely going to be used in association with them. And it is then more likely to draw upon them than other models which haven't been primed. Because priming influences what we're thinking, causing us to focus on things within prepared mental models, priming is not just about referencing information quickly, it also carries a lot of weight in influencing decision making.[20]

When improvisors are present and spontaneous, there is even more likelihood that priming will affect the response of other improvisors, because the mental models that are being primed are assigned more weight due to the conscious not doing very much work at all. When an improvisor makes reference to death for example, other concepts around death are more likely to come out in the scene.

A study by John Bargh et al in the mid-1990s titled *Automaticity of Social Behavior: Direct Effects of Trait Construct and Stereotype Activation on Action* showed that participants who were shown words relating to elderly people,

---

[20] Yes, those marketers that we love so much have been using priming in advertising to influence us for years!

were primed with not just the idea of the elderly, but also with attributes of the elderly. While the researchers were careful not to refer to slowness as an attribute of the elderly, the participants were still primed with slowness as a behaviour. Once the experiment was over — in reality it had just begun — the participants took even longer to leave the building in which the experiment was held, than participants who had not been primed with elderly people.[21]

A more recent 2016 study titled *Semantic representations in the temporal pole predict false memories* by Martin Chadwick et al showed how priming may be used to embed false memories. When the authors showed lists of four commonly related words — for example Snow, Warm, Winter, Ice — in more than half the cases the participants would remember from a bigger list, both the given words as well as associated concepts — in this example Cold. The word cold had been embedded as a false memory, as it was not amongst the original four words.

Priming affects improvisation in a number of ways, including its use in warm ups, and is a contributor to the effect that we call group mind, both of which we'll cover in detail in later chapters.

Beginner improvisors tend to mimic their scene partners, with accent copying being particularly common, because not only does it suggest that the scene may be set in a specific part of the world, but it also gives weight to a mental model of the common character traits of a person with that accent. This is often a caricatured model of those traits however, because a lot of styles of improvisation train improvisors to use caricatures by default. Does a player have a hint of a French accent? Suddenly their scene partner is smoking and using a heavy caricatured French accent as well. This is partly to do with listening and agreeing as an improvisor, but is also an effect of priming. Some of these effects are good because improvisors can quickly be on the same page, but, mimicry itself can be a problem. We mimic partly because we're being primed unconsciously by our scene partner, making it more likely that we'll also take on those attributes. Mimicry also has a lot to

---

[21] There has been some controversy over Bargh et al's experiment in recent years, with some researchers — in the minority — being unable to reproduce the paper's findings. More recent studies have also shown that the speed of exit may be linked with whether the participants like or dislike elderly people.

do with a system in our bodies called the mirror system, which we'll look at later.

Priming also works with depth of focus. When a person has either a narrow, or a wide and high level focus on something, they will be primed for that degree of focus. So if an improvisor has a narrow focus and is discussing for example a character's choice of nail polish, then if their attention changes to an unrelated topic, they are more likely to maintain a similar level of narrow focus for the new topic. And of course, the converse applies, high level focus primes high level focus. As the Chicago method improv and Johnstone's impro can tend to be more narrow or wide focused respectively, improvisors in each of those styles are more likely to maintain that degree of focus over the course of a scene.

Priming can also happen before a performance, as improvisors are bringing their short term memory experiences of the day into the space, and are then talking amongst themselves before they are due to perform. This has both the effect of bringing people onto the same page, but also limits the scope of the performance because they are being primed for certain mental models. There are even warm up exercises that can either reinforce or reverse this effect. For example, "Stretch and Share", where players form a circle and each leads a physical stretch while describing what they did that day. And we amaze ourselves at the wonder and magic of improvisation when our show was all about dental hygiene, when completely coincidentally, Lucy had just that day been to the dentist!

There is one catch however. Priming only works when the person being primed is unaware of it, or at least they aren't self-monitoring — being very conscious of what they're doing and feeling. Priming is an unconscious and automatic behaviour that is happening inside us all the time, unless we are aware that it is happening. It can explain some of the more seemingly magical things that happen in improvised performance that seem like extraordinary coincidence or mind reading. However, consciously thinking about priming may negate some of these effects.

Internalising the domain

When you think about improvisation theory — like literally thinking about it — you're training your mind to think about how it works. Like riding a bike, learning to read body language, or learning the skills of a trade, the idea is that you internalise information so that it may be used by the unconscious, so that it becomes what we often call second nature or instinct[22]. Internalising information means that the unconscious is mostly working with this expert knowledge instead of the conscious.

But internalising is much more than it sounds. The word internalise gives the impression that facts are being simply copied from the conscious to the unconscious, when this is obviously not the case. Information comes into the unconscious and goes through a process of analysis, transformation and "bedding in" into various mental models. This includes patterns, feelings, values, opinions, techniques, motor skills, and all sorts of things that may or may not end up as conscious thought. We internalise much more than we think we do.

I can't explain exactly how I ride a bike, all the muscles to use, and how to balance to keep it from falling over, and I'm pretty sure nobody ever explained this to me either. But somehow I've internalised how to ride a bike, and my brain has internalised the muscle memory which allows me to repeat riding a bike whenever I wish. Through the experience of constantly trying to do it, I've never actually had to consciously think about how it is done, let alone explain it. That's because I never consciously learned to ride a bike, my unconscious did.

Internalising in this way is referred to as "internalising a domain".

Studies have shown that major breakthroughs in certain artistic or scientific domains usually come near the end of a process whereby the person has internalised that domain. For example, in order to add a new theory to the domain of mathematics, there's a large amount of prerequisite information that you'd need to internalise about mathematics in order to do so. This is why a PhD takes so long to obtain, because the domain needs to be internalised before any new ideas or insights can be realised.

In his 2008 book *Outliers: The Story of Success*, Malcolm Gladwell popularised the idea that 10,000 hours of practice will make you an expert in something. Gladwell wasn't the first to discuss the idea, but he was certainly the one who brought it to the modern zeitgeist. It then didn't take long for improvisors to

---

[22] Including for use in thin slicing.

start calculating the number of hours they'd spent improvising, to see if they could call themselves an expert.[23]

The origin of the 10,000 hour rule is a paper by Anders Ericsson, Ralf Krampe and Clemens Tesch-Romer in 1993, *The Role of Deliberate Practice in the Acquisition of Expert Performance*, which amongst other things studied the average number of hours of practice performed by top level violinists — roughly 10,000 — as compared to other violinists — roughly 4,000 — all of whom had begun playing at the age of five. More recent studies have shown that this effect is only valid for domains where the rules are very specific, such as games with simple rules, and not the high level ideas such as the success of The Beatles or Bill Gates as claimed in Gladwell's book.

The original paper's abstract states that "Many characteristics once believed to reflect innate talent are actually the result of intense practice extended for a minimum of 10 years", but even so, Ericsson disagrees with Gladwell's interpretation of his study. Whether the 10,000 hour rule is true or not, and the evidence seems to suggest not, 10 years has been shown to be an average amount of time that academics become expert enough in a domain to achieve a PhD or to present new and original research. So perhaps there is some something to it after all.

Improvisation is complex, but it is just another domain. We want to internalise improvisation knowledge, so that when we improvise, these skills are already in place and we don't need to think about them. Being present and in the moment won't make us an improvisor unless we've already internalised the required improvisation skills.

Internalising improvisation works through both the practice of improvising, and with knowledge of improvisational theory. Both are required in order to reinforce each other. The theory guides the improvisor in what to improve, and the practice contributes to the understanding of the theory. This also partly explains why improvisors go through not just plateaus in improvement, but also regular dips — two steps forward, one step back — as it takes time to internalise different aspects of a domain, refactoring mental models as part of the process.

---

[23] The irony being that theatrical improvisation is supposed to be egoless.

Simple examples of where internalisation works without us realising it include: accepting offers, advancing the scene, specificity, and not denying the discovered reality of the scene. These are skills most improvisors take for granted — depending on the method — because they were internalised early in their training. Improvisors don't just do anything that pops into their heads without thinking, and they aren't simply spontaneous without control. As improvisors we are spontaneous while guided by an unconscious, which knows a lot more about good improvisation than our conscious does, because we have internalised improvisation. The unconscious provides more informed and detailed versions of the reality of the scene for the improvisor to use than the conscious ever could. The unconscious is doing the improvising, and our conscious is simply along for the ride.[24]

But internalising improvisation isn't as simple as absorbing everything about improvisation. It's also about focusing on related areas of improvisation, understanding the relationships between them, and knowing why things are the way they are. For example, most of us have internalised how to ride an escalator, with the specific muscle movements and balance techniques that are different from those we use when climbing stairs. We're not usually aware of this until we walk on an out of service escalator that's not moving and our leg movements suddenly seem clunky. Technically, a not moving escalator is a set of stairs, but our balance and body movements tell us that it's not. We're primed for an escalator, so we prime the internalised mental model we have for using one, and it doesn't work too well when the escalator isn't moving.[25]

Using escalators and stairs are two different things, and we learn them as such. We don't learn them together as if they're variations on the same idea, we learn them as separate things. They both have steps, they both take you up and down, and at the beginning and end of their use you must be walking. But aside from that, the mental models we have and the motor skills we use for each are completely different.

We learn and internalise skills like this so that they become automatised, they become an automatic response to situations we've learned along with

---

[24] We'll look at this when we cover *flow* later, but improvisors can often improvise a scene while consciously just watching a scene unfold, with mostly just the unconscious doing all the work.
[25] If you haven't experienced walking on a stopped escalator, then I'd recommend you do so, it will make this whole paragraph make a lot more sense.

the skill. And we no longer need to think about them much in order to do them or to be experts in them.

Improvisation is the same. We need to internalise not only improvisation skills, but the knowledge of which skills go into which methods or models of improvisation and especially when to use them.

For example, when improvising slow grounded scenes, most players will likely begin a scene slowly with limited information — called a soft initiation — and gradually discover the scene[26] with our scene partner. Yet when improvising shorter scenes, we'll more likely begin with lots of information quickly — called a hard initiation. When the style of improvisation changes, we're going to have difficulty making the different initiation types — soft or hard initiations — instinctual with each style, at least initially, and will have to consciously remind ourselves each time before improvising. Whereas if we only ever do one style of improvisation, then we'll very quickly internalise the initiation style that we need so we're no longer consciously thinking about it.

Like escalators vs. stairs, softball vs. baseball, netball[27] vs. basketball, sprinting vs. marathon, and like different football codes that look the same but aren't, to become expert and make our actions instinctual, we need to understand both the domain being internalised, as well as the bounds around it. The same problem occurs in theatrical improvisation, where historically there has been an assumption that all improvisation is the same.

And finally there's the practice aspect of internalising improvisation. It's fine knowing the theory, but getting out and doing it is just as important. Often academics know a lot about their chosen area of expertise, but do not have much useful practical experience outside of academia. Likewise a sporting coach often knows more about a particular sport than the athletes they coach, but that doesn't mean they're any good at that sport themselves.

Louis Pasteur said that "Chance favors the prepared mind". In the case of improvisation, regardless of the domain in which it is applied, this is certainly true. Improvisation requires internalised expertise in order to work.

---

[26] Discovering a scene from the initiation is called an organic initiation, and starting with an already planned premise is called a premise based initiation, of which both may be either soft or hard initiations depending on the amount of information given.
[27] A game played mostly in Commonwealth countries by women, which is like basketball, but you can't dribble the ball.

Cognitive load

There is only a fixed amount of processing power in the brain, and this is only allocated to conscious thinking as it is needed. The amount of processing going on in our conscious at any one time is called cognitive load. The more conscious thinking we do, the more cognitive load we have. And the more brain power we have allocated to it, the less power that's allocated to the unconscious working on draft mental models of reality. The reverse is also true, in that the less cognitive load we have, the more power there is to give to our unconscious, and the more information that will be drawn to the attention of our conscious. This sounds a lot like what we want when we improvise, right? We want our instincts to do the work, not our thinking caps.

This is also why for example we might have difficulty solving a problem while consciously thinking about it, whereas the answer may more than likely be in our unconscious already. How often have you had difficulty with a problem, and then found the answer almost like magic the next morning? All our processing power is being put into thinking about the problem, with little being allocated to the unconscious solving of it. By reducing the conscious thinking and filtering, the other areas of the brain can have more input, or can create more significant draft versions of reality. Turn off the thinking, and you can access more useful areas of your brain that conscious thinking takes processing power away from.

We solve problems overnight because sleep causes the mind to start cataloguing mental models, filing away the medium term memories, and dumping the short term ones. Dreams are a by-product of this process, and are combinations of various memory artefacts, which if you remember them the next morning, can usually be fairly easily traced back to significant events of the previous day. This mental model analysis also contributes to the next morning problem solving effect.

Analytic focus & experiential focus

In the late 1990s, it was discovered that the brain constantly switches between two possible conscious focal states, or modes: analytic focus[28] and experiential focus.

Analytic focus is the logical processing of information — often called "elaborative processing" — and is the passing of information through various filters in our mind in order to interpret and understand it, and then adding a subjective interpretation to it. When our brains are in this mode, we're consciously thinking about stuff. For example, as I type this, I'm wondering if I've explained it clearly enough. Then I start to think about how much you might know about improvisation and whether I should be using improvisation terms to make it clearer. In the end I don't have enough information to really know, so I start second guessing and constantly changing my mind about it, and in fact I've reread it at least 20 times now to make sure I've got it right. I have an analytic focus, I'm thinking about stuff, and I often try to think too far ahead when I don't have enough information to know for sure. You could say, that I'm *in my head.*

Experiential focus on the other hand is not thinking, but experiencing things, letting your senses soak up everything that's around you, like a big sensual sponge. As I stop to consider what I've written, I instead put it out of my head and sense the warm air coming up from the heater under the table on this cold day. I feel my feet bent at an odd angle against the floor through my socks, and I hear the background buzz of the fan in my hard drive. I'm experiencing everything around me. I'm not judging, I'm *not thinking*, *I am present* and I am here *in the moment.*

Analytic focus utilises the conscious thinking and filtering aspects of our brains, and due to cognitive load means that the senses and other unconscious systems aren't contributing as much as they could. By moving out of analytic focus and into experiential focus, the unconscious is allowed more influence on our conscious actions. Or as dancer Ruth Zaporah says in her 2014 book *Improvisation on the Edge*:

---

[28] Research into these modes also often refers to analytic focus as "narrative focus". This shouldn't be confused with narrative in respect to story or storytelling, it's just an unfortunate coincidence.

> *The practice of improvisation [allows us] to embody the arisings, and with imagination to actively engage with the images, thoughts, feelings, and sensations as they arise. This engagement demands a clear perception without the constraints of attachment and identification, both of which blind us to the true nature of each moment.*

An example of how analytic focus is bad for improvisation, comes from a 2012 study looking at the effect of analytic and experiential focus in dealing with anger. *The Effects of Analytical Rumination, Reappraisal, and Distraction on Anger Experience* by Thomas F. Desnon, Michelle L. Moulds and Jessica R Grisham, examined the behaviour of 120 students who were asked to recall an anger inducing memory. They were then asked to either: ruminate — an analytic focus on negative experiences they've had in the past — ; use cognitive reappraisal — a method for reappraising an emotional experience in order to understand and move through it — ; or be distracted by some other stimulus. They found that rumination maintained anger, while the other approaches diminished them. Anger is one of those emotions that is a natural enemy of improvisation, as it raises the heart rate and blood pressure, and impairs the brain's ability to process information, control behaviour or be present.

Thinking in improvisation isn't all bad though, nor is analytic focus. In fact theatrical improvisation — as opposed to other domains like dance improvisation — requires both analytic and experiential focus, not just in workshops and rehearsals, but also in performance, something which we'll look at in more detail in a later chapter.

Analytic and experiential focus have only recently been proven by science, but have been known to Zen practitioners for thousands of years. Meditation in fact is a tool for clearing of the mind of analytic focus, and preparing a pathway to experiential focus.

Meditation and mindfulness

Mindfulness and being present in the moment is most often associated with meditation and Zen Buddhism — or at least it was when I was growing up

— which means it was often ignored or avoided by many creative people who did not have a religious bent — much like yoga was until the 1970s.[29]

Meditation is a simple sectarian mind tool that just happens to have been discovered by Zen Buddhists and incorporated into their belief system, much like drinking wine and chorus singing for example have been incorporated into other religions. Meditation allows us to be present in the moment while at the same time being hyper–aware.

There are now many scientific studies which not only prove that mindfulness and meditation effects are real, but that their use has real clinical effects when treating illnesses such as depression and eating disorders such as anorexia nervosa. It has been discovered for example that people with depression tend to spend more time ruminating, and that conversely this is a leading cause of depression. Meditation and other mindfulness tools allow them to spend more time in experiential focus, thus reducing their time in analytic focus and reducing their exposure to depressive states. In fact clinical trials have shown that mindfulness generally has greater success with treating depression than other popular approaches, including medication.

To be present means to be here in the current moment. The current moment is right now, not five minutes or five years ago, and not what might happen a minute or a year from now. It is just the now.

Mindfulness is the intentional acknowledgement of the emotions, thoughts and feelings in the now, without any emotional or analytical judgement of them. And meditation is a mind technique which allows us to be mindful, which teaches us to be present in the moment, noticing what is going on in the now, but without being judgmental of it.

The most common form of meditation begins by forming a focus on what's referred to as a prime stimulus — the most common being your breath, a chant, or some part of your body. Whenever you have a conscious thought outside this prime stimulus, you notice that it has appeared, and you then consciously let it go away. This process causes analytic focus to switch off and minimises conscious thinking, and as we now know, turning off conscious

---

[29] These misunderstandings are still prevalent, because while my mother did yoga with a group of other school mothers over 40 years ago, a few Christian parents at my daughter's school recently had other ideas. They complained that the free yoga class for children was religious and should not be taught outside of Buddhist scripture class.

thought allows the conscious to sample more of the unconscious. This in turn causes more of the unconscious to become conscious, usually highlighting thoughts that have been repressed or which were affecting you but you were unaware that they were doing so. In a way, meditation makes the inner game of tennis, conscious.

Meditation trains our mind to do three things: to *not think*, to *pay attention* and to *switch attention*. For improvisors, these are three of the core skills upon which improvisation is built, and yet they are the least often acknowledged skills for beginner improvisors.

Meditation aside, improvisors do typically over time end up being present and in the moment, even if they don't realise that they are. This is usually due to a combination of trial and error, practical performance experience, and exercises which induce presence without specifying that this is what is actually happening. And many improvisors don't realise that most of their warm up exercises are doing the same thing as meditation: making them present, making them pay attention, and making them more able to switch attention.

The great thing about mindfulness is that it has additional effects aside from putting you in a good state for your unconscious to improvise for you. These include reducing anxiety and rumination over challenging or threatening events — such as improvising in front of an audience. Mindfulness gets our conscious filtering and control systems out of the way, and it removes uncontrolled emotion which induces conscious thinking, thus relaxing us and allowing us to once again let go. Conversely, theatrical improvisation has also been used to treat anxiety and depression[30], due to the mindfulness it induces.

Studies have shown that the more experienced meditators are, the faster and easier they are able to switch into a state of mindfulness, which is great for improvisors and one of the reasons why many experienced players don't need too much warm up before they perform. And as you meditate, you learn more about meditation's effects, and you begin to learn how to induce those effects more quickly, eventually to the point where you often no longer need to meditate in order to do so.

---

[30] *Second City* in Chicago for example, runs Improv for Anxiety workshops.

Mindfulness is a cognitive state that is very important for improvising. Meditation can train you to be mindful, but so can years and years of performing improvisation. Together however, they will give you more insight into mindfulness and the effects it has on improvisation.

Exploring in the dark

Most of the well known early practitioners in the development of improvisation as we know it today, did not understand how improvisation works in our minds, or which internal processes are utilised when we improvise. They followed the traditions of their forebears and the results of their own experiments into what did and did not seem to work.

All of the above concepts, theories and processes work together in allowing us to improvise. They provide the beginnings of a platform upon which improvisation may occur, and begin to explain why the experiments of those early practitioners either worked or did not. We'll look at a lot more of the science in later chapters, but in order to continue, we now need to know what improvisation actually is.

What is improvisation?

So theatrical improvisation is just making stuff up right?

No.[31] Far from it.

In *Whose Improv is it Anyway?*, a study of gender, race and power in the Chicago improv community[32], Amy Seham defines improvisation as a combination of and fluctuation between "making do" — being consciously creative within the limits of what we've been given — and "letting go" — the surrender of conscious control — allowing us to channel artistic or divine inspiration. A wordy yet appropriate definition which fits nicely not just for improvised comedy, but for all types of improvisation, whether it be music, sculpture, painting, dance, public speaking, or other forms of applied improvisation.

---

[31] Yes, I do realise the irony in not saying Yes to the very first question we ask of improvisation.
[32] Some in the Chicago improv community feel Seham's book is overly selective, choosing groups that fit the premise of her study, while ignoring the many groups or initiatives which did not. In recent years however some of the big schools have taken strong action against gender bias and the ill treatment of women, showing that regardless of whether such initiatives existed at the time, there were still problems. Aside from that, her book still gives great insight into the development of improv in Chicago and improv theory in general.

Michael Gellman, a director with *Second City* and author of the book *Process: An Improviser's Journey*, says improvisation is the craft of *acting without text*, which is a more tangible definition of what we do with theatrical improvisation. The ability to improvise is certainly a craft, but it could also be argued that enacting the craft is an art form, and therefore it can also be art. But acting without text also includes improvising dialogue within written scenario plays which could be formally blocked — the actions planned out — in rehearsal.

Both are good definitions that improvisors would agree with, however neither of them gives us a real sense of what improvisation actually is. Seham's is more of a lofty academic definition, and Gellman's is more of an open ended "everything is acting" approach. And being simple statements, neither of them have much practical use as a working definition of improvisation.

Going back further, in their 1967 book *Improvisation*, John Hodgson and Ernest Richards state that improvisation is "a means of exploring in which we create conditions where imaginative group and personal experience is possible." This is also a good definition, but to the uninitiated could also include activities such as group therapy for example.

Hodgson and Ernest go on to say that improvisation is "the spontaneous human response to an idea or ideas, or a set of conditions." It isn't, it's more than that. But in conjunction with our science so far, this leads us to our starting point and first key skill required for improvisation.

Spontaneity

> *Invention is not the same as spontaneity. A person may be the most inventive without being spontaneous. The explosion does not take place when invention is merely cerebral and therefore only a part or abstraction of our total selves.*
>
> *— Viola Spolin*

> *Too much structure, too many tight rules, and a sense of significant and fearful consequences should those rules be broken all inhibit spontaneity. On the other hand, too little structure and too much ambiguity also*

> *raise anxiety. [..] So, there's a window, just a bit of structure, that creates an optimal circumstance.*
>
> —Jacob Moreno

> There tends to be **an element of surrender in spontaneity** as well as innocence, and this results in an expansion of consciousness. To do this in the present moment involves relinquishing excessive censorship in the mind's functioning, and it requires a corresponding opening to the inner impulses, intuitions, and inspirations. For example, remember a time when you danced to some music with a sense of abandon. For the most part, you probably recall it as some of your better dancing. Singing with gusto and enthusiasm produces similar results. Indeed, a good deal of the modern training of artists in various fields consists of freeing their spirit within the boundaries of mastering their medium.
>
> —Adam Blatner in *Foundations of Psychodrama.*

Often, we hear improvisors referred to as being spontaneous. And improvisors often say that spontaneity is improvising. Core chapters in both of Keith Johnstone's books *Impro: Improvisation and the Theatre*, and *Impro for Storytellers*, are titled *Spontaneity*, and Viola Spolin refers to it specifically in her work. There are even improv groups around the world with variations of the word spontaneity in the name. Yet how often do students hear the term in improvisation classes?

Jacob Moreno used the term spontaneity as early as 1924 in his book *The Theatre of Spontaneity*, and then went on to use it in his development of psychodrama. Moreno has actually used many definitions of spontaneity over the years, as his experiments continued to explore its nature and effects.

One of his early definitions was:

> *Spontaneity operates in the present, now and here; it propels an individual towards an adequate response to a new situation or a new response to an old situation.*

Moreno felt that improvisation — as opposed to spontaneity — was the use of rehearsed characters and responses[33], and so the term "spontaneity" was used instead of "improvisation" throughout psychodrama theory and practice.

The most common dictionary definition of spontaneity is, the instant and unplanned reaction or response to an unexpected impulse. And an impulse is often defined as something that causes an involuntary instinctive action. So, spontaneity is the process of doing stuff without conscious thinking or planning. In other words, spontaneity is when we let our unconscious, drive our impulses.

In psychodrama this is a good thing. Whatever is buried or repressed within us, we wish to make conscious through our spontaneity. But in theatrical improvisation, this is just the beginning of the process. Instead of unconscious personal impulses, we want our unconscious training in progressing improvised scenes to be driven by our spontaneity.

Anyone can be spontaneous, but only trained improvisors being spontaneous can perform a good quality improvised scene. Improvisation is the instant and unplanned reaction to unexpected impulses. But in most artistic domains that use improvisation, those reactions are coming from a highly trained and expectant instinct — they're not just random spontaneity.

It's not uncommon to hear improvisation teachers say something akin to "Don't think! The scene is right there in front of you, in the moment!", which is probably true for them, because they've internalised improvisation and how to progress improvised scenes. But for the student improvisor, the scene is not right there in front of them, because they haven't yet internalised all the skills or experience required to see that "the scene is right there in front of you".[34]

Theatrical improvisation isn't random or uncontrolled, it is an internalised learned craft. It is acting without text, and making do while letting go of some conscious control. It utilises a trained instinct and an informed

---

[33] Moreno was writing this in the 1920s after only a few years of experimenting with improvisation, and with none of the theory that was developed for what we now call theatrical improvisation. And yes, some contemporary improvisors do still use stock characters and responses.

[34] Beginner improvisors often seem random or uncontrolled when improvising. This is because they've learned to be spontaneous, but not yet perfected the techniques required for progressing entertaining scenes.

unconscious, with some conscious thinking thrown in as needed. Improvisation is a full cycle creative process and requires a large number of varying brain functions to work well. Don't be fooled into thinking that improvisation is simply making things up in the moment — it is far from it.

So, what is improvisation? Improvisation is a process through which spontaneity allows trained practitioners to respond to new challenges. This is true for many performing arts, including acting, dance and music, but also for applied improvisation, including its use in business. You can't improvise dance, without knowing how to dance, and you can't improvise in a business, without knowing that business. Likewise, you can't improvise theatre, without knowing acting, comedy, and how to progress an improvised scene.

Theatrical improvisation then, is the process through which spontaneity and the unconsciously learned crafts of acting, comedy and scene progression, allow us to act out new unwritten and unrehearsed comedy and drama.

Presence

When we improvise we want to be listening, almost hyper-attentive to what's happening around us. We want to be able to draw upon that information as much as possible, we don't want to be thinking very much, and we also want the ability to switch our attention as things develop and change. This gives our trained unconscious all the information it needs in order to improvise. Not so co-incidentally, this is also a common scientific definition for "mindfulness" or "presence".[35]

Presence is often referred to in improvisation as "being in the moment", "being present", or "not being in your head" — the negative of the Viola Spolin phrase "being in your head". Being present is critically important when improvising, because through it we find spontaneity. Surprisingly though, it is often not taught to beginner improvisors or described in books on improvisation, and many improvisors begin their journey into improvisation as thinking comedians, instead of present actors.

When I learned to improvise, I was never taught to be present. In fact I didn't hear the phrase "being in your head" until I'd been improvising for a number

---

[35] There have been a few scientific papers over the years which have attempted to define "mindfulness". The most useful I've found is the 2004 *Mindfulnes: A Proposed Operational Definition*, by Scott R. Bishop et al.

of years. And even then it wasn't very well known in our community which at that point went back almost 20 years.

By being in our head, by thinking as we improvise, we're utilising a selfish part of the brain that filters out ideas. It makes judgements based on real life emotion and sensual inputs, instead of letting the unconscious react in the moment with its improvisation training. We're judging the tennis return, instead of letting our unconscious react and respond with our internalised tennis training.

When we're thinking, we're inventing. And when we're inventing, we're not fully listening or utilising the full power of our mind. Not only that, but our scene partner who is expecting to respond to a scene partner who is present and using their trained unconscious, must instead respond to our conscious thought processes. We're not building together in the moment as improvisors, and this is difficult for them because they're not trained to respond to a thinking improvisor. Not only doesn't it work very well, but it's also unfair.

Retroactively correcting core improvisation skills like being present, is difficult, because it means consciously changing or unlearning internalised skills and knowledge. This requires not only teaching new skills, but teaching them strongly enough so that they replace the old ones in the brain and muscle memory. Particularly so for presence, because it is the core mind technique we use to listen and respond in the moment.

This all fits in with our understanding of presence very well. By turning off the conscious decision making, we draw upon more of the power of the unconscious. While improvising a scene, being present gives us more information and more power to discover the scene.

This is also where we struggle against our brains as a prediction machine, which can be great for us as individuals working our way through life, but not so much for improvisation. Unconscious prediction of motor skills and internalised improvisation skills are certainly beneficial, but it's the predicting of the future that gets improvisors into trouble. That's when we're in our head and not being present. Being present means the only thing that's important is what is happening right now at this very moment.

Different methods and styles of improvisation utilise different mixes of the conscious and unconscious, and being present in the moment. Typically, grounded Chicago method scenic long-form tends to be more present, due to it being open ended acting. On the other hand, short-form games and some game of the scene style improvisation tends to be less present due to rules and playwriting — or at least for those without extensive experience internalising them.

The term "playwriting" was first introduced by Viola Spolin in her book *Improvisation for the Theater* and means pre-planning a scene, or the next part of a scene, in your head while it happens. It's writing the play yourself, instead of discovering it through improvisation.

Either way, being present is the enabling mechanism for improvisation. It allows us to improvise with more information and power than is possible by conscious thinking alone. By not thinking, and trusting ourselves, the processes we've internalised for improvisation will kick in and the unconscious will flow spontaneously out of our head. And much of it may well surprise us.

Fear of failure

We can understand non-improvisors being afraid to perform in front of an audience. But as improvisors with at least a few levels of training under our belts, we're supposed to dismiss this, because it's fun and because it's what we've been trained to do: be present and spontaneous in front of an audience.

But if there is a natural enemy of improvisation, it is fear, or to be more specific, anxiety. Anxiety sneaks up on us. It often starts small, no more than a quick thought, but because we have no filters while improvising, it can quickly escalate into panic. With all of our training in how to make a scene work, anxiety is still the main thing that can quickly derail a scene, even if we know consciously what we need to do to fix the scene. Anxiety makes us think, activates what's called the DMN or Default Mode Network in our brain — we'll look into this in more detail later — makes us conscious, and breaks our unconscious improvisation skills. And the process that we need to follow in order to stop thinking and be present again — to remind ourselves to be present — is ironically a thinking process! And so the cycle continues and our ability to recover worsens.

So what causes anxiety on stage? We've been trained to trust ourselves so that we can perform in front of an audience, and to accept that we are able to entertain an audience, regardless of our level of ability. Even the newest improvisors can entertain an audience to a certain degree, and most improvisors can remember at least one scene they've done which was good. So objectively, the ability to improvise isn't the issue. We also have no real conscious control over improvisation, because we're supposed to be present in the moment, free from judgement and analytic self focus. So if we know we're good enough, and we know we can perform without having any control, surely we shouldn't feel anxious?

Fear and anxiety in improvisation comes in many forms, and often goes beyond the level experienced as stage fright or "fear of public performance". Viola Spolin says that stage fright is the "fear of being judged", and that can certainly be the case. But it's also more than that.

Sure, we could be anxious about another cast member, or a respected audience member, or even an unrespected audience member, and their judgement of us. But also there's the ultimate fear of not being able to improvise — because after all, we go on stage with nothing, like literally nothing.

Improvisation is an inexact art. We are consciously affected and manipulated by the work we're doing, and there are always going to be moments where players feel out of control or have no ideas with which to continue the scene.

The problem is that we incorrectly associate the idea of having nothing, with having no skills. That's because we don't realise that the product of improvisation is not a scene, it is the process of improvising.

We think we go on stage with nothing, and then suddenly we must deliver a scene from that nothing. That's a huge ask, akin to say building a house from nothing, or curing world hunger. But that's not true at all. We go on stage with improvisation training, but we don't deliver a scene, we deliver the process of improvising. We don't know what the scene will be, but we go on stage with so many internalised skills that we may not even need many of them. We're usually over prepared to engage with the process of improvisation. We don't go on stage to immediately make up a scene, that's stupid, anyone would be anxious about that. No, we go on stage to follow the improvisation process, and for that we are exceptionally prepared. We go on stage prepared to improvise, and that's the art we make. The process of improvisation is our art, not a scene.

So what is a scene the product of? A scene is a product of everything else in the room. The players, the audience, the room, and what's in everyone's heads. All of this is beyond our control, it's nothing we can control as an individual. We don't make scenes. The improvisation we're making does.

In Jimmy Carrane and Liz Allen's 2006 book *Improvising Better*, the authors discuss audience approval and the fear of significant audience members judging us on stage. Whether it be a respected audience member, a highly regarded improvisor, an acting scout, director, teacher or someone in a position of power over your future as an improvisor or even your day job, improvisors often become anxious or panic over whether they'll give their best performance, and what other people will think. Obviously this is a bad state to be in, and improvisation will suffer accordingly, leading to more panic and more suffering.

Carrane and Allen call this the improv committee, a perceived committee in the audience which you must try to please. They then say that "The improv committee resides in your head"[36]. You can't possibly know what anyone in the audience is thinking or looking for, so there's no point in trying to figure it out. The improv committee resides in our heads, it doesn't exist in the audience, we invent it while we are on stage. They have an even better phrase which helped me for many years as I was working through my own fears: "It's hard enough to be in your own head, let alone someone else's."

But fear of the improv committee isn't really fear of an audience member or their thoughts. It's the fear of not being able to improvise well enough, which is simply triggered by the recognition of the audience member. The moment you see or hear that the audience member is in the room, the unconscious pulls up mental models of that person. Will I get that role? Will I get picked for a team? Did I take their advice from class? And once you have an offstage thought, and a stressful thought, it's more likely that you'll have more, primed and ready to go. Improvisation is like that, you literally and metaphorically follow the fear, and once you start thinking about it, you quickly end up with: what am I doing, I can't even improvise!

---

[36] According to Jimmy Carrane, this most likely originated with Liz Allen.

When we improvise, we expose ourselves on stage, and often this can create scenes that have close connections with an improvisor's real life. For example, we see an ex-partner in the audience, and suddenly the scene starts duplicating our relationship with them. Embarrassing. Or we see our boss in the audience, and worry that she'll figure out we went above her head last week without her knowing, and look, the scene is about going above her authority. Embarrassing.

It is impossible to be in someone else's head, or your scene partner's. You can't even be in your own head. You are trained to improvise, and the process of improvisation that you create, will look after the scene for you. That's what is meant by the common improvisation phrase "you are enough".

The quality of improvisation we produce is dynamic and transient. It changes almost randomly for many different reasons. It could be we've just had a bad day at work, or our scene partner is thinking about someone in the audience, or the audience is different to what we normally expect, or any other of the almost infinite number of things that could affect a show. As our experience as an improvisor increases, our expectations as an improvisor also increase, and we expect that each time we go on stage, we should be better than our memory of our last performance. Because the quality of improvisation goes up and down, if we perceive that our performance is worse than our previous performance, then we will feel as though we've plateaued or gone backwards. This is not actually the case. We're unconsciously lying to ourselves that we should be better than we actually are, because improvisation isn't an exact process of steps to greatness, each show better than the last. Sometimes improv is awesome, other times it's not. There are hundreds of things effecting how good your scene will be, and very few of them are directly to do with you.

But like everything else, beginner improvisors learn over time not to be afraid. They will begin to internalise self–trust, and will learn or devise tools to minimise fear, and that will be that.

Presence and spontaneity are part of the foundations upon which improvisation is built. Once an improvisor has moved past the anxiety, then the presence and spontaneity may be refined and focused into the core principles of improvisation: listening and action.

Listening and action

There are two main activities we perform while improvising: listening, followed by action. These are the core principles of improvisation, because they're mandatory in order to improvise well.[37]

When we listen, we're listening to more than just dialogue, and we're listening with more than just our ears. We're also watching very carefully with our eyes, looking for body language — including facial expressions — and behaviours. We bring all of this listening together both consciously and unconsciously, to determine what is going on in the scene and with our scene partner.[38]

If improvisation happens in the moment, without thinking, then listening and immediacy of an action in response are critical skills. Listening gives us the information about the scene which we need in order to respond — it's not about thinking, it's about experiencing, paying attention and being able to switch attention. And responding with an action immediately is how we contribute back to the scene, our scene partners and the audience.

We can't 100% listen and 100% action at the same time, so how do we optimise both our ability to listen, and our ability to respond with substance and immediacy?

Leveraging the unconscious

> *Start 'cold', and where will the ideas come from? From you, and then there's a chance that your inner demons may be released, and that's the price you pay for being an artist.*
>
> — Keith Johnstone, *Impro for Storytellers*

Improvisation is all about having experiential focus. When we're improvising with analytic focus, we're thinking about stuff, we're in our head, and we're not experiencing, we're not *listening*. And because we're not listening, we're

---

[37] You can of course improvise by taking actions without listening, but it would be crap.
[38] This is often referred to by improvisation teachers as "active listening", however active listening is focused on understanding what was intended by the other person, and often includes repeating that understanding back to them. Improvisation has no such restriction, and wrong interpretation is often what makes an improvised scene come alive.

not experiencing what is happening in the scene, we're second guessing what's happening around us. We can't think and listen at the same time, even though we often think we can.

And when what's around us is other improvisors, then we're thinking about what the other improvisors are doing and what they're possibly thinking. And then regardless of which mode they're in, nothing we can think about will help us figure out what they're going to do, because we can't read minds. Meanwhile, our scene partners have moved on, as has the scene and the information critical to its continuation, our useful participation in it, and often our confidence as well.

With experiential focus, we don't need to know what our scene partners are thinking. We're sensing, we're experiencing, we're *listening*. But if we're in experiential focus, doing all this listening and experiencing, how do we then think about things we need to think about as we improvise? The point is that we don't need to think, we want to minimise as much of the thinking as we can, so that the unconscious can take over. Our brains analyse roughly 11 million bits of information per second, and only 40 of those bits are conscious thinking. That's a staggering amount of brain power to leverage if we can let the unconscious do much of the work for us.

When we first learn basic improvisation skills, there's a critical moment when we're given the option of consciously recognising a switch to experiential focus, or sticking with analytic focus and surviving on wit. These modes aren't named in class, and their existence is rarely acknowledged or even known by level 1 teachers. When the first real improvising exercise is given, often in the form of a game which requires either discovery or invention — such as "Name things not as they are" or the "Present Game"[39], or some exercise where we have to think of something first before we step out or take a turn — then we have to make a choice whether to think, or to experience and let the unconscious do the work. Those who are thinking about what things aren't, or what the present might be, begin to reinforce analytic focus as part of their instinctive improvisational play. They begin to internalise

---

[39] There are several variations of a "Present Game". I'm referring to the one Keith Johnstone invented that he calls "Presents". At first a player physicalises the size of something they are giving, and their scene partner then receives and names the present. The second stage is then the giver not actually physicalising anything and the receiving player physicalising and naming what they've received.

thinking as part of improvisation, and are usually not able to tell the difference or consciously switch between the two modes. [40]

I met a Zen meditation practitioner once, who'd just gone through a beginners' impro course for the first time. She was fascinated that impro seemed to be as she called it, "meditation in practice". More concerning though was that while she was able to identify the use of experiential focus, her impro teacher never mentioned it or what her mind should be doing while improvising, and that most of the class remained in analytic focus. That's right, one of the important things that is not usually taught in improvisation 101, at least outside the main improvisation hubs, is how to actually let go and be in the moment, instead of thinking up witty things.

It's common in improvisation schools to let the less experienced teachers teach the level 1 course. This is a big mistake. The most important moment in our improvisational career, is when we first let go, we become present in the moment, and we switch to experiential focus. And then there's that first night after class when we dream like we've never dreamt before. That's experiential focus in action. That's improvising. And it's too important to be left to an inexperienced teacher, because the longer this is delayed, the more that thinking becomes habit and the more difficult it becomes to reverse.

So, in summary, when listening, we want the unconscious to pull in as much information as possible. To do this we need to be as present as possible. And when we perform actions, we want this also to be mostly handled by our unconscious. Or at least we want to leverage as much of the unconscious as we can. And in order to do this, we also need to be — as we've already seen — as present as possible.

---

[40] The first part of the "Present Game" is actually a bad exercise for learning how to be in the moment and how to best support your partner. By giving an unnamed present, you've already written ahead in the scene to a point where a present will be opened, and not only have you given your scene partner possible lines to recite, but you're also forcing them to name what you want that present to be based on the size and shape you've mimed. I know it's a useful exercise, but there are better exercises that don't undo core principles. It is somewhat ironic that often the term pimping — which is what this is — is also taught in beginner levels.

Justification

Elaine May[41] used to say that an actor's job is to justify[42]. This isn't particularly true for solo spontaneity or experienced improvisors, because the solo and experienced unconscious tends to automatically justify. For beginner improvisors however, who are still learning spontaneity, justification is a conscious recognition that what just came out of their head is slightly — or greatly — disconnected from what came previously, and is their attempt to connect those two ideas. This is a conscious process. For example:

> MARY: Here's my wallet. Take my husband.

In this case there is an unspoken connection between "Here's my wallet" and "Take my husband", which may not immediately make sense to the players. In hindsight, after clarification, it will be obvious what the connection is, but it's possibly unclear at the time it is said. Mary could clarify — justify — these two ideas with the line "Because I'll pay you anything you ask to just take him away." In all likelihood this was what Mary unconsciously meant in the first place, and just jumped a bit too far away from what was expected, without putting the correct words to the thought.

Here's another example. Tracy walks across the stage through a mimed chair that Amy had previously placed there. To justify this, she might say:

> AMY: You moved my chair again! Stop doing that!

Or if there was no opportunity for her scene partner to move it, she might say:

> AMY: And I've had enough of your mimed furniture! Practise in your own room for a change.

They're not great lines, but are an attempt to justify the disconnect between walking across the stage and having not integrated the idea that there is a chair in the room.

Justification can be triggered by anything from small to large disconnects, and it can cause anything from small to large changes in our understanding of the scene and its scene content, regardless of the size of the disconnect.

---

[41] An actor, part of the comedy team "Nichols and May" along with Mike Nichols, and discoverer of early improvisation techniques.
[42] According to Del Close in Jeffrey Sweet's book *Something Wonderful Right Away*.

For example, if a character suddenly changes their age — large disconnect — then this could be justified as they always seem to act younger than they are, which most likely leads to a small change in our understanding of the scene and its scene content. Or for example, if a character slightly changes their accent — a small disconnect — then this could be justified as them being a spy or imposter, which leads to possibly a large change in our understanding of the scene and its scene content. As we become more experienced improvisors, the disconnects we contribute tend to become smaller, what we perceive as other players' disconnects also become smaller, and the justifications we contribute often become bigger.

In short-form improvisation some theatre games set up players to try and connect two or more disconnected ideas on purpose.[43] This isn't justification, it's just the connecting of two ideas that are unrelated.

For example, two players may be challenged to start a scene in an airplane cockpit and finish in a hair salon. It may turn out that this is an airplane cockpit themed hair salon, or there is a hair salon in the back of the plane, or even the airplane crashed into the hair salon. These aren't justifications, they're story connections. The justification may well be the mimed flight controls and how to justify them being mimed in a hair salon:

> FRANK: That's what I love about this salon, it's the small details. The control yoke and the rudder pedals make you feel like you're really flying, and they adjust the intensity of the blow dry at the same time!

But typically, justification isn't the forced connecting of disconnected ideas. In the above cockpit/salon scene, the scene progresses from a cockpit to a salon, and there's no justification required along the way. The goal is to improvise from one idea to the other so that it all makes sense with no justification required.

Justification is a retrospective clarification of how one idea, move or offer, leads to another idea, move or offer, and is usually from an unconscious that jumped too far ahead. In real life conversation, saying two disconnected statements would most likely confuse or bemuse the listener, but in

---

[43] Ted flicker of the 1957 St. Louis *Compass Players*, used to play a game where the audience would suggest an opening line and a closing line for a scene. Depending on how disparate the lines, this could involve a lot of justification. Similar games have been adopted for short form improvisation over the years.

improvisation we use justification to connect the ideas so the listener — the audience — isn't distracted, confused or bemused by the disconnect.

When we collaborate with other people, the problem is compounded, and players — particularly beginners and intermediates — find themselves justifying disconnected trains of thought, not just disconnected ideas, and not just those coming from them, but also from their scene partners.

Justification is what we use to translate unconscious stuff we didn't know was coming and which doesn't perfectly fit with what we have already. We listen, we respond, and we justify anything which doesn't fit.

Agreement

Everything we've looked at so far applies to the individual improvisor. Even when performing solo, being present and spontaneous, listening and performing actions, and justification, is the process each improvisor follows. And what comes out of our unconscious are the responses that fit the rules that we've internalised.

These aren't rules in the sense of improvisation rules we learn in class, but the logic we've internalised as we've learned how to improvise. It's like the riding a bike analogy — there are rules for balancing and riding a bike, but they're too many and too complex to consciously recognise them.

In order to apply some kind of structure to what comes out of our unconscious, we apply a general rule of accepting or agreeing to everything as it appears. This skill also becomes internalised when improvisors are first learning their craft. We agree with what has come before, we accept that it is the truth, and we don't deny it.

When collaborating with others, not only are we accepting or agreeing with our own responses, but also with those of our collaborators. This can be a big hurdle for newer improvisors who aren't used to collaboration, or who are often ego driven. This is also a problem in applied improvisation, where for example people in business teams don't always see agreement as a collaboration skill.

Improvisation is about listening, agreeing and responding. When more people are included within the process, their responses and the art as a whole must also be listened to, agreed and responded to. When an improvisor bulldozes[44] or brings in their ego or control, improvisation is no longer a collaboration, but a solo performance with support players whose main skill becomes second guessing what the bulldozer wants them to do.

When we talk about collaboration in improvisation, agreeing to a shared truth of what has already been revealed in a scene, a phenomenon called group mind often comes into play. Group mind is an effect often seen when groups of people work closely together on a shared creative task. In order to understand group mind though, we first need to look at a mechanism within our bodies called the mirror system.

Mirror neurons

Neurons, are cells found throughout the body which process and transmit information through electrical and chemical signals, and are important for the operation of our brains, central nervous system, spinal column and other systems. In 1992, Giacomo Rizzolati discovered that a certain type of neuron in macaque monkeys caused the monkeys to mirror the behaviours of not only other monkeys, but also humans. Later studies showed that this mirror system also exists in humans, and that not only does it make us mirror the *actions* of others, but the *emotions* of others as well.

Research into mirror neurons has exploded in the last 20 years. We won't do it justice in just a few paragraphs, so let's just look at the main concepts that can affect us when we improvise.

Studies show that one person's behaviour, such as tapping their foot or rubbing their hands, has a priming and mimicry effect on other people. They are then more likely to mimic the original person's behaviour. The yawn copying effect is an example of this, in that when we see other people yawn, we yawn too. In fact even the thought of yawning can make us yawn.[45] Although in the case of yawning, there are additional influences beyond priming and the mirror system that are still being researched, that make yawning a unique case.

---

[44] To bulldoze in improvisation, is exactly as the term suggests: to take control, dominate and ignore the responses of other players. Keith Johnstone was the first to use the term in his sixth *Theatresports* newsletter in 1994, subsequently republished as *The Book of Moose* and in *Impro for Storytellers*.

[45] I kid you not, I've actually started yawning right now as I write this.

Recent studies have also looked at "tactile empathy", the idea that watching someone being touched, activates the same neurons in the watcher, as the ones being activated in the person actually being touched. In 2003 a study showed that people who inhaled obnoxious fumes and screwed up their face in disgust, fired the same neurons in the olfactory area of the brain, as people who watched people being disgusted. There is strong evidence that this is the cause of empathy, the mirroring of actions, which causes someone watching to have the same emotion as the person actually performing the action. Empathy is critically important for theatre, and we'll spend some time on this later.

Taking this further, some studies have suggested that mirror neurons can mirror intention, and that by watching someone's actions, we can mirror the intention which caused their action. The classic example of this is a study where a hand would pick up a teacup from within different environments, such as a tea party in progress, or a finished tea party, meaning they were either picking it up to drink from it, or picking it up to pack it away. Different neurons would fire for each intention for the person picking up the cup, and the corresponding neurons would also fire in a person watching the hand pick up the tea cup. The watcher's mirror system was detecting the intention of the person picking up the cup.

Studies also show that we heighten mimicry. When a person A pinches person B for example, person B's impression of the pressure of the pinch is greater than the actual pressure of the pinch. So when B is asked to respond by pinching at the same pressure as they were pinched, they actually pinch back with greater pressure.[46]

It is believed that this mirror system evolved to help us learn and fit in with others. Babies have been shown to mimic facial expressions in other people for example, as most parents would already know. And the empathy aspect means that not only do we mimic in order fit in, but we also mimic when we *feel* that we fit in. Another study has also shown that we mimic more in social groups that we feel a part of, and less in groups that we don't, such as different ethnic or religious groups for example. This most likely evolved from the tribal era in order to teach us which groups we belong to.

---

[46] I wonder how many wars have been started this way.

WHAT IS IMPROVISATION? 65

Unlike priming, the mirror system kicks in automatically and almost unconsciously, whether we're aware of it or not. Not only that, but when we watch other people doing things, we already automatically know what they're doing or how they're feeling, and we often feel as though we want to do them too.

Group mind

The phrase "group mind" conjures up images of magical or supernatural out-of-body experiences, where a group of players can build amazing scenes or entire shows that no mere mortal could equal.

Other common definitions of group mind include: my scene partner and I think the same way; my scene partner and I both know what should or will happen next; we all think the same way at the same time; we can count to 20 without talking over each other, but only after we've tried a dozen times and failed; or, knowing exactly what our scene partner is about to do.

All these definitions are bad for improvised performance. I don't want to be thinking the same thing as my scene partner, or even the same way as my scene partner. Vibrant, dynamic and exciting scenes come from the differences between players, not the similarities. We each bring our knowledge, experience and point of view to improvisation, and it is the interaction between players trained in improvised techniques, that generates great improvised performances. I want to discover new things with my scene partner, not simply give life to what is in my own conscious.

And then there's the mystical definition that something inexplicably magical happens to a group when they perform. In *Truth in Comedy* it states that:

> The ImprovOlympic workshops constantly prove that a group can achieve powers greater than the individual human mind. Scenes created have turned out to be prophetic, and ESP has actually occurred on stage. Players are able to speak simultaneously, at a normal rate of speed, saying the exact same thing, word for word. Some teams became oracles on stage, answering the great questions of the universe, one word at a time, leaving audiences chilled and astonished.
>
> Audiences have witnessed the group mind linking up to a universal intelligence, enabling them to perform fantastic, sometimes

> *unbelievable feats. It only happens when the group members are finely attuned to each other, but it almost seems like they are tapping into the same universal consciousness that enables individuals with special abilities. Somehow, we are able to connect to it — and all improvisers know the value of connections!*

The claim that ESP — Extrasensory Perception, the ability to read minds and be psychic — is a bold one indeed, considering that ESP is pseudoscience. But in those early days, and in such an artistic or new age influenced community, it's easy to see how some may have come to that conclusion.

But group mind does exist, and we regularly experience it when we improvise. Viola Spolin referred to it, if not by name, in her 1963 book *Improvisation for the Theater*:

> *A healthy group relationship demands a number of individuals working interdependently to complete a given project with full individual participation and personal contribution. If one person dominates, the other members have little growth or pleasure in the activity; a true group relationship does not exist.*

And…

> *A group of individuals who act, agree, and share together create strength and release knowledge surpassing the contribution of any single member. This includes the teacher and group leader.*

Spolin didn't explain what exactly causes group mind or the exact effects, but she did recognise that it exists and that it does improve the quality of improvisation.

When I first looked at group mind, I put it down to coincidence and wishful thinking, because when you think about it, how often does your troupe *not* have something magical happen? Probably quite often. Coincidence is like that, it's an exception masquerading as a rule. Group mind could be the exception to the rule that it is difficult to have 8 people work really well together, so when it randomly happens, it seems magical.

Another take on this is flow. Flow was first described by Mihaly Csikszentmihalyi in his 1990 book *Flow. The Psychology of Optimal Experience*. He defines it as a period of intense internal concentration and total immersion in an activity, with positive motivation and focus, a centring of attention, and a loss of self-consciousness. When players feel that they are in flow, this can feel like everything is happening around them according to a plan which they control, and that the outside world no longer exists for them. This can make them feel like the rest of the team is also working the same way. But flow is for the individual, not the group, and often one person can feel in flow, but the rest of the group do not. So, while it may contribute in some cases, group mind is not just flow.

Human beings love patterns. We're wired to recognise patterns, we look for similarities in everything we do, and by default we assume the patterns we see are true until proven otherwise, even if we are imagining them. We understand the world by matching the patterns that we detect, with the mental models we have in our heads. For example, we have a mental model of what a house is: it's probably a building, with a main door and windows, and it is intended for people to live in. The concept of a house is different from a flat or a unit or a place of work, even though they often look alike. When we see something, our unconscious flips through the models we have in our head, looking for matches, in this case a house. A tent, or a flat that has been converted into a house, are also arguably houses, but will depend on what we have in our head as a rough mental model for a house, and that will be different from person to person.

A chemical that affects our ability to detect patterns, is dopamine. Dopamine is a pleasure chemical which is released in our bodies as a reward for experiences such as eating, orgasm, and success, and it is also believed to be one of the main chemicals associated with addiction. Dopamine release is a signal to the brain that we are having an important experience that should happen again, and again, and again.

Dopamine has also been proven to increase our ability to see patterns when there aren't any, which makes sense in an odd sort of way. It also indicates that warm up exercises with a group success goal, such as many of Spolin's theatre games, can lead to improved pattern recognition — through her transformation exercises — and thus group mind. This also hints at some interesting dopamine generating warm up exercises before a show. But whether you eat, orgasm or go the more traditional route of counting to 20, I leave up to you.

As improvisors, we're aware of group mind, and so we're already primed for recognising things that look like group mind. Did two actors speak the same line? Did they both start a scene about death? We recognise patterns in openings, other scenes, and life in general, especially so in a format like *Harold* when the players are also already primed for pattern recognition. And most improvisors have just spent the last hour together before a show anyway, so there will be more chance that there will be subject matter priming and even coincidences that look like priming.

For example, if divorce comes up several times in a warm up, then everyone in the group is primed for divorce. This doesn't mean that divorce will definitely come up in a performance that follows, but there is a bigger chance that it will. If a scene was initiated where a couple have negative emotions toward each other, they seem like they are married, and seem to live in the same house, then divorce certainly has more chance of coming up than anything else. Not only is it more likely to come up, but both players would be more likely to jump on the idea, seeming as if they were possibly mind reading. Or… as if they had group mind.

Priming also works over the course of a scene, so if divorce comes up, then divorce primes the improvisors for other mental models related to divorce, such as marriage or children. Children may then prime us for something else again, and so on throughout the scene, each time seemingly having group mind. And when priming introduces associated concepts — see earlier when we discussed priming false memories — a group of improvisors can even converge on a single primed concept that hasn't been specifically discussed. For example if concepts related to divorce were brought up, yet divorce wasn't, then divorce may still be primed as a primary associated concept.

The exercise "Stretch and Share" — where players stretch while sharing stories about their day so far — is popular in show warm ups, but it is basically a priming exercise. So if that's the case, is it really a good exercise for a warm up? It depends on what kind of show you're doing, and whether you wish to be heavily primed or not as a group before a show.[47]

The mirror system also contributes a lot to group mind. If we're mimicking other players, then we're more often than not in the same location, or the

---

[47] I tend to use "Stretch and Share" in class to improve the feeling of group mind amongst students, but not in my shows where I want less priming before the show.

same country, or have the same emotion, or have similar character traits, or similar initiations, or similar emotions, etc. This is particularly interesting when talking about group games which generate themes, and sound and movement openings where the focus can be extremely narrow, and thus the chance of behavioural mimicry is very high. Strong mimicry leads to more of a sense of belonging, which leads to more confidence and presence, and more mimicry, and so on.

A 2011 study by Lior Noy, Erez Dekel, and Uri Alon titled *The mirror game as a paradigm for studying the dynamics of two people improvising motion together* had two experienced improvisors perform a "Mirror" exercise then "Follow the Follower" — two Spolin games where two players face each other and first one leads and the other copies their movements, and then they both follow and nobody leads. The study showed that when one of the players is nominated as the leader and the other the follower, the delay between the actions of the two players was greater than if there was no leader. The range of the speed of movements was also less when one was leading, and there was additional variation or noise in the follower's actions. This meant they were copying each other more accurately when there was no leader at all. Let's just consider this again. When there was no leader — they were following each other — the reaction times were faster than when there was a leader. One of the researchers' conclusions is that when there was no leader, the players were often not just copying each other, but predicting each other's movements.[48]

Although mimicry is great for group mind, it's not ideal if it overpowers the scene itself. For many years I would mimic the accent or voice of my scene partner if they initiated with an accent or different voice. It is quite common for newer improvisors to be affected in this way, to copy the accent, status or character of a scene partner, because they haven't yet internalised turning off mimicry in improvisation. This kind of mimicry works well if you're using it to specify something about the scene, such as a location, or shared family background. But if the scene partner was using it to reflect something that's unique about just that character, then the mimicry could overpower parts of the scene that contradict the accent. For example, if the scene was located at

---

[48] For the technically minded, the response times were often as low as 40 milliseconds between the two players when there was no leader, which is way too short for a follower to simply be following a leader.

a security desk at an international airport, we don't want every customer to be the same ethnicity as the security officer.

Mimicry of movement can also be an issue, as character traits, status and variations in depth of stage can all be negatively affected by copying the movement of scene partners, often turning a scene into more of a mirror exercise. While group mind is a good thing, it's not when it begins to take over or water down the uniqueness of a character, or the dynamics of a scene.

But there is more happening in group mind than just priming and mirror neurons, and probably more than science currently knows. We will look at another contributor a bit later when we look at scene analysis and "emergent interactive frames", but to do that we first need to look at another aspect of group mind — one that allows us to predict its potential effects. We turn to something called systems theory and complex adaptive systems.

The idea that a system can be better than a sum of the parts was discovered initially through economics and the analysis of the depression in the 1930s, and then explored in detail in the 1940s and 1950s. Systems theory describes what happens when a number of elements or components which operate by themselves, come together and operate as a single system. A motor vehicle is such a system, as is a chemical, as is a group of people in a brainstorming session[49], and so is an economy.

There are a number of different types of systems, but there are two main categories, simple systems and complex systems. Simple systems have a simple path of cause and effect which allows us to figure out what the system does by looking at its component parts. A microwave oven and a motor vehicle are simple systems, because we can look at the components and figure out what the system does. Simple systems can be reverse engineered to discover how they work and what their component parts are, and therefore they can be designed from first principles.

Complex systems on the other hand, are systems where you can't figure out what they do by looking at their component parts. The stock market for example is a complex system, as is an insect colony, and a group

---

[49] Brainstorming is also a great example of improvisation in practice. Participants are encouraged to be spontaneous and use their unconscious to generate as many ideas as possible, with no filtering or questioning until after all ideas have been documented. It's also an example of where we don't necessarily want group mind effects.

brainstorming session. In particular, we're interested in complex adaptive systems, which are complex but also adapt their behaviour over time. Complex adaptive systems are called such because they are diverse, are made up of multiple interconnected elements, have the capacity to change and learn from experience, and they can't be reverse engineered to first principles. You can't look at a complex adaptive system, and figure out how it was made.

Improvisation is a complex adaptive system, and is therefore more than just the sum of its parts — the players. We can see this in practice when we try to analyse how an improvised scene works and everyone has their own opinion of the scene and what went wrong — or right. And if we know that an improvised scene or show is a complex system, then there's a whole bunch of other interesting effects and aspects of complex systems that also apply to improvised scenes and troupes.

Firstly, they can't be reverse engineered, so we can't design the perfect improvised scene or show from first principles, which will disappoint quite a number of improvisors who prefer playwriting to responding in the moment. We can get close, but an improvised scene is not like a house or a car that we could design from first principles. Human beings are flawed and unpredictable for a start, so anything we do that involves our own actions in the result, will already be short of ideal. *Theatresports* and *Harold* for example, have been refined over many years through exploration to be the forms they are. They weren't suddenly written down as a one–off design to be followed by the letter from day one. But this is one of the great things about being human that actually helps with improvisation: human beings are random and spontaneous.

More significantly though, the observable effects of a complex system — a process called "emergence" — allow us to better understand improvisational technique. Emergent effects are what we see when a system works so well that surely it must be magical. It is the stuff we see that we could never have imagined if we'd only seen the individual components of the system. It is what the authors or *Truth in Comedy* were seeing as ESP. Looking at an ant for example, we can't tell that a giant colony of millions of little ants could build the complex ant hills which house their nests. Or to be more scientific about it, emergence is the production of additional results and effects caused by the sum of the parts, but which are not attributable to any clearly traceable component. And for this reason, it can often be viewed as quite magical.

Emergence is what allows improvisation troupes to be greater than the sum of their parts. Priming shared mental models, internalising shared models of improvisation, and interaction frames — which we'll look at later — all lead to group mind. Emergence is the effect we see as a result.

The amount of emergence in a system is commonly based upon the number of components and their interactions. In the case of an improvised scene, this will increase over time as more information is added and clarified, meaning that group mind is more often felt later in scenes than earlier, which often contributes to why longer scenes seem more magical — at least the good ones anyway. Many of the interactions in a scene may be negligible, not useful, or may create noise that prevents emergence. However, rehearsal and performance allow the troupe to refine and better their group play, thus increasing the amount of useful emergence. This is why regular training and performance in the same group creates better performances, because working together builds a better complex system, which leads to more emergence or group mind, even if we can't see exactly why this is happening.

We can optimise emergence in several ways. Firstly, the system must be self-regulating and self-organising, not merely directed via hierarchy or by a single component of the system. This is effectively what Viola Spolin was referring to in the quotation from *Improvisation for the Theater* about working together as a group. Creativity, capability and skill all improve when the group builds together, integrating the abilities of everyone into the group. Wow, sounds like theatrical improvisation doesn't it?!

The diversity of a complex system is also important, as it increases flexibility by making it resilient to environmental changes. This feeds innovation, due to the varying combinations and interactions between the component parts. This is particularly true of an improvisation troupe, where the more varied the players are, the more innovative the troupe often is, and the more able to prevent bad scenes and discover better and more varied scenes.

Another interesting effect of such systems is amplification. We see this when improvisors focus on something in a scene, and it tends to amplify over the life of a scene. We also saw this effect when looking at mirror neurons — mimicked responses typically heighten the mimicry. This is useful and evident when improvising a game of the scene in the UCB method for example, where amplifying and heightening are important, but can also be seen in other styles and methods. In the case of Johnstone's impro, story and perceptible offers of action tend to amplify throughout a scene. In the case of Chicago related methods, relationship and the detail of "Yes, and…" can become amplified. This is also why initial work on a form or technique tends to exaggerate the specific skills or techniques we're working on, before we notice and pull them back somewhat as things begin to come together.

Whatever goes into our mind, often comes out again in a scene. We know this from priming, and if we're working on certain skills or scene content, then that's being reinforced over and over again, causing it to be more prominent in a scene, or amplifying it.

But priming and amplification don't just happen with the improvisors on stage. In his book *Impro for Storytellers*, Keith Johnstone talks about circles of expectation, the idea that what happens on stage, sets up a loop of expectation with the audience. So, if the improvisors asked the audience for a location to begin their scene, then the audience would have certain expectations of what they would see in that scene. For example, if the scene was set in a library, then the audience would not expect the characters to be cooking or playing table tennis, and they may also be annoyed that they weren't doing things you would expect in a library, or at least making use of the fact that they're in a library. The characters may later open a book and have its contents come to life, as that may be expected, but not if the library is simply the false entrance to the hero's hideout or there are no references to books in the scene.

The audience has expectations that should be met, and through the use of listening, space and object work, shelving, call backs and other techniques, improvisors learn to internalise the satisfying of the audience's expectations. This in turn also leads to improvisors sharing ideas and outcomes, which once again looks like the fabled group mind. As with the above library example, although the scene could go anywhere, there is a higher chance that the scene will involve a book, or some kind of interaction with a librarian or between librarians, because that's the nature of what the audience and players expect.

Group mind is an effect caused by numerous brain functions, of which priming, the mirror system and emergence are only three. As improvisors however, we prefer to see it as described in *Truth in Comedy*, a magical mystical experience and universal intelligence that comes into being, empowering a team of creative people to build something greater than the players themselves.

Intuition guiding action

In *Making sense of improvisation*, a 1997 applied improvisation paper by Mary Crossan and Marc Sorrenti[50], the authors define improvisation as "intuition guiding action in a spontaneous way." This is the most accurate definition I've found in any earlier work on improvisation, and it fits perfectly with what we've discussed so far about defining the nature of improvisation. But what about the mechanics behind this guiding action of intuition?

Improvisation, including the comedic aspect of it, works because a number of differing brain functions happen to work together in particular ways. Improvisation isn't magic or supernatural — it's a wonderful by-product of the cognitive operations of our minds, most of which originated before we had the capacity to think and speak. In a way, improvisation could be considered itself a side effect, an almost random craft created by connecting together a number of contributing brain systems. And with this side effect, a number of key practitioners happened to stumble across varying methods for harnessing it, and turned it into a craft and art form.

Improvisation is an awesome evolutionary mind hack.

We become present, we become spontaneous, we listen, and we respond. With these simple steps we are able to improvise. And by agreeing to what we discovered, justifying anything slightly awry, and responding in ways which work better for scene progression than others, we are able to enact the process of theatrical improvisation. And through improvisation, we are able to build complex dramatic and comedic scenes, grounded in real life and truthful behaviours, but with the capacity to go well beyond.

---

[50] Crossan and Sorrenti's paper discusses the links between improvisation and organizational learning.

1600s to 1920s

Acting and theatre have been around for millennia, sometimes scripted, sometimes guided by a story or rough outline of a scenario, and sometimes completely improvised. But theatrical improvisation didn't really take off as an art form, because scripted or predefined narratives tended to become better each time they were performed, so why bother to improvise them?

For the very few literate civilizations — such as the ancient Greeks — these works were fairly easy to document and accurately reproduce[51]. But for everyone else, at least up to the 18th century, narratives had to be passed on by word of mouth, and this is what helped lead to the initial development of theatrical improvisation.

Commedia dell'arte

Commedia dell'arte is a partially improvised comedy form popular initially in Italy from the mid–16th century, that then spread to the rest of Europe. *Commedia* uses predetermined scenarios and a set of stock masked characters

---

[51] This is why many more plays come from literate civilizations than any other — they had the ability to archive culture with the written word.

with which to play them. Each character has a specific personality, costume and mask that is the same across much of the history of *commedia*.

Commedia troupes would tour Europe performing these predetermined scenarios, with actors often finding themselves being typecast and playing the same characters time and again, building up stock lines, gags and techniques for that character. The more they improvised these scenarios, the more likely they were to simply repeat the same actions and lines over and over again. Often only the newer performers would add spice or newness to the art — as they were still exploring and learning their trade. The more experienced actors would have their kit bag of lines and actions that they would usually repeat over and over again, knowing that they would always work well with an audience.[52] Often stories would be changed to fit the culture or politics of the town they were playing in, but this would also usually be plotted out before the performance.

Commedia was performed in public — usually just in the street — which caused additional problems that were partly solved by the use of a mask. The origin of the mask isn't clear, but the result is that the viewer is unable to lock on to recognisable facial expressions — scientifically called micro-expressions. By using a mask, the audience is less distracted by all manner of street activity and noise, and better focuses on the unchanging and unnatural face of the character. Masks pull focus. And in order to better convey emotion and intention, as well as pull some of the focus from the audience staring too much at the mask, *commedia* players became more physical in their portrayals.

A number of changes in culture and technology contributed to the downfall of *commedia* as a popular entertainment, and it gradually morphed into theatre and music hall over the next few hundred years. Once literacy improved, actors were able to read scripted plays without the need for improvisation in order to follow a scenario, and the intentions of playwrights were able to be captured and remembered in detail. And with the invention of indoor theatres, outside distractions were removed and artificial light was

---

[52] Unfortunately, this hasn't changed much in the modern era, where in some improvisation communities players still pull from a kit bag full of scripted characters and moves that they've used countless times before.

able to be focused on where the audience should be looking, thus removing the practical need for masks.

Commedia dell'arte is often held up as a precursor to theatrical improvisation, however there is no direct link between them. The idea that theatrical improvisation comes from *commedia* is often attractive to us improvisors, because we feel we have some kind of creative connection to a classical past. But *commedia dell'arte* was of its time, and ended because we found better ways to make theatre.

Later practitioners often used elements of *commedia* in their work — for example David Shepherd cites *commedia dell'arte* as one of the inspirations for his co-founding of *The Compass Players* and his work on improvised scenes from a play, and it was even referenced in early advertising for their shows. But these influences arise mostly from the more idealistic *commedia dell'arte* that we've partly invented in our own heads — the *commedia* which was completely daring, immediate, improvised and in the moment, and is a seemingly classical copy of the same theatrical improvisation we have today.

These days, most improvisors have never been on stage before learning theatrical improvisation, and have careers such as in law or I.T., but for some reason we all still feel the reverence of a time honoured and much esteemed yet idealistic tradition, which goes back through the ages. And although many improvisors would much rather watch lowbrow broadcast TV than Shakespeare[53], we all still oddly enough consider ourselves to be poets and geniuses. However, like *commedia*, we do also know how to heighten the hell out of a penis joke.[54]

Music Hall, Vaudeville, Überbrettl

Since 1737, the most significant theatres in the U.K. were effectively controlled by the government and monarchy. New plays had to be submitted to the Lord Chamberlain for approval, before receiving a license for performance, and even then, only a handful of theatres were allowed to stage spoken drama. Reasons for rejecting a play were initially at the Lord

---

[53] Academic discussion continues on whether Shakespeare's works were highbrow or lowbrow back in his day. They have since become highbrow however, because their language is now considered highbrow.
[54] Obviously neither you nor I would actually do this!

Chamberlain's will, but in 1843 changes were made to the law which required the Lord Chamberlain to provide a good reason for doing so.

In the early 1800s, saloon bars began appearing in pubs, providing light entertainment for drinkers. Because they were providing musical entertainment — hence the term "music hall" — they were able to bypass the theatre laws covering the performance of spoken word plays, and due to their clientele, these were often risqué or political in nature. When the law changed in 1843, licensing became more flexible and spoken word performances were often added to music hall bills, making music halls much more popular, with many eventually changing into actual theatres. Licensing and censorship laws for spoken word theatre in the U.K. continued until 1968, when they were finally revoked.

Keith Johnstone notes that this censorship — in particular the requirement to submit a script to the government for approval — prevented improvised drama from being performed in the U.K., and partly contributed to why his *Theatre Machine* troupe often toured Europe. However, this censorship only applied to certain theatres, and other practitioners had already experimented with improvised theatre in the U.K. well before 1968, and had even written books on improvised theatre practice.

By the 1880s, music hall had spread to Europe and in the U.S. had become vaudeville. In France, and in Germany from 1901 with Überbrettl — translated as "super cabaret" — theatres began appearing presenting acts consisting of poetry, song, drama and sketch comedy of a mostly left wing political commentary against the governments and popular parties of the time. And while World War I interrupted cultural life across Europe, the interwar period revitalised artists, including Jacob Moreno's work on improvisation in Vienna in the 1920s, which we'll look at soon.

European movements of the early 1900s

The early 1900s in Europe were an avant–garde melting pot of art, social and political movements and unrest, leading to enormous amounts of artistic output and political action, including two world wars and the testing and subsequent failure of several significant political systems.

From this melting pot came the Italian futurist movement in 1909, which quickly spread to other European countries as far away as Russia and England. Futurists believed in the oncoming revolution of technology and machinery, and actively celebrated and promoted aspects of this future, including speed, strength, violence and industry. Futurist artists came from many artistic domains, including writing, painting, sculpture, fashion, architecture and theatre, thus inspiring later movements across a wide range of artistic endeavours.

In 1915, leading futurists Filippo Marinetti, Emilio Settimelli and Bruno Corr published their theatre manifesto titled *The Futurist Synthetic Theatre*. This manifesto called for a revolution in theatre, calling the theatre of the time passé and not worthy of continuing, and that the new theatre should be immediate, brief, and not pander to the lowest common denominator, or spoon feed audiences with expectations of tried and true theatre formulae.

On improvisation, the manifesto[55] reads like a call to action for theatrical improvisation over the next century, and called the new theatre:

> *Dynamic, simultaneous. That is, born of improvisation, lightning-like intuition, from suggestive and revealing actuality. We believe that a thing is valuable to the extent that it is improvised (hours, minutes, seconds), not extensively prepared (months, years, centuries).*
>
> *[..]*
>
> *The Futurist theatre will be able to excite its audience, that is make it forget the monotony of daily life, by sweeping it through a labyrinth of sensations imprinted on the most exacerbated originality and combined in unpredictable ways.*

Somewhat ironically, the manifesto also included scripts for a number of short 1-3 minute futurist theatre scenes. Whether they were "born of improvisation" and were able to "excite its audience" is unclear, but on a quick reading, fairly unlikely.

One of the many movements to spring from Futurism was Dada, effectively a protest movement against the existence of movements. Dadaism began around 1916, railing against the logic and reason of modern society, which amongst other things, had led to war and the capitalist classes. Dadaists embraced spontaneity and rejected the art of meaning, often producing

---

[55] Text reproduced from the 391 website, http://391.org

irrational, nonsensical or protest works against other movements. It is an amusing irony that Dada was therefore also protesting against itself, and it was often said that "Dada is anti–Dada".

Futurism, Dadaism and other avant–garde movements of the 20th century contributed in many ways to the later development of theatrical improvisation as we know it today, and specifically Jacob Moreno's *Theatre of Spontaneity* in 1922.

Russian revolution in theatre

Up until the late 1800s, actors would use manufactured physical embellishments and flamboyance to convey emotion and intention. This was born from the fact that acting performances were usually performed with the house lights on, due to them not yet having the technical ability to light a stage as we do today. Performing in the light meant there were more distractions to draw an audience's attention, and audiences often spoke amongst themselves as a performance was in progress. Conveying emotion and intention through physical movements was simply necessary for audiences to understand the performance. As technology improved, and with it the ability to light a stage, actors simply continued using these embellishments as part of their craft.

In the early 1900s, Russian theatre went through a revolution against this style of acting, that then lead to naturalistic acting and many of the techniques we still use in theatre production today.

Konstantin Stanislavsky was a Russian actor and later a theatre director, who opened the *Moscow Art Theatre* (MAT) in the late 1890s, and went on to develop a more thorough and detailed process of directing. As part of Stanislavsky's "system", a play is analysed word by word for intention, and the resulting acting is rehearsed and blocked in detail before performance. Through this script analysis, a series of beats or "units of action" are defined where motives and objectives change over the course of the play. Improvisation is also used in rehearsal, and the actors discover emotional experiences for their character which drive their physicality and psychology. All of this makes the actors and the play itself, more naturalistic.

Vsevolod Meyerhold was a young actor working with Stanislavsky in the early years of these experiments, and he and Vladimir Nemirovich–Danchenko — Stanislavsky's co–founder at MAT — rejected Stanislavsky's use of improvisation. Considering this, it wasn't until Stanislavsky developed his theory of Active Analysis near the end of his life in the 1930s that he fully embraced improvisation. Meyerhold went on to directing, and developed a system called "Biomechanics", where certain body positions are used to portray specific emotions and character types. As with Stanislavsky, Meyerhold believed that emotion was key to naturalistic acting, and developed his system to compliment Stanislavsky's theories. However, he believed that the physicality of the actor would lead to the experiencing of emotion, whereas Stanislavsky believed that the emotion should come first.

Yevgeny Vakhtangov was another of Stanislavsky's actors at MAT. He was influenced by Stanislavsky and Nemirovich–Danchenko, as well as Meyerhold, and in fact was able to resolve the differences between Stanslavsky's and Meyerhold's methods. One of his important theories with respect to how improvisation works, is that of bringing yourself to a role. He believed that an actor's performance is influenced not just by the rehearsed character and its objectives and other adornments, but also by how the actor personally feels before they go on stage. The character is a combination of what the actor did that day, the actor's personality, and the character's objectives.

Vakhtangov took this further and encouraged actors to use their mood and experiences as part of their acting. The first thing an actor should feel when they walk on stage, is their current state of mind, followed by their mood affected by the next thing in the play. He thought that this brought a unique immediacy and richness to the character, thus requiring very little warm up, and a more naturalistic and believable style of acting.

Another of Stanislavky's students was Mikhail Chekhov — the nephew of Russian playwright Anton Chekhov. Chekhov's early work on Stanislavksy's affective memory or emotion memory — using an actor's memory of an emotional event — led both Stanislavsky and Chekhov to see the limits of this method. This led to Stanislavsky's later Method of Physical Actions — which we'll come back to later — and Chekhov's Psychology Gesture. Psychology Gesture is a technique for using specific gestures discovered in rehearsal, to instantly invoke the psychological state of a previously rehearsed character. Chekhov was also a great believer in improvisation as a way to discover and explore a character.

Jacob Levy Moreno

Jacob Moreno was born in 1889 in Bucharest, Romania. In 1895 his family moved to Vienna, where he stayed until leaving Vienna University in 1918 after nine years of study in medicine. He then moved to the town of Bad Vöslau in Austria to become what we now call a family doctor or GP, before moving to the U.S. in 1925[56].

In the early years of university, Moreno began working with children he found playing in a local park, leading them through telling stories and playing games, many of which utilised spontaneity and improvisation. Similar to Keith Johnstone almost 40 years later, Moreno rebelled against the limits and values placed on children by both parents and teachers, and gave the children opportunities to challenge themselves, be creative and think outside the bounds often imposed upon them.

For a while he also started a children's theatre, presenting both written and improvised plays, where he noticed that when the children rehearsed[57]:

> ...the first time they were fresh, they were creative, they were wonderful. The more often they repeated that performance, the less spontaneous they became.

Moreno began thinking about spontaneity and the theatre, and realised that actors are typically subservient to the text and direction of a play. Presuming that spontaneity in theatre is a good thing, Moreno wondered if a completely improvised theatre would allow it to be more creative and exciting. With the start of World War I, and an increasing concern by parents and authorities regarding their children's rebellious and almost disciple-like behaviour

---

[56] Sources vary on exactly when Moreno moved to the U.S. including 1925, 1926, 1927, 1935 and 1938. The most likely date of leaving Vienna is 21 December 1921, according to René Marineau's book *Levy Moreno 1889-1974: Father of Psychodrama, Sociometry and Group Psychology*. His most likely arrival date in the U.S. is some time in January 1926, according to the book *Impromptu Man* by Moreno's son Jonathan Moreno. Crossing the Atlantic by ship in the 1920s took roughly a week, and if you include overland travel from Vienna, then in all likelihood Moreno emigrated from Vienna in 1925 and immigrated to New York in 1926. Together with receiving his licence to practice medicine in the U.S. in 1927, this probably explains most of the discrepancies. Not that it's particularly important for the future of improvisation.

[57] From an interview with Moreno's wife Zerka Moreno in Steve Capra's 2004 book *Theater Voices: Conversations on the Stage*.

around Moreno, he stopped working with children.[58] He had however firmly begun to think about the nature of spontaneity as an actual state of the mind.

By 1918, Moreno was part of the Vienna literary and intellectual scene, and started a journal titled *Daimon* to provide an outlet for publishing their work. Moreno would have been aware of futurism and other movements at the time, and possibly the *Living Newspaper* — which we'll look at soon — both of which would have influenced his — soon to be a reality — spontaneity theatre.

In 1922, Moreno formed an improvisational theatre company called *Stegreiftheater*, which translates vaguely to English as *Theatre of Spontaneity*. He rented a hall in which to perform, and the company would present improvised plays several times per week for the next few years, becoming a popular attraction for audiences in Vienna, yet not so much for theatre reviewers.

In the *Theatre of Spontaneity*, actors and audience members would improvise theatre without an author or director. Possibly influenced by the Futurists' *The Futurist Synthetic Theatre* manifesto[59], Moreno's theory was that many arts lost their impact and importance the more time that was spent creating them, and that scripted theatre was basically out dated and stale by the time it appeared as a performance. By removing the author and director, and empowering both the actors and the audience, theatre could be created instantaneously at the moment it was originally envisioned.

In reality, Moreno would come prepared with story outlines and had often written lines of dialogue for a roughly 20 minute long play, for which he would then cast his characters from both his acting troupe and members of the audience. As the play progressed, musicians would improvise music and visual artists would paint backdrops during the performance as required. But if an audience member disagreed with the performance, or wished to make a point, they could stand and challenge the performance and optionally take the place of the actors or propose changes to the play.

---

[58] Had he been female, like Viola Spolin, perhaps history would have been different.

[59] There is no evidence that Moreno was aware of the manifesto, but considering it was published 7 years earlier, that aspects of the manifesto can be found in his *Theatre of Spontaneity*, and the fact that he moved in similar circles and once edited a literary journal, it is very likely that he was.

Moreno initially had issues with performers not knowing when to speak during improvisation, so he developed a system of signals for actors to indicate to each other when they were beginning and ending key events, such as entrances, exits, main speeches and pauses. Signals would include sitting down or standing up from a chair, or holding hands, which if not part of the prewritten scenario, had to then be integrated into the scenario in order for it to work. But the idea of signals seems to have been dropped after the group had been working together for a while.

He believed the on–stage work was collaborative, but he also believed that characters should alternate taking the lead over the course of a scene. He also developed a system of written notation whereby he could document or even pre–plan a performance, which included where the actors should stand, who should take the lead at any one time, and the key events and interactions between the characters.

Moreno also discovered that spontaneity required a warm up process, and plotted his shows and scenes so that the most significant part of the performance would happen as the actors reached their highest level of spontaneity. Oddly enough, he seems to have not considered warming them up by improvising before the show, so that they were fully spontaneous when the show started. He also originally used clichéd character types — possibly copied from *commedia dell'arte*, although he was highly critical of *commedia* — but then later dropped them and allowed the actors to develop characters themselves.

Through his two years of workshops and public performances, Moreno discovered a number of modern improvisation techniques, and while his writing now seems rather naïve knowing what we know about improvisation, it is fascinating to read about his discovery of game and opposing intentions for example. In the case of game, he discovered that players should have a game to be played within the scene. This is similar to the techniques of modern sketch writing and the UCB method of improvisation, and is also discussed in the book *Truth in Comedy*.

Theatre of Spontaneity performances included improvised plays, spot improvisations — single scenes — based on themes, and a version of *Living Newspaper* — improvising scenes based on the news of the day — all of which are staples of modern day theatrical improvisation, yet were very new in 1921. Moreno's *Living Newspaper* was originally called *Dramatized Newspaper*, but by 1947 he'd changed the name retrospectively to *Living Newspaper*, possibly to better associate it with the more popular *Living Newspaper* movement. We'll look at *Living Newspaper* in more detail in the next section, and its links to Chicago improvisation.

The *Theatre of Spontaneity* was so new, that reviewers refused to believe that it was improvised. If the show was good, they assumed it had been written and rehearsed, and if it was bad, they assumed that improvised theatre simply did not work. How they thought it was all planned is unclear, because the shows seem like they would have been fairly chaotic. Moreno was directing the show while it was in progress, with both the actors and the audience actively involved in the process. Actors were initially guided by his system of signals and had to think about lead taking, stage position and often pre-set lines of dialogue and blocking, and the audience could jump up and challenge or change what was happening on stage at any time. Surely the success rate was random at best.

During *Theatre of Spontaneity*'s run, Moreno began to involve himself with his actors on a personal level, often experimenting with therapy techniques he would later develop into psychodrama. Two such cases stand out which had a significant effect on Moreno for years to come. The first was with an actor couple named Robert and Diora, who seemed to be in a happy relationship. But one day in 1924 Diora left Robert, leading him to commit suicide the next morning.

The second incident involved an actor named Anna Hoellering, and her husband Georg Kulka who would watch each performance from the front row of the audience. After a particular show, Georg told Moreno that their marriage was full of anger and physical abuse, and asked if Moreno could help. In response Moreno gave feedback to Anna on her performance, encouraging her to take more risks and embrace harsher more active characters outside her comfort zone. It seemed to work, and Moreno's notes say that the couple went home that evening in "ecstasy"[60]. But a few years later they divorced, and in 1929 Georg committed suicide. While neither of these suicides can be directly attributed to Moreno, he always felt that he could have prevented them if he'd paid more attention, and this may have significantly contributed to his move toward improvisation as therapy.

---

[60] This seems to be fairly universally accepted as meaning "had amazing sex".

One of Moreno's best actors was László Loewenstein, whom Moreno renamed Peter Lorre, and who went on to a Hollywood acting career with roles in *Casablanca*, *The Maltese Falcon*, *Arsenic and Old Lace* and many others. While the *Theatre of Spontaneity* would have certainly helped his acting technique, Lorre was already considered a good actor by then — at the age of 17 — and most likely improved the *Theatre of Spontaneity* in return. However, it was here that Lorre developed the rehearsed facial expressions that he was later known for in Hollywood, and that Moreno was so against. His time with Moreno is rarely mentioned in biographies.

In 1924 Moreno published a book titled *The Theatre of Spontaneity*, documenting his experiments with the theatre, before moving to the U.S. in 1925. The book remained relatively unknown outside of German speaking countries until the English translation was published in 1947. However, Moreno continued to work on spontaneity theatre in New York after immigrating, at the same time as trying to build his psychotherapy and psychodrama practices.

Moreno began demonstrating his spontaneity theatre techniques around town, in churches, schools and public halls, before forming a new *Impromptu Theatre* company based at Carnegie Hall. There was much publicity before their first of several public performances in 1931[61], but the reception was mostly negative, leading to a quick end to *Impromptu Theatre*. But Moreno's work still attracted the attention of actors and other artists, many of whom were well known at the time or who went on to have successful careers in the theatre world. And it is this early work and his prolific work load that so influenced the New York acting scene. Amongst other projects, he worked with theatre and acting schools on spontaneity, started a journal titled *Impromptu* in 1931 which contained articles on spontaneity theatre and psychodrama, and had substantial influence on people such as Stella Adler, and companies such as The Actors Studio and Martha Graham's Dance Company. To list how deep Moreno's contacts and influence goes, would take too long, and it would be much easier to simply defer to the most comprehensive — but not complete — history of this time in the book *Impromptu Man*, by his son Jonathan D. Moreno.

---

[61] Thus Jacob Moreno most likely holds the record for the first improv show in New York.

Living Newspaper

The *Living Newspaper* is an improvised show format, where improvisors improvise scenes inspired by that day's news stories. Rarely referred to by name, and originally unrelated to improvisation, it became the basis of one of the most popular improvisation show forms of the 20th century, and has a history going back to the early 20th century. Until the advent of immediate personal communication such as SMS and social networks, no other theatre format could better demonstrate the immediacy of improvised theatre.

In 1919, the Russian government created the *Living Newspaper* to disseminate Soviet news and propaganda. The news was literally read to the public while moving picture images and actors were at the same time used to support the commentary. The *Blue Blouse* theatre collective was created in 1923, which continued to spread across Russia, and by its height in 1927 boasted over 5000 such troupes.

Whether Moreno's 1921 *Theatre of Spontaneity* was influenced directly or indirectly by the *Living Newspaper* or conversely whether Moreno's work somehow influenced *Living Newspaper*, is unclear. However, in the 2000 paper titled *Living Newspaper. Theatre and Therapy*, author John Casson makes strong cases for both.

The concept of a *Living Newspaper* was popular around the world throughout the first half of the 20th century, because it narrated the news in an era without television or video — something the Greeks and Romans were also doing back in their day. Thus, we see slightly different versions of it appearing throughout.

We see it in Moreno's work, in Russia's propaganda, in other countries across Europe, Asia and South America, as well as in cities across the U.S., both as independent and as federally funded workers' theatres through the WPA — Work Projects Administration, a federal U.S. agency for public works.

The *Living Newspaper* influenced David Shepherd in the development of theatrical improvisation, with him originally wanting to open a workers' cabaret theatre. This led to Shepherd's founding of *The Compass Players* — that coincidentally also opened its show with a *Living Newspaper* set which incorporated news events as scene suggestions. *Second City* even later considered developing a TV show titled *The Living Newspaper*[62] around 1961-1962. The technique was also used in Britain variously over the years, including in workshops by the writers' group at the Royal Court Theatre in London which ran from 1958 to 1959, of which Keith Johnstone was a member.

In December 1970, Brazilian theatre director Augusto Boal started developing his *Newspaper Theatre* in São Paulo, with his *Nucleus Two* group of the Arena Theatre. This is the first theatre form he developed that later became part of his 1974 book *Theatre of the Oppressed*. *Newspaper Theatre* is a set of ten techniques for using the current news in theatre performance, and while most of the techniques require research, analysis and preparation, one is for using improvisation to immediately act out the news. Boal had been part of a psychodrama group from 1967 to 1968, so he was also familiar with Moreno's work.[63]

It is impossible to identify the inspiration for any of these *Living Newspapers*, partly because there were so many of them, but also because it is — perhaps simply retrospectively — such a simple, obvious and popular idea.

---

[62] According Joan Rivers in Jeffrey Sweet's book *Something Wonderful Right Away*.
[63] In Boal's autobiography *Hamlet and the Baker's Son: My Life in Theatre and Politics*, he says that the idea for *Newspaper Theatre* came from some earlier work of his and Arena Theatre playwright Oduvaldo Vianna Filho's. This possibly refers to their work with the Centro Popular de Cultura — Brazilian Centre for Popular Culture — a left wing organisation for grassroots cultural initiatives which existed just before and after Brazil's military coup d'état of 1964.

Spontaneity science

Moreno and other early practitioners began to explore the nature of spontaneity, a precursor of today's theatrical improvisation methods. Moreno's actors were already trained in acting and theatre, so all they had to focus on was how to be spontaneous and how to apply that to their craft.

Training ourselves in being spontaneous is different from training ourselves to improvise. Spontaneity is required first, which then allows the unconscious to use the scene progression and theatre techniques that it has learned and internalised. Yet many of the exercises we use today in improvisation, teach us both spontaneity and scene progression at the same time, making them difficult to use in other non-theatrical domains without being adapted in some way.

For example, a scene painting exercise will help with spontaneity, scene initiation and scene progression skills. The spontaneity aspect may be useful for training improvising jazz musicians for example, however the visualisation and storytelling aspects may not. Recognising this, gives us insight into how theatrical improvisation exercises can be adapted into other domains including applied improvisation. And in order to be able to do that, we need to better understand spontaneity and its causes and effects.

Dual Task Processing

Only in recent years have we begun to understand how our brains process tasks, how they prioritise them and how many they can handle at any one time. The problem is called dual–task processing, because it happens while performing two or more tasks at once. For many years there were two competing theories of dual–task processing: a serial processing central bottleneck theory; and a parallel processing capacity sharing theory.

The serial processing model theorises that each task is queued at a central processing point in the brain, and each task is processed as it comes to the head of this queue, one task at a time. In research literature this is referred to as the psychological refractory period or PRP, because experiments have shown that two cognitive tasks can take longer to perform at the same time than if they were performed one after the other. This is because there is a delay in the queue while the first task completes. With this theory, it is not possible to perform any more than one task at a time, and it is the speed of the processing, and the breaking down of larger tasks into smaller subtasks, that gives us the impression that we can. Multitasking for example, is really dividing attention between multiple tasks, breaking them down into individual subtasks, and the brain then processing them one at a time. Our brains don't process two tasks literally "at the same time".

Other studies however have showed that our brains are able to perform some tasks at the same time, in parallel, without either task having to be queued at a central processing point. Within this model, there are still questions about whether the brain simply splits processing evenly amongst the tasks, or whether it provides some tasks more brain power than others based on some kind of priority. This parallel model is referred to as the capacity sharing model, even though there are questions about how brain capacity is being shared.

In the mid to late 2000s however, a combined model began to be proposed which accounts for the anomalies between the two models, and explains a number of other observable effects with how we process cognitive tasks. The idea is that a central processing point does process single tasks from a queue, but then other tasks or subtasks which utilise other parts of the brain, such as sensory inputs and outputs or memory, can process in parallel, either while they are in the queue, or after they've been processed at the central processing point.

In their 2006 paper *Dynamics of the Central Bottleneck: Dual-task and Task Uncertainty*, Mariano Sigman and Stanislas Dehaene refer to this as a hierarchical model of cognitive architecture. They say that there is a hierarchy for processing, that many tasks are handled one at a time, but other brain systems that provide functions that aren't required by the current task, can still process tasks in parallel. Not all systems can parallel process their own tasks, but most can process one task while another system is processing another task. Visual attention — turning and looking at something that catches our eye — for example, can't parallel process with identifying what we're looking at, but visual attention and memory recall can.

The more interesting part of this for improvisors, is that as we process the same two tasks over and over, our brains learn how to process them faster, because it builds a mental model and cognitive muscle memory that can be repeated each time those two tasks need to be processed. This means that the more we perform the two tasks, the less time they need to spend with central processing, and the more they can be handled by other brain systems in parallel. Basically, you can train yourself to perform two tasks in parallel, by continually performing them serially — one after the other.

A classic example of this is patting your head and rubbing your stomach at the same time. At first you'll find this difficult, potentially with a high cognitive load — lots of thought processing — but later you'll find it easy and be able to perform other tasks, even while patting your head and rubbing your stomach. Drummers are a classic example of this, using all four limbs to control different parts of a drum kit all at the same time.

The more practical improvisation example of this is theatre games, and more particularly, theatre games or scenes with a number of different game rules. The more we play a game, the easier it becomes. This means that playing the same games all the time is going make the games easier and less risky, which could be a problem if the point of the show or improvisation is taking risks in front of an audience. When challenge and risk are helping to drive the audience's interest and response, this will negatively affect the quality of the show.[64] Unless of course the improvisors then begin to fake risk, which is also a fairly common occurrence.

Divided Attention

Divided attention is the conscious focused attention on more than one thing at the same time — for example holding a conversation while watching a kettle boil. And because each focused attention is a processing task, it is affected by the dual-task processing effects described above. Even though we think we're paying attention to two or more things at the same time, in our brains we're actually switching back and forth between them.

Increased divided attention can cause cognitive overload due to what's called interference. Because the queuing and processing mechanism in our brains can't keep up with the required cognitive load, this slows down the conscious processing, meaning that it has less filtering and control over the unconscious and other subtasks within the brain. As a result, we become more present and there is less rumination and less of that inner critic that constantly talks to us inside our heads. This is why many theatre exercises involve divided attention — concentration on two things at once — because they induce presence while teaching our brain the patterns it needs to better parallel process these tasks the next time it is presented with them. The originators of these exercises realised that divided attention had an effect on presence when the attention was split between two tasks which use the same functions within the brain. They didn't know the reason, but they knew the effect.

This has an impact on improvisation because it means we can train our brain to optimise certain tasks. Think of a theatre game which has divided attention, such as an "Alphabet" scene, where each successive line of dialogue must start with the next letter of the alphabet. Because attention is divided between keeping track of the alphabet and lines of dialogue, at the same time as performing an actual scene, this causes cognitive dual-task processing overload, as the players are switching attention back and forth between the two tasks.

Cognitive overload reduces conscious processing. But the more we perform or practise this type of scene, the more we learn to parallel process it, the

---

[64] Keith Johnstone suggests that players should be given the opportunity to master difficult games, and that it is the scene content that engages the audience, not the risk or mechanics of the game. I'd suggest that it is all of these things.

better we get at it, and the less conscious involvement we need to perform it. This contributes to why a lot of short-form improvisors — such as in *Theatresports* or *ComedySportz* — get bored with games after a while. Once you've learned the trick, and optimised it in your brain, there is less work required to perform it. Games like this can then get to the point where it's more like going through the motions than anything else. Considering a lot of short-form is about watching improvisors struggle with divided attention, this can diminish the entertainment value of short-form performers who have been doing it a long time, as there is no audience perceived difficulty involved and improvisation looks safe, boring and even rehearsed.[65]

There is also scientific evidence that consciously thinking about a problem or a skill, can negatively affect our ability to perform actions. In 2002, researchers Beilock, Carr, MacMahon and Starkes showed that golfers who focused their thinking on putting a ball into a hole, actually did worse than when they had divided attention and were also performing a listening exercise. Again, this is because the cognitive overload causes the conscious to reduce its control over the unconscious skill of putting, allowing the more skilled unconscious to have more control of actually getting it in the hole.

Both Keith Johnstone and Viola Spolin were aware of divided attention, although they weren't aware of how it really works and its full effects. Johnstone wrote about divided attention in regard to the hat game, where you perform a scene while trying to pull the hat off the other player's head during a scene. He said that part of the mind plays the scene, while the other part watches the hat, and that players needed to be able to make this split in order to protect their hats. While his focus seems be on training people to use divided attention to induce presence, what he's actually doing is training people to be able to pull off hats while playing a scene. At the end of training, players can pull a hat off someone's head and play a scene at the same time, which effectively then makes the exercise redundant and not as much fun — although it has taught them what presence feels like. I'd suggest that not learning the trick of the hat game actually makes it more fun than learning

---

[65] I've seen a lot of long time short-form improvisors build a fake persona for the stage which pretends to perceive risk, in an attempt to better excite an audience. Maybe a better idea would be for them to branch out and experiment with other forms and styles instead. Real risk and the excitement of the unknown is often what brought them to improvisation in the first place.

it. Divided attention is a fun state to be in, so why perfect theatre games and no longer have that sensation.

A lot of Spolin's work is very much about divided attention and its use in making actors more present to invoke the power of the unconscious. Spolin's games all have a "focus" or goal, which is often a problem to be solved. But while there is a focus, there are still other skills required in each game, such as acting, speaking, gibberish, object work or other game rules. By dividing attention between the primary focus and the secondary skills and rules, we become more present. But many of the same issues apply as in Johnstone's hat game, in that the more we play a game, the better our brain is able to multi–task those specific skills. Whether we consider this as cheating at the game, or as becoming better at a new skill, depends on why we're using the exercise to begin with.

The Default Mode Network (DMN)

The brain contains many different regions and processing centres, which together make up the operation of our minds and bodies. Many of these regions work together as connected systems or networks that implement high level brain functions. Many of these are only activated when needed, an example being the mirror system which we looked at previously.

Scientists use a technique called functional magnetic resonance imaging, or fMRI, to scan the brain and visualise changes in blood flow during cognitive tasks. By watching blood flow, they can identify which areas of the brain are being activated, deactivated, connected and disconnected during these tasks.

One of these networks, discovered in 2001 by Marcus Raichle and his colleagues, is called the default mode network or DMN. The DMN is active when we're not actually doing anything, but is deactivated when we're performing a goal oriented task. Originally called the intrinsic or task-negative network, the DMN is basically our default waking state. When we begin to process a task, the DMN deactivates and the extrinsic or task-positive network (TPN) activates instead. Later studies have shown the existence of a number of other resting state networks like the DMN, related to memory and motor skills. But it is the DMN which is most useful for our purposes.

When the DMN is fully activated, we enter a state of introspective thought. Thinking about ourselves and other people, recalling and thinking about the past, thinking of the future, day dreaming, mind wandering, and other non-goal oriented cognitive tasks. All bad things for improvisors. In depression for example this can lead to rumination, and so DMN modulation techniques have been developed to prevent spending too much time or focus in this mode. Meditation is just one example of this, because mindfulness deactivates the DMN. Sleep deprivation also reduces activity within the DMN when it is activated, but we'll cover sleep in a later chapter.

When the task-positive network (TPN) activates to start processing goal oriented tasks, the DMN doesn't fully deactivate. There is still some limited activity that is useful during task processing, but for all intents we say that the DMN has deactivated. Likewise just because the TPN is active, doesn't mean that the DMN can't partially activate and compete for cognitive function, which can positively or negatively affect the ability of the TPN to complete its task. So for example if we are tidying up the lounge room, the TPN activates, and if our mind wanders, then the DMN reactivates, impairing our ability to quickly finish the tidying up.

When we improvise, we don't want to be thinking or ruminating, so we want to deactivate the DMN, or reduce the activity within it. Traditional meditation and mindfulness exercises train our brains to deactivate the DMN. This doesn't mean that the TPN must then be active, it just means that the DMN and its self analysis and thinking behaviour is not. Meditators and improvisors do however deactivate the DMN and intentionally activate the TPN for focused attention processing and their trained theatrical improvisation processes respectively.

Improvisation isn't about not thinking. Improvisation is about trained task processing using a trained unconscious, while in a state of mindfulness.

Memory of the future

In 1985, Swedish neuroscientist David H. Ingvar coined the phrase "memory of the future" in an essay titled *"Memory of the future": an essay on the temporal organization of conscious awareness*. Ingvar identified the brain's ability to retain memories of possible predicted futures. He posited that if the information for events in the past — such as motor skills, sounds, or mental models — are stored in memory, then information related to future events must also be stored in memory. Otherwise we would not be able to comprehend the future, and the body would not be able to act on any information from the past or present.

It is thus often suggested that the brain is simply a prediction machine. And that its main purpose is to analyse and predict what will happen in the future and to prepare for any possible actions that these predictions may require. The memory of the future, is the remembering of possible outcomes and actions related to those predictions.

One of Ingvar's examples is the interpretation of speech, whereby past knowledge of speech recognition is used to predict intended meanings of words and sentences before they are complete. For example, if someone were to say to you "Evil can be cold and calculating", the brain has already predicted the intended meaning of "cold" as soon as it is spoken and before "calculating" ultimately clarifies it. Ingvar also gives the example of humming a known melody, where recognition is used to predict upcoming notes that have not been consciously remembered.

The unconscious is not just acting in the now, it is also predicting and acting on the future. And for improvisors this is a bad thing. Turning this future prediction off is difficult for new players, but being spontaneous and in the moment, using the techniques we've already discussed, is how we prevent this from happening. We want to build in the moment using spontaneity, not predict the future and forward plan the path to getting there.

Flow

Mihaly Csikszentmihalyi's "flow" is often misunderstood. The dictionary definition of flow is often of something continually moving or streaming, but that's not the flow we're talking about. Then there's William James' 1890 term "stream of consciousness" — the depiction of a streaming out of continual thoughts — which often confuses the matter even more, and is often the interpretation used by improvisors.[66]

For Csikszentmihalyi, the term "flow" is used to describe a period of intense internal concentration and total immersion in an activity, with positive motivation and focus. It's a centring of attention and a loss of self-consciousness. When in flow, it can seem as if the world ceases to exist, time

---

[66] Stream of consciousness is often applied correctly when discussing improvisation, but is also often confused with Csikszentmihalyi's flow.

stops or slows down, and we feel like we're on autopilot. If you don't know if you've experienced flow or not, then you possibly haven't, because flow is an extremely positive, pleasing and satisfying experience that you would certainly remember. It is not just when ideas are "flowing" or when there is good concentration and focus.

Flow is also a state in which the experience is an end in itself, where an extrinsic reward isn't driving the experience. The term for this is autotelic, something with a purpose that is itself. For many people, theatrical improvisation is an autotelic experience, because we do it regardless of the reward, the career opportunities or the threat of failure. And often we even do it in spite of these.

Most of us improvisors have memories of moments of flow, scenes we were in, shows we were in, or some other improvised process where we were completely focused. It seemed like the world around us was not just paused but no longer existed, while we performed almost in slow motion. Much of this is actually due to cognitive overload. The brain begins to ignore functions which don't contribute to the current activity, such as monitoring time or sensory inputs we can temporarily do without. This gives us the feeling of otherworldliness.

The term flow was coined and popularised by Mihaly Csikszentmihalyi in his 1990 book *Flow. The Psychology of Optimal Experience*. While the book was the culmination of decades of research, and human beings have been experiencing flow throughout history, the idea of flow was not popularly known at the time. It quickly spread to sport and popular psychology.

Csikszentmihalyi found that one of the conditions for flow occurring is that there is a skill-challenge balance in a particular activity. The challenge to the individual must be high, but the skill level must also be high enough to be able to actually perform the activity. Flow is the individual performing at their optimal ability, hence the title of his book. This makes sense from a cognitive overload perspective, because using all your abilities will stretch the capacity of your brain. But this also means that you must continually find new challenges in order to engage flow, because flow leads to optimal performance, which generally improves ability, meaning that optimal performance will possibly be at an even greater level next time in flow. If an activity is easy, then you become bored, or if the activity is too difficult, then you become anxious and frustrated. Only in balance does flow occur.

But here's the twist. The skill-challenge balance isn't a balance of the individual's actual level of skill and the actual level of challenge. It's the individual's *perceived* skill level and their *perception* of the difficulty of the challenge. So long as they think their ability is high and that it matches how difficult they think the activity is, then they are preconditioned for flow, regardless of how good they really are or how difficult the task.

As far as I'm aware, no research has been done on flow in improvisation, at least not in published academic research. The only relevant study is a paper by Jeffrey J., Martin and Keir Cutler in 2002, *An Exploratory Study of Flow and Motivation in Theater Actors*, which supports a number of general flow theories, but also adds some non-sport related theory.

Martin and Cutler recommended that teachers and directors match the acting skill levels of acting students with role difficulty and to make sure that the actors' goals match their ability. This would have a higher chance of inducing flow in students, which leads to more intrinsic rewards for optimal performance. This then spawns other effects like more motivated actors and higher class retention rates. This all also applies to theatrical improvisation too, but doesn't really tell us about the behaviour of flow while in performance.

Fear and anxiety

Fear is only as deep as the mind allows.

– Japanese proverb

Fear leads to anger. Anger leads to hate. Hate leads to suffering.

– Yoda in the film "The Phantom Menace"

Fear is an emotional state caused by the perception that something is a risk to us or to something we hold dear. This doesn't mean that the something is definitely dangerous, just that the brain thinks there is a chance that it might be. This then triggers the fight or flight response, where our body prepares what it needs mentally and physically to either run away or stand and fight.

Fear is often confused with anxiety, which is similar to fear, but instead of being a reaction to a perceived real danger, it comes from apprehension about an imprecise or unknown negative experience. Fear is usually a known threat, whereas anxiety is concern that something negative might happen at some point. Usually the fear of improvisation is actually anxiety, and is the result of a feeling of being pulled into something bad and unavoidable, something that we don't know if it will be a problem. Anxiety can't be fixed by moving out of danger, it's a constant concern about the unknown.

One type of anxiety, called social anxiety, is anxiety caused by the thought of being evaluated by others. Numerous studies have shown that people with social anxiety more often regard themselves less able to socially engage with others, have an expectation that they will perform badly, and they incorrectly think that other people treat them less positively. These map pretty well with common fears that improvisors have, such as regarding themselves as not as good as others, thinking that other people don't think they're very good, and having an expectation that they may improvise badly.

With fear, once the fight or flight response is triggered, the autonomic nervous system begins making physiological changes to the body. Anxiety has much less of a response than fear, but many of the same changes can certainly occur. This can include any number of the following: loss of peripheral vision; loss of hearing; dilated — enlarged — pupils; increased heart rate; increased blood pressure; increased blood sugar; increased sweat; constriction of blood vessels to stop blood flow in non-essential areas of the body; an increase in blood flow and tension in the muscles; and a constricting of the neck and back muscles. This last one is interesting because it causes the body to slump into a protective shape similar to the foetal position, which then begins to restrict the vocal chords.

In response, the brain switches to analytic self focus and peripheral vision, presence decreases, narrow focus increases, and the default mode network deactivates and the task positive network is activated. These obviously aren't particularly good conditions for an improvisor to be in. Basically, for an improvisor, fear and anxiety really suck.

Jacob Moreno actually discovered this, that anxiety limited spontaneity, and that less anxiety meant more spontaneity. Stanislavsky also wrote about muscular tension and physical tightness — both being effects of anxiety —

in his book *An Actor's Work*, saying that this then affects our physiology, as well our memory and thinking.

Not only does anxiety negatively affect our ability to improvise, act and perform, but the reverse is also true — the more confident we are, the better we are able to improvise. But then as improvisors, we know this already.

We'll look at some ways to reduce anxiety in a later chapter.

Conditioning

Most people have heard of Pavlov's dog, Russian physiologist Ivan Pavlov's experiments, which he published from 1901 to 1903, regarding the conditioning of dogs. Dogs need saliva to help swallow and digest food, so in preparation for eating they begin to salivate whenever they anticipate food. Pavlov noticed that his dogs would often salivate at the sight of his assistants who would usually feed them, even without any sensory detection of food. He went on to discover that he could train the dogs to present themselves and salivate at the sound of a simple bell and nothing else.

At the same time, a psychology professor named Edwin Twitmyer, discovered the same thing. But instead of using dogs, he found that he could train people to simulate the reflex action caused by a hammer tap just below the knee, by using only the sound of a bell. For comedians, it's truly unfortunate that by a simple luck of the draw, we've ended up with Pavlov's dog instead of Twitmyer's hammer.

Conditioning research has expanded in the hundred odd years since, and we could spend several weeks understanding the current research alone. Suffice to say that fear conditioning is just one of the many branches that have come from conditioning research.

Fear conditioning

Fear conditioning is the association of some kind of stimulus, say a noise, a smell or an image, with that of fear. Not only does it become associated with it, but it becomes an uncontrolled response. Evolutionarily it is assumed to come from the learning of associations with danger, allowing us to better predict it and for the fight or flight response to kick in sooner. A specific example could be a deer learning that a certain sound of grass moving indicates that a big cat — a lion, cheetah etc. — is nearby.

Fear conditioning is learned through repetition of association, similar to any other conditioning or such as with Pavlov's dogs. An ordinary neutral stimulus is given, say the sound of a bell, or a certain image is shown, while at the same time a painful negative stimulus is given, such as a shock or other fear causing event. Follow up studies have suggested that the neutral and negative stimuli may well need to be completely unrelated to cause the conditioning, but this has yet to be fully proven.

Once fear conditioning is in place, it will usually continue until the brain decides otherwise. Because conditioning is based on remembering stimuli and their associations, it was originally thought that you can forget conditioning over time, however it has subsequently been shown that conditioning can only be removed by laying down new memories over the top of the older conditioned ones. This means that the new memories must be strong enough to not only compete with older memories, but to completely replace them. Scientifically this is referred to as extinction, or causing the conditioning to become extinct.

Post–traumatic stress disorder (PTSD), often seen in war veterans and sexual assault victims amongst others, is believed to be a state of shock caused by a traumatic event. Trauma and stress cause changes in the brain which prevent it from making the conditioning become extinct. The sound of a car backfiring or helicopter rotors amongst war veterans is a classic example of this — the shock of war prevents them from letting go of their traumatic experience, so they remain conditioned to their response.

Different amounts of certain brain chemicals such as cortisol and other types of glucocorticoids, can make people more or less susceptible to PTSD or fear conditioning. Recent experiments have even shown that these chemicals injected at the time of or directly after such a traumatic incident, can reduce or prevent the fear memory consolidation of PTSD or fear conditioning. These chemicals are being looked at as possible future drugs for military personnel, and people regularly in stress related situations. Another technique for preventing this condition is sleep deprivation. Sleep deprivation of up to 5 hours, after the fear conditioning of mice, has been shown to reduce or prevent conditioning. Whereas between 5 and 10 hours does not.

What this means for humans however, we don't yet really know. I'm certainly not suggesting injecting all level 1 improvisation students with cortisol each time they perform. But sweet sugary foods and trans fats are just some of the types of food which cause cortisol levels in the body to spike, and thus may reduce some of the effects of fear conditioning.

Most people who quit improvisation do so right after level 1, and a lot of this is related to fear and anxiety management — which shows how critical level 1 curriculums are and how good level 1 teachers need to be. So, if improvisation training focuses more on fear and anxiety in early classes, then perhaps at some point improvisors will no longer have to figure out ways to combat their fear. Of course until the 1970s, theatrical improvisation was mostly the domain of actors and comedians, both already absolved from the effect of fear and anxiety, at least while on stage anyway, so what can we be doing now, to repeat what they did back then?

1930s to 1940s

By the mid–1940s, theatrical improvisation as an artform all but ceased. Jacob Moreno had begun to move on to develop psychodrama — although he would release an English translation of his book *Theatre of Spontaneity* in 1947 — and Keith Johnstone and the Chicago theatre and arts community was still a decade away from discovering improv. It is at this time that Stanislavsky in the 1930s developed some of his most innovative techniques which used improvisation, and Viola Spolin in the 1940s developed many of the core improvisation techniques which would later be used to build the Chicago improv method.

Active Analysis

Stanislavsky died on 7 August 1938, but in his final decade he revised his theories to include the Method of Physical Actions and Active Analysis. From his earlier experiments with Meyerhold, Stanislavsky began working with physical actions as a method for finding a character's psychological state. He believed that the psychological and emotional state of a character drives the physical actions of that character, but also conversely physical action drives the psychology and emotion. By focusing on the physical actions of a character, as a series of steps through a play, the actor may more easily elicit a deeper psychology of the character.

Following on from the Method of Physical Actions, Stanislavsky's final work was on Active Analysis. His earlier work used actor and cast read throughs of the script in early rehearsals, at which point the text and characters would be analysed, and the conclusions used to influence the development of the production. In Active Analysis, the actors don't see the script until late in the rehearsal process, and in rehearsal they instead improvise actions through the play guided by the director. This allows the actors to better find and explore their characters and psychology first, before finally being provided with the actual lines to be spoken.

These later theories weren't fully documented by Stanislavsky, and may not have been fully explored before his death, both of which contribute to them not being very well known until the last 20 years or so. However, with the rising popularity of modern day improvisation, and more information being published on Stanislavsky than ever before, more directors are now beginning to use this technique for the production of scripted plays.

Viola Spolin

Viola Spolin was born in 1906, and in 1924 she enrolled in the Recreational Training School at Hull House in Chicago, which was run by Neva Boyd. Boyd was using improvisation games, drama and storytelling as teaching techniques, and was influenced by the work of Jacques Copeau. Copeau was a French actor and director, who in the early 1900s integrated physicality and improvisation into actor training, and had developed exercises and games to this end. Boyd's teaching had a lasting influence on Spolin, who by 1939 — at Boyd's suggestion — was drama supervisor for the Recreational Project for the Works Progress Administration of Chicago. This was the same WPA that was producing *Living Newspaper* projects across the country.

She began developing drama programmes for children, devising her own games and exercises which ultimately appeared in her 1963 book *Improvisation for the Theater* — coincidentally the same year in which Neva Boyd died. *Improvisation for the Theater* was compiled in the 1940s and 1950s from her own exercises, and with later editions including some of Boyd's games from her 1945 book *Handbook of Recreational Games*.

In 1942 Spolin moved to Hollywood, and in 1945 she founded the Young Actors Company, where she taught child actors with her still developing system of theatre games. It was here that much of *Improvisation for the*

Theater was written. In 1955, her son Paul Sills asked her to return to Chicago for the start of the *Playwrights Theater Club* and *The Compass Players*, and while this delayed publication until 1963, Spolin said that it was not until she saw her system in use professionally at *Second City* from 1959 onwards that she was able to rework her book into the form that it is today.

Spolin discovered the use of divided attention to invoke presence and induce spontaneity. She also discovered that not all divided attention is equal, in that divided attention requires multiple tasks of the same type, such as for example two verbal tasks or two physical tasks, in order to divide attention. This is now known as dual-task interference, which we looked at in the previous chapter.

Spolin's focus was on the use of spontaneity to engage intuition and playfulness. What this actually means is using divided attention to induce presence and allow spontaneity to tap into the unconscious. She believed that creativity is all about transformation[67] — "Creativity is not rearranging; it is transformation"[68] — and that theatre games each with a specific focus, allow people to work together spontaneously and intuitively to solve problems, allowing the mind to discover a transformation between two states. Transformation in Spolin terms is a change from one thing to another, for example from one emotion to another, or from one mimed object to another. What many new improvisors do, is consciously plan or look for the opportunity to change, whereas Spolin's games — with correct side coaching — encourage the change to be discovered spontaneously.

From a scientific perspective, transformation is the pattern matching we go through in order to identify various mental models, and then the priming of those models. For example, in her exercise Transformation of Objects, players pass around a mimed object, which will hopefully transform into a different object while each player is handling and heightening the original object. Once we're aware of the pattern matching and priming effect, it's often possible to feel the process as it occurs. By handling a space object, suddenly another object will appear in the mind as a quick transition. The new object is quickly primed in our mind and the old object is then let go. Objects can seem to almost magically transition from one object to another, without any conscious prompting. But again, this requires good side

---

[67] Obviously Spolin's use of the term "creativity" isn't the academic one we now know.
[68] Quoted from Viola Spolin's book *Improvisation for the Theater*.

coaching for the players to induce transformation and not simply invent a new object.

Spolin also popularised a number of now commonplace teaching techniques, such as each exercise having a single focus[69], side coaching, who/what/where initiations, and pause vs. freeze. For the uninitiated, her work is often considered as a simple list or encyclopedia of theatre games, but her discoveries such as those above, as well as divided attention and intuition, are the foundation techniques upon which the Chicago method of improvisation was built — regardless whether she developed her theatre games or not.

Students also often find it difficult to understand her games, because they're now used for teaching aspects of theatrical improvisation and acting that were not her original intention. A good example of this is Spolin's "Space Walk" exercise, which has since been adapted into many variations that are no longer focused on her idea of "space substance".

Spolin originally called her work "recreational theatre", and was influenced by the work of Jacob Moreno, who was by the 1940s living in New York and still working with improvisation and the theatre, as well as exploring spontaneity for therapeutic work. Spolin said that her work was often called "sociodrama", a technique developed by Moreno for acting out plays as group therapy.

Method acting

For six months in 1923 and again in 1924 — coincidentally the year David Shepherd was born, and the year Viola Spolin began training with Neva Boyd — Stanislavsky's *Moscow Art Theatre* (MAT) toured the U.S., presenting plays in almost a dozen cities across the country. The impact on American acting was almost immediate, helped by the fact that a number of the MAT's actors stayed in the U.S. after their run, and started giving workshops and building schools based on Stanislavsky's methods up until that time.

---

[69] Early versions of *Improvisation of the Theater* referred to "point of concentration" or "POC", but this was later changed to just "focus". Considering the word "focus" can apply in many different circumstances, "point of concentration" would still seem to be the better and more obvious choice.

This ultimately led to Lee Strasburg's development of what is now known as "the method", an acting method based on the misinterpretation of parts of Stanislavsky's earlier system.[70] The method builds on Stanislavsky's emotion memory or affective memory, which brings stronger emotion and realism to the actor's portrayal of a character. Other American actors and directors also uniquely reinterpreted and adapted Stanislavsky's system, and "method acting" is now used as a general term for most American methods influenced by Stanislavsky's system.

The 1930s and 1940s were the calm before the storm. Moreno was applying improvisation to medical practice, and he was still giving workshops to key theatre practitioners in New York. Viola Spolin was in the process of developing her ground breaking techniques, and there was a revolution in American acting. When theatrical improvisation finally exploded in the 1950s, many new techniques had to be invented to support it as a practical method of improvising scenes in front of an audience.

---

[70] Academics still argue over whether method acting is the same as Stanislavsky's system, or miscommunication of his work. The current weight of opinion is that it is the latter.

Approaching scenes

Much of what we've looked at so far, also applies to general improvisation and not just theatrical improvisation. We become spontaneous, we listen, and we respond with actions which come from our trained unconscious — our internalised skills in improvisation. What distinguishes one domain of the arts from another, is the internalised history and experience of our improvising.

In the case of musical improvisation, this might be the specific jazz improvisations a musician has been involved with, along with theoretical knowledge of music and the subtleties and nuances of the specific instrument they're playing. In theatrical improvisation, this is our history and experience of theatrical improvisation, both on stage and off, and the rules our unconscious has assembled to allow us to progress improvised scenes.

But different domains of improvisation also use different amounts of the conscious vs. the unconscious. Ultimately, as an ideal improvisor, our unconscious will be doing all of the work. But the practice of improvisation is rarely at the ideal level.

Thinking

As beginners, we are almost constantly thinking as we improvise. And during training that's mostly a good thing. Only by actively thinking about what we're doing, along with putting it into practice, can we learn and internalise improvisation. Once internalised, we can let the unconscious do the work instead, and then we can start thinking about the next thing we wish to learn. The best improvisors are always learning, and unless they're doing exactly the same style of show every night, there will be things they are constantly thinking about in their improvisational ability. Not as actively as beginners, but certainly to some degree.

Getting the balance right between thinking and not thinking can be difficult. I spent my first 2 years thinking almost the whole time I was on stage. What should I do next? What's my scene partner trying to do? What's something funny I can push the scene towards? What template that I've been taught does this scene look like? Now I know better. When I want to, I can be using almost 100% of my unconscious to do the work, I will respond in the moment to everything that is happening now, and my conscious will sit back as an informed audience member and just enjoy the scene.

But I rarely do that. Instead I'm thinking maybe 20% of the time, working on internalising new skills, figuring out how better to work with new scene partners, making the odd conscious choice in a scene, sensing audience responses, and generally trying to improve my ability and enjoyment. When I'm improvising and just sitting back watching and having fun, this can cause conscious thoughts about how much fun I'm having. I'm not thinking ahead or thinking about what to do, but I am thinking while I'm not thinking.

We'll look at game of the scene later, but it's worth considering part of the UCB method in our discussion on thinking. The UCB method breaks a scene down into two parts: the base reality at the beginning of the scene; and the game part for the rest of the scene. I heard an interview a few years back with an experienced UCB improvisor who said that the game heightening part is the sketch writing part of the scene, and that writing a sketch is a conscious thinking process. It's crazy that experienced improvisors can still think that thinking ahead, or playwriting is a good thing. The game or sketch writing part becomes more of an internalised unconscious skill over time, but if you're actively thinking ahead, you fall into the same traps that all other thinking ahead falls into: namely, bad improvisation.

Yes, thinking happens, so let's not be precious or fool ourselves that the scene is always there unconsciously in front us and that our conscious is completely blank. Nobody improvises that way, it's an unattainable ideal, even though some of us think we do. If we are thinking then that's OK, we should just make note of it and see if we can do less of it next time.

On the other hand, we should certainly be thinking while in class or at rehearsal, as that's where we learn the skills that we want to internalise.

Choices

One of the stronger arguments against letting the unconscious do all the work in improvisation, is when we talk about choices. *Truth in Comedy* talks a lot about choices, and about always taking the active choice, the choice which leads to something happening. Yet it also talks about letting the unconscious do the work. Choice by nature is a thinking decision–making process. Choice is the weighing up of different options and deciding which one to go with. So how do we reconcile this contradiction with leveraging the unconscious?

Keith Johnstone doesn't refer directly to choice, because he believes that the unconscious should be allowed to express itself without having to consciously choose anything from a list of options. He said that:

> the inspired improviser is the one being obvious, the one who accepts their first thoughts, not weighing one idea against another.

Much of Johnstone's impro system involves removing anxiety, engaging with a stream of consciousness and making bold unfiltered offers to advance a scene. His work teaches improvisors to internalise a balance between making bold and active choices which are also obvious choices, and makes this — the stream of consciousness, advancing and progressing story — a key part of his method. Spontaneity comes first, then scene progression techniques are built from there, which contributes a lot to why Johnstone based scenes can sometimes get crazy and absurd.

Many improvisors who've worked with Del Close, speak of him calling for the third choice when directing scenes. The reason is that the first choice was usually too crazy, jokey or bland, the second more relevant, but the third being a better active choice. In both *The Compass. The Improvisational Theatre that Revolutionized American Comedy* by Janet Coleman and *The Funniest One In The Room* by Kim Johnson, Close recalls "take the unlikely choice" as being a phrase of Elaine May's, which is understandable considering that one of the St Louis Kitchen Rules is to take the active choice. The St Louis

Kitchen Rules were developed by Elaine May and Theodore Flicker in 1957 as early principles of Chicago method improvisation, and we'll look at this in more detail in the next chapter.

In her book *Art By Committee*, Charna Halpern says Del meant that the first thought is usually a knee-jerk reaction, the second is usually better, and the third is probably the best and the most intelligent. Some have instead said that the first choice is usually too obvious, the second too crazy, and the third somewhere in the middle. And in his book *Theatrical Improvisation, Consciousness, and Cognition*, Clayton D. Drinko says that Close wanted players to slow down in the early days so they could consider second and third choices, which would be more creative and unique.

Regardless of the origin of the phrase, Close would keep asking for different choices until a good choice was made, and this is now referred to as taking the third choice, even though the original intention may have been simply to look for later more active choices.

The problem with choosing is that it is a conscious act. So are we now supposed to stop being present and think about our choices?

In the Chicago method, conscious choices serve two main purposes: they're training wheels through which scene progression is learned, and they ground scenes by providing some conscious filtering. By learning about choices, by making choices in a scene, we're training our unconscious to see options that work better. We are internalising active choices, in the same way that Johnstone's work simply assumes active choices, and we're discounting some of the crazy absurd choices. When students first learn to improvise, the Chicago method teaches scene progression and spontaneity at the same time, hence the need for learning about choices early and before learning to be completely spontaneous.

While conscious choices may still need to be considered and taken on stage, the ideal is that they no longer need to be. As an improvisor gains more experience, the need to think and make conscious choices becomes less and less. Not because we aren't making choices, but because the unconscious learns how to do it by itself. Choosing between options becomes internalised, something that's given more focus when training in Johnstone's methods.

So by all means be aware of choices and train in the act of making active choices, but the end goal is the internalisation of this skill to immediately take the best choice, so that we're no longer consciously doing so.

At this point it's worth mentioning a training exercise called "New choice!", which is often used as a short-form game. An offstage director calls out "New choice!" and the improvisors must change their last action to something different. This seems like it has been based on Close's direction on choice, but the origins aren't clear, as the exercise has also been presented as a Johnstone technique. The exercise itself is useful — because it trains you in active choices — but it is often used as a short-form performance game where the new choice is often used as a comedic device. Because changing choices mid-scene often changes what's already been invested in the scene, this works much better with Johnstone's short-form impro than the Chicago method, due to it often being more frantic, having a focus on story, and the absurdity curve. As a short-form game, it may provide some initial amusement for an audience new to improvisation, but it is best used as a training exercise in choices.

Rules, guidelines and principles

At this point we also need to talk about rules. Because once we begin learning methods for progressing scenes, we need to figure out what we must and must not be doing in scenes, what we should and should not be doing, and what other options we may or may not have available to us. So should we follow rules in improvisation?

When we talk about rules, we're not talking about the rules of an exercise or a game in the short-form or theatre games sense. We're talking about statements which guide the way we improvise, such as "Don't deny the reality of the scene" or "Support your scene partner".

Mick Napier was the first improvisation teacher to popularise the idea that there are no rules, even though he wasn't the first to teach it. His book *Improvise: Scene from the Inside Out*[71], opens by explaining that rules about how to improvise were most likely developed over time by people identifying

---

[71] The book *Truth in Comedy* by Charna Halpern, Del Close, and Kim Johnson, was written ten years before Napier's book, and similarly talks about rules, stating that ultimately "There are no rules". However Napier was the first to concentrate on this core idea and is now the principle reference for it.

bad scenes, and then figuring out what these bad scenes had in common. His point being that things that are common in bad scenes may not necessarily be the cause or effect of bad scenes, and they may even exist in good scenes. Playing by a set of rules may force you to only discover a subset of all the possible scenes that do work, and you've therefore excluded a whole bunch of great scenes that clearly break those rules.

Rules for improvisation go back to at least Jacob Moreno in the early 1920s as he explored how improvisation worked. There were rules developed in the late 1950s for the Chicago method[72] of improvisation, but they were more about the core principles of improvisation than a set of rules — though they were still called rules. More recently in their book *The Upright Citizens Brigade Comedy Improvisation Manual*, UCB state that their "rules" are required in order to improvise in their style. And much like UCB, Keith Johnstone in his two books defines most of the rules required for his impro method, and following those rules is required as part of improvising within his system.

While Napier states that there are no rules, he then goes on to give some new rules to follow, such as: hold on to what you've got; look after yourself first; and don't overload the beginning of a scene with lots of exposition. No wonder improvisors find Napier's book inspiring, but then often go back to boxing themselves in with rules.

"Look after yourself first" is an interesting theory, and at face value seems to contradict the whole point of improvising: accepting others people's ideas, building on them, and supporting them without ego. Napier's point is that by looking after yourself first, you're giving your scene partner information to work with. This is often misunderstood to mean taking over the scene, or "bulldozing" in Johnstone parlance, or indulging the ego, but it's not. It's about building a foundation upon which a rich scene can be built together. Most theatrical improvisation classes teach much of this anyway when they look at building a character with physicality, emotion and point of view. Therefore most of what Napier is doing is simply extending what is already taught, clarifying it's utility and labelling it.

---

[72] Specifically, the St Louis Kitchen Rules at the St Louis *Compass Players*, but the original *Compass Players* as well as *Second City* also developed rules of improvisation.

When Napier, Johnstone and UCB are talking about rules however, they're not all using the same definition of the word "rules", and that's what makes it confusing for newer improvisors. Instead, I prefer to use the terms "core principles" and "guidelines", to be more specific about their intent. They aren't fixed classifications, but they're useful for refining the more generic and even less specific term "rules".

Whether an instruction on how to improvise should be considered a core principle — how improvisation works — or a guideline — to keep this in mind as a general case — is up to the improvisor and the method or style they're improvising with. But generally, core principles are mandatory, they exist to make improvisation work, and guidelines are what most people still call rules: optional training wheels for beginning improvisors.

Even within the various improvisation methods there are contradictions about what you should and shouldn't do, how often to apply them, and in what circumstances. So improvisors will often flog a guideline — formerly "rule" — to death until they understand it or are sick of it, at which point they'll either internalise it and integrate it into their play as a skill they can draw upon when needed, or give it up as no longer useful. But not all guidelines are equal, just as not all styles and methods are equal. And not all guidelines apply in all styles and methods.

In Napier's case, "hold on to your point of view" sounds like a rule. It's not a core principle of improvisation, because there are lots of theatre games you can play without doing so. Longer scenes will also eventually require changes in point of view[73], and if that's the case then how long must a scene be before being allowed to change point of view? So this now seems more of a guideline to be followed to improve our chances of improvising a good quality short long–form scene. Point of view was derived as a way for unscripted characters to focus on an intention or objective. This comes originally from script analysis, an acting technique invented by Stanislavsky for breaking down scenes into beats and character objectives. So it is actually more of a core principle of acting and scene work than an improvisation guideline or a core principle of improvisation itself. But a character's point of view according to Napier should be kept for the duration of the scene, whereas scripted scenes

---

[73] Napier does say that longer scenes should still maintain the same point of view, and explains why. That's his opinion based on the improvisation he teaches and performs, and we will look at point of view in more detail later.

do not have such a restriction. This does seem a bit contradictory when we consider Napier's original argument that excluding scenes based on certain criteria — in this case character point of view carried through an entire scene — is a bad thing.

Guidelines are training wheels. When we learn to ride a bike, we use training wheels to learn the easiest skills, and to take away the need to learn the more complex skills such as balance. The training wheels allow us to focus on pedalling, sitting on the seat, steering and braking, and understanding the individual limits of each. But training wheels also reinforce the idea that the bike remains upright and balanced while performing all of these other actions. As the training are gradually raised, balance is slowly introduced, and once the training wheels are completely removed, not only are we learning about balance and unlearning fixed stability, but we're also learning that there are less limits to the skills we've already learned. We can now lean the bike at an angle, while standing up on the pedals and turning the handle bars at an angle, and this allows us to steer more acutely than when the bike was upright with training wheels. While we have mastered the basics, removing the training wheels opens us up to all the possibilities we didn't have with them on, including those that contradict what we originally learned about balance and steering.

Improvisation is the same. Newer improvisors are given an environment where they are learning skills such as stage presence, voice, character, story, emotion etc. in scenes controlled by guidelines that hopefully give them a better chance of not having to worry about the quality of the scene, and thus anxiety creeping into their play. After a time, the wheels come off and the improvisor can explore the vast expanse of possible scenes, while having a basic knowledge of improvisation that will keep them from going astray. Or at worst, would leave them fearful or untrusting of their ability to improvise.

The problem with this is that the guideline may become internalised as a core principle. However this is a matter for teachers to address in the way they introduce and facilitate such exercises.

Different teachers and different methods will tell you different things about specific guidelines, regarding whether they should be followed or even if they actually exist. But core principles and guidelines are important, not because they should be either followed or ignored, but because of the knowledge that is derived by understanding them, regardless of whether they're valid or not, and regardless of whether you use them or not.

"Don't ask questions" is a great example of this. When I was a beginner improvisor, we were taught a theatre game called "Scene With/Without Questions", where we would improvise a scene either with every line being a question, or without any questions at all. The theory was that asking questions was bad, because it made our scene partner do all the work in providing detail, so improvising a scene without questions would train you not to ask questions. But as I learned later, asking questions isn't the point, it's the lack of contribution to the scene that's the point, and that questions are a more common opportunity for improvisors not to contribute.[74] This often comes from our anxiety as an improvisor. If we don't know what is going on, then we tend to ask about it. "Why are you here?", "What are you doing?", "What's that?", they're all questions designed to inform us so we can reconcile our misunderstanding. And in improvisation, questions make the other player fill in most of the information for the scene. Therefore "Scene With Questions" is the better exercise, because it teaches us to ask the kinds of questions which also contribute information to the scene.

For example, the initiation "Why are you here?" gives some information about the context of the character being here. Their scene partner feels that their character is not expected to be here, but the line has given them little else to go on. They end up having to provide that information instead of the original player.

"Why are you here Wendy, you're supposed to be at work" is obviously a more useful question, because it contributes more information, but "Wendy, I wasn't expecting you home so soon. Ummm... Have you met Jack, our plumber?" contains pretty much the entire premise for the scene. This kind of hard initiation is only going to work in certain styles, such as short-form or in scenes which are required to start with a premise.

---

[74] Keith Johnstone refers to a Questions Only Game in his book *Impro for Storytellers*, but aside from that the origin of such games is unclear. Perhaps this is why there has been such a misunderstanding of the point of the exercise, along with a thirst for new games that newer short-form improvisors generally have. *The Improv Handbook: The Ultimate Guide to Improvising in Comedy, Theatre, and Beyond,* by Tom Salinsky and Deborah Frances-White discusses the misuse of this exercise in much more detail.

So not all questions are empty of information, and it's certainly possible to perform a good scene composed entirely of questions.[75]

But who cares? Whether you use it as an exercise in asking better questions, or as a hoop to jump through for a naive audience, the more useful insight from "Don't ask questions" is the understanding of what it means. By internalising our understanding of how information is conveyed and received in a scene, through the understanding of what "Don't ask questions" means, we become much better improvisors.

Another example of training wheels guidelines is the five levels of relationship between characters. Depending on the source, there are roughly five different levels of relationship: strangers; colleagues; friends; family; and lovers. Each relationship conveys a degree of closeness between the characters in a scene. And closeness more often defines how vulnerable and willing the characters are to open up with emotion, and truth and stakes, which is what we want in a scene.

Lovers for example will be completely open in a scene, making them the easiest of relationships to turn into an entertaining, emotionally-driven scene. Strangers on the other hand will most often have a reservedness to them that can prevent them from opening up and being emotional. They protect themselves from the emotional intrusion of people they don't know, and end up mirroring the emotions and evasiveness of their scene partner.

We don't want our characters to be reserved and protected, we want emotion and stakes. And that's more likely happen the closer the relationship is between the characters. By simply defining a character as a sister or divorced wife, the improvisors and the audience immediately feel the intensity[76] of the scene — something which would be much less likely if the scene was between

---

[75] It's not uncommon these days to hear the don't ask questions rule debunked, yet here we are still talking about it. Napier made it extremely clear in *Improvise: Scene from the inside out*, and UCB thought it important enough to mention in their *Comedy Improvisation Manual*. This aversion to questions can at least be traced back to *Truth in Comedy* by Del Close, Sharna Halpern and Kim Johnson, where questions are discussed in some detail in the section on initiations and game moves, although they never say it is a rule.

[76] Improvisors TJ Jagodowski and David Pasquesi use the terms heat and weight to break down the relationship and intensions of the characters at the top of a scene, with heat being the relationship between them — including the intensity and closeness of that relationship — and with weight being the interaction between the characters that happened just before the scene started — what the scene is continuing on from or being influenced by.

two strangers. Obviously portraying these characters is not about simply labelling them as sister or divorcee, it's about the emotion and point of view that the characters in that relationship might have.

The other issue with relationship levels, is the discovery of new things about the characters. If the characters have only just met, then much of the scene will be character exposition, the characters are learning about each other instead of playing the scene about the relationship between them. Strangers more often have not known each other for very long, which makes it even more difficult where there is emotional distance and reservedness, as well as ignorance of their scene partner's character.

But true lovers and friends can raise other problems for improvisors, such as more tolerance, less miscommunication and less friction. As we get to know people better, we test the boundaries of what we can say and do. The first time we criticise a friend for a choice they make, is a high stakes action, but if the friend is close enough, then they'll accept it graciously and become a closer friend. The next time this happens, there will be less stakes, and as we become closer, there are much less possible high stakes issues between us. We go through these cycles of friend testing until we find the closest distance between us which works for both of us, each time reducing the stakes of our possible interactions.

So, for medium experience improvisors, dynamic relationships somewhere between colleagues and lovers may be the better option. But for beginners, it may be better to choose characters who are close and familiar with each other. As we get better at improvising, we learn how to emote and engage with an audience with characters who are less familiar. This makes it easier to make scenes work at any distance, and subsequently we no longer need to care about the distance of a relationship.

While these relationship guidelines are valid for both the Chicago method and Keith Johnstone's impro, Johnstone also developed additional techniques — such as his work on status transactions and other techniques he discusses in *Impro: Improvisation and the Theatre* — that he felt made it easier to define and play a relationship between strangers. In fact one of his key intentions in developing his system, was in order to allow relationships between strangers.

Transaction scenes are another example. Transactions usually involve strangers talking about a transaction — such as buying something from a shop — and not dealing with the emotional engagement that comes with their relationship. For this reason, many improvisation teachers recommend against doing transaction scenes. But it's not the transaction that's the issue, it's the emotional reservedness of strangers and the talking about a transaction that are the problems. And if you work around those, then many transaction scenes can indeed be brilliant.

A scene between a father shopkeeper and his delinquent son the customer, has a great chance of being a good scene, or even better if the status is reversed and the father is the hard on his luck but happy customer and the son the more successful but unhappy shopkeeper. Take off the transaction scene training wheels and you can have some great scenes, even between strangers. In fact many of *Monty Python*'s best sketches are exactly that, transaction scenes between two strangers, where the dialogue of the transaction drives the characters, emotion and comedy forward.

Rules and guidelines are useful because we internalise the knowledge we gain by understanding them. Don't throw away guidelines because they're training wheels or because they limit the number of possible great scenes. Throw them away because the reasoning behind them has been internalised, and the guideline is no longer needed.

Discovering the scene

As we've previously alluded to, beginner improvisors often think about improvisation as "making it up". The problem with this phrase is that it gives the impression that we're inventing, which implies thinking. Improvisation however isn't about inventing or thinking, it's about responding immediately to the now, the current moment, without any planning.

Strangely enough, it is not unusual for improvisors to briefly discuss where the characters' lives would have gone after they left the scene, particularly in a scenic long–form where you spend quite some time in a particular character — which is odd if you consider that it is really just a made up scene with made up characters.

As with our Zen practitioner earlier, when I first learned to improvise, I wasn't taught not to think. Sydney isn't one of the big improvisation hubs, but we do have a long history of improvisation, and yet it took me several years to figure out that it is not about thinking. In fact, I don't remember being in any single workshop or class in my first 5 years of improvising where I was ever told not to think.

Of course you *can* plan and invent while improvising if you wish, and there are a lot of short-form troupes around the world that do this. But it is not improvising in the purest sense, and it is not going to give you the best results. For beginner improvisors, trusting in "not thinking and that everything will be OK", can be difficult to accept.

Vast amounts of information are flowing out of an improvised scene, to which improvisors are responding in the moment, which in turn generates even more information for the improvisors to respond to. So if multiple improvisors are responding immediately to everything that's happening, there's not only no time to think ahead, but it is impossible to think ahead because you never know what the other improvisors will do at any given moment. Yet it is not uncommon to hear improvisors saying they were trying to steer a scene toward a certain point, or they were trying to include an idea they had into the scene.

A better way to consider improvisation, is as a process of discovering the scene that's already there. There are an infinite number of scenes that you could possibly be in at any moment, you just need to wait and see which one it is. At first this sounds weird, because we are still making it up as we go, and nobody has yet written down every single possible scene there is. So why do we care how we approach the unfolding of a scene?

The use of the word *discovery* has some interesting effects on how we process information, and this is what makes it a good approach.

If we consider that we're simply discovering something that has already been invented, then psychologically there is less pressure to invent something new, less pressure to be in control and there's a sense of fait accompli. In his book *The Paradox of Choice – Why More Is Less*, Barry Schwartz suggests that:

> *When people have no choice, life is almost unbearable. As the number of available choices increases, as it has in our consumer culture, the autonomy, control, and liberation this variety brings are powerful and positive. But as the number of choices keeps growing, negative aspects of having a multitude of options begin to appear. As the*

> *number of choices grows further, the negatives escalate until we become overloaded. At this point, choice no longer liberates, but debilitates. It might even be said to tyrannize.*[77]

This is what happens when we invent in our scenework, the sheer number of choices overwhelms us, and we begin to depend upon tricks and playwriting — the writing of the scene in our head. This includes tricks such as stock characters that have already been practiced time after time, black–out jokes — jokes which end a scene with the lights quickly fading out — that are known to go down well with an audience, and a focus on what the self wants to do, instead of what the scene and scene partner need.

Discovering the scene puts us in a mindset of wanting to see what happens next, without having to force it to happen or to make up something up. Discovery is about discovering the next little thing, and the delight we have when that next little thing is discovered, without us having to do any work to make it happen. Trust that the scene is already there, and it will happen regardless of what we do.

The Cone of Candidate Scenes

When we begin to improvise a scene, before anything else happens, there are an almost infinite number of scenes that we could possibly play. Every scene that could possibly be played, could potentially be this very scene. After the first few seconds however, the number of scenes that this could potentially be, greatly decreases, especially once we get to more significant information from the scene, and the circles of expectation with the audience also kick in. For example, if I start a scene as a female character, then all of the scenes that don't have women are no longer possible.

As a scene progresses, the number of candidate scenes, scenes that this could possibly be, decreases. So if we're near the end of the scene, we still don't know which of the many possible scenes which contain for example a dog, a spatula and the spoken dialogue "It is damn it!" this scene is, but it is one of them. Is it the scene with all those things plus the death at the end? Or is it

---

[77] Schwartz tells the story of how he went to buy a regular pair of jeans, only to find that the number of different types available was huge, and that the more he explored the different options, the more convinced he was that there was a pair that would be perfect for him. The number of choices increased his confidence that there was a perfect choice, even though there wasn't, which in turn increased his negativity about not being able to find that perfect choice.

the one with the wedding proposal? Only at the end of the scene do we know which of the almost infinite number of scenes this actually is.

The moment when we have the most information about what happens in a scene and what that scene is actually about, is when the scene ends. And the point when we have the least information about what the scene is about, the point where we have seemingly endless possibilities and tangents to explore, is at the very beginning. Why would we plan anything at the top of a scene and wreck one of the more exciting things about improvisation? That this scene can go anywhere, and there's everything yet to play for! Any guessing or thinking before the scene ends is wasted effort, and anyway, we'll have more than enough time for thinking about the scene and tearing it to shreds once it is over.

This is one of the most exhilarating and addictive things about improvisation. Not the end goal of completing the scene, but what we will discover if we just let the scene take us along with it.

1950s to 1960s

The mid–1950s to early 1960s is a unique time in the history of theatrical improvisation, as it transitioned from a scenario–based art form and acting and sketch devising technique, into a performance craft for improvising new scenes on stage and from scratch. New techniques had to be invented to allow a scene to progress while improvised, and new uses were found for improvisation in the processes for creating theatre.

Viola Spolin

In 1955, Spolin returned to Chicago to conduct workshops at the *Playwrights Theater Club* and later *The Compass Players* and *Second City*, which led to her publishing her book *Improvisation for the Theater* in 1963. From there she started a game oriented performance and actor training company named *Game Theater* with her son Paul Sills in Chicago in 1965, and she continued to run both public and private theatre company programmes until her death in 1994. Her work has continued to have a significant impact on improvised theatre to this day.

David Shepherd

David Shepherd was born in 1924. And while improvisation pioneers such as Keith Johnstone, Del Close and Viola Spolin receive much of the credit for the development of modern theatrical improvisation, it is Shepherd who almost singlehandedly kick started many of the movements and groups that pushed improvisation forward in the U.S. Shepherd's influence can be found in the *Playwrights Theater Club*, *The Compass Players* and *Improv Olympic* in Chicago, the *Canadian Improv Games* in Canada, and countless other improvisation based projects to this day. He may also have indirectly influenced the development of *Theatresports* via the popularity of *Improvised Olympics* and *Canadian Improv Games* in Canada.

Shepherd had been to Europe and seen their politically inspired cabaret[78], and by 1952, he'd decided to create a workers' cabaret theatre in the U.S. — a theatre produced, directed and acted by regular working people. Moving to Chicago with $10,000[79] family inheritance money, Shepherd quickly realised that regular working people did not have the same interest in a community theatre. Instead, he soon found himself at the University of Chicago and their burgeoning intellectual and arts communities.

The Compass Players

In the 1930s and 1940s, the University of Chicago went through a revolution under the guidance of president and then chancellor Robert Hutchins. His changes included more focus on philosophy, intellectual discussion and pursuits, and classic texts. He also removed the minimum age restriction for enrolling in an arts degree, meaning that so long as you could pass the exams, you could be admitted to the programme at any age. This led to an influx of younger, more arts focused students, often with more socialist leanings.

It was in this environment that the *Playwrights Theater Club* was founded in 1953 by a group which included Paul Sills and David Shepherd, with Shepherd providing financing of $7000. Shepherd had been impressed by Sills' direction and his use of Spolin's games — which had yet to be published — and thought they could eventually work together on his dream of a professional cabaret and theatre company with social commentary. *Playwrights Theater Club* wasn't that dream, but it was a start.

---

[78] In Janet Coleman's book *The Compass. Improvisational Theatre that Revolutionized American Comedy*, she says that Shepherd was in Europe studying cabaret, however other sources including Coleman, state that Shepherd was simply visiting Paris on his way back from India to New York.

[79] Sources vary on whether it was $10,000 or $15,000.

By 1955, Shepherd was unhappy with the direction of the group and felt it was presenting highbrow productions to a bourgeois audience. But it wasn't until the Chicago Fire Department closed down their theatre for being a fire hazard, that the *Playwrights Theater Club* disbanded, leading to Shepherd's founding of *The Compass Players*.

In Coleman's book *The Compass. The Improvisational Theatre that Revolutionized American Comedy*, she says that Sills' Spolin workshops had shown Shepherd that individual beats of a play could be improvised and sustained based on a "where" and a physical activity. Shepherd is referring to a beat as a scene, and not as a Stanislavskian unit of action, but still, in this case this would seem to be the beginning of a method for improvising scenes from a play.

Shepherd's idea for *The Compass Players* was to improvise a performance based on a rough outline of a story or play, which they called a "scenario", similar to *commedia dell'arte*. By using scenario plays and improvisation, they could effectively write, produce and perform a brand new play every week. Initially they wrote and performed a new 1 hour scenario every week for 10 weeks. Feeling the strain of constantly coming up with and working on new scenarios, this soon turned into performing each scenario for a few weeks, and then for a few months at a time. As they became better at improvising scenes, the scenarios began to have less importance, and the show became more of a revue, with sketches devised through improvisation, and games around which they could improvise.

By 1957 the Chicago company had ended, and a St Louis company of *The Compass Players* was set up consisting of Nancy Ponder, Jo Henderson, Ted Flicker as director/producer, and a 22 year old Del Close who was then new to improvisation. They were later joined by Severn Darden, and then Mike Nichols and Elaine May, who replaced Jo Henderson. While the various groups that performed as *The Compass Players* only existed from 1955 to 1959, it is the 1957 St Louis company that began to truly treat improvisation as an art in itself.

The St Louis Rules / Kitchen Rules

The St Louis Rules were developed by Elaine May and Theodore Flicker while with *The Compass Players* of St Louis in 1957[80]. They are variously known as the Westminster Place Kitchen Rules, the Boarding House Rules, the Landesman Kitchen Rules, The Compass Rules or just plain The Rules. This is due to them being developed in the kitchen of Fred and Paula Landesman, who owned the mansion they were staying in at 4411 Westminster Place, St Louis. Fred and his brother Jay owned The Crystal Palace cabaret venue where *The Compass Players* was playing.

The St Louis *The Compass Players* by then would perform what was then known as "spot improvs" after their main show. The cast would get suggestions from the audience, go back stage for 10 minutes to plan the corresponding scenes, and then they'd come back on and perform them. They'd then repeat the process however many times the audience remained interested.

They noticed that some scenes worked and others didn't, and set themselves to the task of figuring out why. Over a two or three week period — sources vary, even quotes from the cast members vary, often even from the same cast member — they figured out a set of rules which would make a scene work.

May and Flicker would spend each morning analysing the previous night's show to figure out what went wrong, and to see if any first principles could be identified. They would then bring the rest of the cast in for rehearsal, and use exercises they'd come up with to better understand the principle. They would then test the idea in that evening's show.

While the St Louis Rules were a key turning point for Chicago method improvisation, and are well known and quoted in certain circles, there is an interesting twist in the story. You see, very few sources strictly agree on what they are.

---

[80] According to Lee Gallup Feldman's dissertation *A Critical Analysis of Improvisational Theatre in the United States from 1955-1968*, The Compass Players at Crystal Palace opened on 2 April 1957, and that Flicker stayed four months before heading back to New York. Considering the St Louis Rules were developed during the show's run, this would date their development to roughly April through July 1957. Gallup Feldman does not mention the Kitchen Rules, so it safe to assume that she was unaware of them or their development.

The first reference in print, is an interview with Del Close in Jeffrey Sweet's 1978 book *Something Wonderful Right Away*. Close says that the whole group came up with three principles of improvisation:

1. Don't deny verbal reality.
2. Take the active as opposed to the passive choice.
3. The actor's business is to justify.

In the same book, Flicker instead says jokingly that the rules are an eight week course, but had to do with three things: place, character and circumstance. Considering Flicker had previously been involved with *The Compass Players* in Chicago, was intimately involved with devising the rules in St Louis, and his mind potentially clearer than Close's over the intervening decades, we'd have to assume that his recollection is more accurate than Close, who was only experiencing his first improvised show when all this happened.

However, in *The Compass. The Improvisational Theatre that Revolutionized American Comedy*, Coleman says that Flicker recalled the Rules as being (paraphrased):

1. Don't deny the verbal or pantomimed reality.
2. It is better to take the active choice.
3. When there is no information given about the scene structure or character's motivation, you are the character in the moment.

But Flicker also says that these were rules already devised by the earlier Chicago *The Compass Players*, and that the rules they devised in St Louis were actually extensions to these. He says that scenes require a Who, a What and a Where, or to put it another way, a place, characters and their circumstances, which sounds a lot like the influence of Shepherd, Sills and Spolin. Amongst other discoveries, they figured out that argument and transaction scenes were to be avoided, and came up with exercises which avoided these kinds of scenes.

If Coleman is correct, then the first three rules were already *The Compass Players* rules from Chicago, and the St Louis Rules are instead the Who, What, Where and scene type discoveries — the type of rules that Napier refers to and that we're now calling guidelines.

And finally, in Kim "Howard" Johnson's 2008 biography of Del Close, *The Funniest One in the Room*, he states that the Rules are:

1. Never deny reality.
2. Take the active choice.
3. It is the actor's business to justify whatever happens on stage.

The most confusing rule amongst various sources is the third. Some see this as simply justifying the current reality, whereas others see this more about character and being in the moment. Close says that May came up with the term justification, after a cast member once said that their character wouldn't behave a certain way and asked "How can I justify doing that?" May replied that the actor's job is to justify, meaning that anything can happen because the character is the improvisor.

Johnson reconciles Coleman and Sweet, saying that the character is the improvisor, and therefore whatever happens on stage cannot not be in character. However, justification is more than that. Justification is an action which gives a believable reason for the next thing that happens in a scene. Walking through a previously mimed table for example, can be justified by saying that the table has moved somehow. And justifying why a character might be doing something, is just another instance of justification.

It would seem that the St Louis Rules aren't as obvious as they're often presented. And if Coleman is correct, then what are commonly stated as the Kitchen Rules aren't even the actual Kitchen Rules. They're the Chicago *The Compass Players* rules, and were devised during the early David Shepherd and Paul Sills years of *The Compass Players*, before Del Close had joined the group. In fact, the Kitchen Rules seem to more closely resemble the rules that Napier so derides.

Second City

After *The Compass Players* had ended in 1959, the idea of using improvisation to generate sketch content for a revue style show continued with *Second City*. The company was founded by Paul Sills, *The Compass Players* performer Howard Alk, and Bernard "Bernie" Sahlins — an actor and previously a producer with the *Playwrights Theater Club*. *Second City* went on to become the longest running comedy show in U.S. history, and is one of the most influential comedy theatre companies in the world today.

Keith Johnstone

By the 1960s, Keith Johnstone had developed his ideas on improvisation into a general theory of how to improvise scenes. To test the work he was exploring in his classes, he formed a group named *Theatre Machine*, which would create a theatre show based entirely on improvised scenes. *Theatre Machine* first presented demonstrations in schools and throughout the U.K., thus bypassing the censorship laws of the time, before moving into public theatre shows and touring Europe. Johnstone would host the shows and set up the scenes, and his troupe of actors would improvise the scenes.

At this point Johnstone started writing his first book *Impro: Improvisation and the Theatre*, which consists simply of 4 essays on improvisation: status — as in status transactions; spontaneity; narrative; and mask work. Johnstone says he wrote most of the essays in a short period in 1966, but publication was delayed until many years later in 1979, because he was unhappy with the essay on mask. Who knows how improvisation would be different today, had he published it a decade earlier. *Impro: Improvisation and the Theatre* was the first popularly available book to dissect status transactions in everyday life, and to present a self-contained method for actors to improvise narrative based scenes.

Johnstone's improvised stories weren't what you'd expect from a play or a novel, because his actors only had a few minutes to perform each story. His scenes were therefore often presented in compressed time. In one example Johnstone gives, a man rows a boat to an island, meets a girl, and gets chased by a bear, all in the space of a few minutes, which has little resemblance to real time or the time as used in most plays or novels. Some have said that because the scenes are short, the story must be compressed in order to fit. In reality, Johnstone's theories on story are actually based on compressed time, as can be seen when improvisors using his techniques perform long–form improv, typically a rather complex story still provides the backbone for a series of time compressed scenes.

Using improvisation in the theatre was fairly common by the 1960s, in both Europe and the U.S., as improvisation had become part of most actor training programmes. And directors such as Michel Saint–Denis — nephew of Jacques Copeau — would travel to various schools around the world and teach acting techniques such as improvisation and mask. In the U.K. for example, John Hodgson and Ernest Richards published their book

Improvisation in 1967, meaning they were probably in the process of writing it several years before Johnstone. *Improvisation* includes most of the requisite theories for theatrical improvisation, such as spontaneity, being in the moment, and listening and responding, although it does not mention status transactions. Both Keith Johnstone and John Hodgson are known to have come into contact with Saint–Denis and his methods leading up to this time. And Robert Newton's *Acting Improvised*, published in 1937, also discusses spontaneity, listening and responding, as well as the practical side of improvising publicly performed plays from scenarios[81] — similar to Moreno in the 1920s and *The Compass Players* in the mid-1950s.

Impro: Improvisation and the Theatre has become a classic text, due to Johnstone's original work on status transactions for scene progression, an all-encompassing method for improvising story-based scenes, and due to his moving improvisation outside of the theatre and acting world and into the public consciousness through *Theatresports*.

---

[81] Presumably Newton was aware of the U.K. government censor rules at the time about not allowing improvised performances in theatres. So either he just didn't care, or assumed his work would be performed in community or workers' theatres outside the areas covered by the law.

Scene progression

With the advent of improvised theatre, practitioners needed a way to be able to progress a completely improvised scene. Writers and directors are still to this day important in the creation of theatre, so how can improvisors progress a scene without them?

Spontaneity by then was mostly understood. We become present and spontaneous, and let our unconscious do most of the work enacting the internalised process of listening, agreement and action, with a little thinking thrown in for good measure. But spontaneity, listening, agreement and action aren't any use unless we have the knowledge and skills for creating theatre.

When using improvisation for developing characters, such as with Stanislavsky's active analysis, character acting skills are required for the unconscious to draw upon. Likewise, for example, with Mike Leigh's rehearsal methods — the actors work with Leigh on character acting and interaction between characters, having already trained as actors. And for developing scripts using improvisation, an understanding of story and plot is required.[82]

---

[82] Not all script writers have a conscious knowledge of story and plot. Many have simply developed that knowledge unconsciously due to their improvisation or other experience.

In theatrical improvisation, we are improvising a scene. And all the spontaneity, listening, agreement and action in the world isn't going to allow us to improvise a scene, unless we already know how to make a workable scene from nothing. To do that, we need to understand and have internalised the skills required for acting and theatre practice, and more specifically the skills for scene progression.

Scene progression is the way we progress an improvised scene. It's what most improvisation training focuses on, along with general acting skills. Yet every method — Johnstone's impro, the Chicago method etc. — has its own unique approach.

Playback Theatre for example, uses a more character based approach, due to the fact that they are usually given a story to follow as part of their improvisation. They are given characters to play with, and are given most of the steps to follow that will progress their improvised scene before they begin the scene.[83] *Playback Theatre* does use some of the techniques we'll look at as part of improvised scene progression, but typically their scenes are prewritten by the story teller and they have no need to make up a new scene from scratch.

Moreno's Psychodrama, one of the inspirations for *Playback Theatre*, also acts out real life situations which have already happened, or which need to happen as part of a client's therapy. And in most cases there is no scene progression, just a replaying, or role playing in order to reach into the unconscious.

When Moreno was experimenting with improvisation in 1920s Vienna, he would come with already prepared story outlines and often written dialogue. This technique continued with groups in the U.S. through to the 1950s, with prepared story outlines in the form of scenarios. These scenarios would be a series of actions which make up the story, with spaces between actions left for improvised dialogue and action.

Lee Gallup Feldman proposed in *A Critical Analysis of Improvisational Theatre in the United States from 1955-1968*, that while "Scenarios and scenes are created primarily through action [..] it is not necessarily the action which

---

[83] Playback Theatre uses set theatre games, called "show forms", which can be used at various stages throughout the show. Some of these leave interpretation up to the improvisors, with little guidance by the story teller. But the less input they are given, the more restricted the forms, so that they are more artistic pieces than improvised scenes. Most long show forms are guided by a lot of detail from the storyteller.

makes the scenes work". The actions in scenarios are the "catalyst [for] performers to meet on common ground". Instead it is the scene work itself which makes the scenario and scene, not the prewritten actions.

As groups explored the use of scenarios in the late 1950s, they began to develop better techniques for maintaining the scenes between actions. This made the actors better at improvising, and the scenes funnier for audiences. This then led to many groups performing just stand–alone scenes. The most important of these groups was the St Louis *The Compass Players*, for being the first documented example of a group doing so. It was also the call to action for Del Close and the future development of Chicago improv.

Once groups began to focus on improvising stand–alone scenes, audience suggestions tended to replace scenarios and prewritten material. At first, suggestions were taken from the audience at the end of the first act, planned out backstage during the interval, and then improvised in the second act based on a premise devised from each suggestion. This process was similar to performing scenario plays — they were improvised from a premise, but with a shorter preparation time and without the time-wasting actions between scenes.

In England, Keith Johnstone's work also began with written works. Members of the writers group at the Royal Court Theatre would improvise alternate scenes for plays, as part of their writing and review process. They too developed techniques for progressing scenes, with Johnstone continuing this work through his acting classes, his *Theatre Machine* touring group, and the early development of *Theatresports* with students in Calgary.

Which brings us to scene progression techniques themselves. As we know, different techniques were developed by different groups, for progressing a scene. If you consider that a play is simply a sequence of beats connected by actions, then surely everyone would have developed the same or similar techniques for how to progress an improvised version?

But we need something more if we're going to use improvisation to create entertaining made–up scenes which have no preplanning or guidance. For example, how do we know what comes next in a scene? And what things, if any, must happen in a scene in order to make it work? And for that matter, what does "make it work" even mean?

Whether we're playing the craziest of short-form games, producing a 22 minute piece exploring a single theme, or trying to improvise a two hour long dramatic play, the techniques we use to get there will be different. And while some practitioners have tried to force fit a single improvisation method to fit all show forms, it never works as well as the specific methods developed for each purpose.

Yes, there are two main mental "models" of scene progression in improvisation: Keith Johnstone's impro system; and the Chicago method. Within these two main models are various improvisation schools — literally school by school — which teach their own philosophy on top of the core principles of their model. Some philosophies focus more on specific attributes which they think are more important, or they may introduce their own principles into the model.

These variations — including individual player skills and artistic elements such as show formats, pace and theme — contribute to what we often refer to as "style". This much abused and multiple definition word was adopted at some point to try to explain the perceived differences on stage, back when everyone thought all improvisation methods and principles were the same.

Instead of calling this "style", let's call it what it really is: "different mental models of how improvised scene progression works", along with the corresponding "methods within those models", taught by particular "schools", each with their own "philosophy" and their own principles and guidelines. All of this together contributes to what we perceive on stage as a specific style.

The two main models of scene progression were developed independently for more than 30 years, on different continents, by people with different backgrounds, interests and influences. The fact that improvisors trained in different methods can work together on stage to varying degrees, is more about spontaneity, being adaptive, and coincidence, than the sharing of similar principles. Because as we'll soon see, the models don't really play well together.

The existence of two distinct mental models and the specific differences between them, can be difficult to explain, because the way we understand improvisation is already internalised into our unconscious. So any explanation is usually taken in the context of what we already think is the truth about improvisation. It's like explaining how to determine gender in the French language, to someone who only speaks English, or detailing how the earth's second moon affects early morning tides. What gender, and what second moon?![84]

When improvisation is taught, particularly when used for comedy, classes typically teach spontaneity, listening, action and scene progression, acting and theatre skills, all rolled into one class. It thus becomes difficult for students to unravel and identify which parts are shared between models, and which aren't. Spontaneity, listening and action are shared between models, as are acting and theatre skills, but scene progression is not.

Before we can understand the differences between the different improvisation models, we need to understand the exact meaning of some of the theory from each. The next few sections are just a small selection of theories from each model.

Offer and acceptance

The terms "offer" and "acceptance" were coined by Keith Johnstone in his first book *Impro: Improvisation and the Theatre*, and if you improvise with his method, then you're probably wondering whether you can skip this beginner's section. Offer and acceptance are the core principles of Johnstone's style of improvisation, and only a fool would deny that offer and acceptance are important or useful. Yet many experienced improvisors will not have heard these terms before.

In Johnstone's model of improvisation, any action the improvisor makes is called an "offer", and agreeing with the offers of other players is called "accepting". Thus the phrase "offer and acceptance". Improvisation begins when we start making and accepting offers, and many of Johnstone's exercises and teachings are based on discrete offers and the acceptance of them — for example, a verbal declaration of a change in story, or by unexpectedly pulling out a gun.

Yet surely offers are being made all the time, and by all improvisors, in the way they stand, move, speak, and emote? If so, then a slight move of a finger

---

[84] Learning that there are two models of improvisation is even more subtle and obtuse than this. A better example might be "specifying gender in the English language" and "how other moons affect the early morning tide", as the uninformed could still interpret them as using male/female and the moons of other planets respectively. Only once we know of grammatical gender and the earth's two moons, do the real meanings of those phrases reveal themselves.

is an offer. Even when a character is standing motionless on stage in the most neutral pose they can, they are still giving out offers. "I'm neutral" is an offer in this sense. "I've been neutral for 5 seconds" is a bigger offer. "I'm still neutral regardless of what you do" is even bigger. There are hundreds of offers being made every second by every improvisor in the scene, some subtle, and some not so subtle.

Once offers have been made, the improvisors in the scene then choose which offers to accept, including the improvisor who gave the offer. The choice of which offer to react to is based on a number of things, the main one being the experience and skill of the improvisor, but it can also be affected by the style of improvisation being used. They can choose to accept the slight finger move offer, or they can wait and accept a larger offer, say the whole body moving or a line of dialogue. Remember that doing nothing while waiting for an offer is also an offer in itself, and by waiting for later offers, the doing of nothing may have been misinterpreted and caused the scene to already move off in another direction.

Offers of this kind are accepted internally by the improvisors as they begin to understand the scene. There is no external indication that an offer has been accepted, we just assume that our scene partners have accepted them — we assume that all offers are accepted and agreed to. A finger movement may inspire a scene partner to see this as a status or emotional change, which is then simply noted by the scene partner. This in turn influences the offers they send out, and the cycle repeats.

For example, actor A moves a finger (an offer), which is accepted and interpreted and agreed to by actor B as a change to higher status. This might then influence their character to be more subservient, which might be expressed emotionally, and then they ultimately initiate their own offers through a line of dialogue or a physical change.

It's not an iterating or repeating cycle however, because there are hundreds of offers every second, coming from all improvisors in the scene. And acceptance isn't synchronised to offers — it isn't offer then acceptance then offer then acceptance etc. — even though many training exercises lead us to think this way. Improvisation is a continually happening process of accepting and integrating information. In fact it's more of an unregulated spewing out of offers triggered by the acceptance of other offers. Improvisors are like lighthouses. They're beacons continually sending out information, regardless of whether each piece of information is received as intended.

But here's the thing. If the above sounds confusing and new, then this is because I've tried to explain improvisation by combining both the Keith Johnstone and Chicago methods. This is often the understanding of improvisation by those who propose that all improvisation theory is the same. But as we can see, it makes limited sense, is part contradictory, and is not what we learned in improvisation 101.

There are no such terms as offer and acceptance in the Chicago method. Not only are there no such terms, but there's also no such concept as offer and acceptance. In the Chicago method, improvisors are acting, they're not making discrete offers. There is the concept of a move, which is more of a distinct conscious choice within a scene, but this isn't the same thing as a scene progressing purely through synchronised offers and acceptances.

In Johnstone's method, offers are clear actions, whether in dialogue or physicality, which advance the scene.[85] These offers are accepted with a responding action or dialogue, and then another offer is made.

Many of the differences between the Johnstone and Chicago models, come from the difference between Johnstone's offer and acceptance, and Chicago's acting and denial, so let's look at that next.

Denial and blocking

To deny, is for an actor to do or saying something which denies the reality of the scene as it has been discovered so far. It is the act of not agreeing with what has already happened. This is one of the closest Chicago method alternatives to Johnstone's offer and acceptance, along with "Yes, And…" — which we'll look at soon. It's not the same thing, but it is similar. In fact, it's closer to another of Johnstone's terms, blocking, which is an offer or action which blocks the advancement of a scene.

One of the problems with both denial and blocking, is that they're subjective. What seems to one player as a strong offer, could be interpreted by another

---

[85] In *Improvisation: The Guide*, a book on Theatresports and the use of Keith Johnstone's techniques in Australia, the author Lyn Pierse calls the stream of hundreds of offers each second "microcues (the slightest nuances)".

player as being a block if they aren't on the same page.[86] And because denial and blocking are subjective, this can cause improvisors to disagree with comments by other players or coaches about their play. But obviously the better the teacher, the better their ability to be objective.

The book *Truth in Comedy* says:

> *Denying the reality that is created on stage ends the progression of the scene, and destroys any chance of achieving a group consciousness.*

The example then given in *Truth in Comedy* is an incident that apparently…

> *[…] occurred during the early days of Second City[87], when Del [Close] and Joan Rivers were in the same company, and it rankles him to this day.*
>
> *One night during an improvised scene, Joan told Del that she wanted a divorce. Del responded as an emotionally distraught husband might, in the hope of getting her to reconsider. "But honey, what about the children?" She replied, "We don't have any children!"*
>
> *Naturally, she got a huge laugh. Naturally, she had completely destroyed the scene.*

While this is given as an example of denial, there's a fine line between denying a scene, and denying an assumed reality. The assumed reality is the reality that a single improvisor sees as their reality of the scene. This is based on their brain as a prediction machine, and the information that has appeared, and also hasn't appeared, in the scene so far. If the improvisor has an expectation or assumption of a reality, then obviously anything that contradicts it is going to been seen as denial. But assumed realities only exist in improvisors' individual heads, so a denial by a scene partner isn't

---

[86] I was once in a scene where a prince was trying to rescue a princess. There were about 6 people in the scene, and near the end people started getting killed, all of them in fact. It felt like a tragedy, and so when the prince and I were the only ones left alive, in a moment of inspiration I killed the prince as I died. But he refused to die. Several times. After the show, the prince said to me "Why'd you do that? I was trying to rescue the princess! It was a scene about rescuing the princess!" Not only was he playwriting, but from my perspective he was blocking my offers, or denying the reality of the scene. But to be fair, it had more to do with him being keen on the player who was the princess.

[87] Rivers was a Second City cast member for about a year in 1961.

necessarily denying the scene, or a denial to everyone watching the scene, it's just a denial to their own reality.

Close could well have followed up with any number of lines of dialogue which would have justified Rivers' line and continued the scene, such as "Don't tell me you sold them into slavery again!" or "You murderous temptress, you said those days were behind you!" or "What?! I'm not even their father?" for example. They're not great lines, but they still justify River's dialogue and continue the scene. Rivers' line is not a denial of the scene, but a denial of Close's reality of the scene.

It is very likely that Rivers indeed did not care about this particular scene, and as is implied in *Truth in Comedy*, said the line purely for a laugh. It is however clear from Rivers' own writings, that this scene could quite easily have come about due to Rivers responding to being type cast yet again in a supporting female role, or as a reaction to what she perceived as Close's arrogance or misogyny. In this case, it is then a question of whether she was consciously trying to trash the scene — in which case the intention was denial of the scene — or whether she was just taking a strong non–stereotypical point of view which she thought made sense — in which case it wasn't denial. Close also recalls this incident in his 1978 interview in Jeffrey Sweet's *Something Wonderful Right Away*, so it was obviously a strong emotional memory for him.

Perhaps this is just a bad example of denial, but in fact good examples are almost impossible to find with any but the most inexperienced improvisors. Most actions taken on stage can usually be justified in some way, used as part of the scene, or could in many cases continue as a better scene. If a male character in the middle of scene suddenly declares for example "Stop calling me Colin, can't you see I'm a woman.", this could potentially be called denial, but there's also any number of scenes where this would make sense. The number of candidate scenes obviously reduces greatly when this happens, but still, scenes can often be continued without too much negative impact.

Denial is often more an intention than an action, and therefore this is really a core principle or rule of improv: You shouldn't *intend* to deny the reality of the scene. If Rivers had fully expected there to be a reality which continued with her line, then her line wasn't actually a denial, it was a strong offer or move. While probably unexpected by most — including her scene partner — and perhaps not a particularly good choice and difficult to justify, it was still valid. On the other hand, if she had no intention of continuing her assumed reality of the scene, and was simply going for the joke, then the line was a result of her intentionally trying to deny the scene, but doing a bad job of denial. Same scene, different intention.

Denial is therefore not usually an offer or move that denies the reality of the scene, because such a move is rare. Denial is really an internal conscious choice, which affects the scene by sending out information which conflicts with the reality that another player has assumed. Some denials are stronger conflicts with the assumed reality than other denials, and these are the ones that are usually referred to when we talk about denials. Denials are more obvious with beginners though, only because they don't have a particularly strong justification skill, and they tend to panic when presented with a reality that they can't yet work through. They may not intend to deny, but panic and the inaction of their scene partner, or limited memory of what's already happened in the scene, makes it a denial. Had an experienced improvisor been in the same situation, it's likely it would not have been as obvious a denial and the scene would have continued.

Small misunderstandings occur all the time, even with experienced improvisors, where the other player's assumed reality is changed by a perceived conflict. For more experienced players, the effect of this is usually that the player will become conscious, think about the challenge to their reality, adjust their mental models, and then continue on with the scene. This is simply justification.

"Blocking" on the other hand, is a Keith Johnstone term, and refers to a set of general actions that can take place in a scene that blocks the progression of the scene. The examples used in Johnstone's *Impro for Storytellers* include denials similar to Rivers' "We don't have any children!", as well as actions that don't deny the reality but effectively roll back a scene a few lines before continuing on. They don't deny the reality, they just prevent useful advancing of the story of the scene.

For example, the following scene in *Impro for Storytellers* doesn't deny the reality of the scene, it just rolls back the scene by a few lines:

> Character A: Like a swim?
>
> Character B: Great!

Character A: Sorry, I forgot – the pool's empty.

If this minor exchange was ignored by the players, then the scene would effectively roll back to before the "Like a swim?" line, and then continue on. This would be a block according to Johnstone, as it is blocking the progression of the scene.

But we don't really know whether this is a block until the rest of the scene plays out, because it could be a scene about the inadequacy of a hotel and its staff. With the UCB method in particular, where the first unusual thing is used to find a pattern for a game, this could be a great start to a scene. In this case it isn't a block, it's the beginning of the game and the emotional stakes, for a hotel that keeps offering activities which aren't available.

Even if this wasn't a UCB method scene, there are certainly lines of dialogue that would continue the scene without denying the reality of the scene, or blocking the progression of the scene, such as "This hotel's not really living up to the standards in this flyer is it." As with Rivers' line, at the time it is delivered it is not clear whether it is a block, and it is only a block retrospectively. Often blocking and denial can only be determined at the end of the scene, and usually in those cases it's more of a lost opportunity than a denial, which can often make scene coaching more subjective.

Johnstone's blocking is about stopping the active story advancement of a scene, and is not about denying the reality of the scene. Acceptance is the agreeing to what the other players are contributing to the scene.

With the Chicago method, there is no equivalent to active advancement of a scene, and therefore no such thing as blocking the advancing action.

Denial and blocking are similar terms, but don't mean exactly the same thing. This can be confusing if you care about what each specifically means, but you don't need to, because you only need to know what one of them means — the one in the model of improvisation that you're using.

The Keith Johnstone and Chicago models

In Johnstone's impro, you make spontaneous offers that are perceptible actions, that attempt to actively progress the story of the scene, which are then individually but implicitly accepted by other players as the scene progresses. You can intentionally block the progression of these offers, but as Johnstone says, blocking is used to "kill stories". Anything which prevents the progression of a previous action, is considered a block and not good for the scene. This obviously then excludes a whole bunch of scenes that could well be good scenes, but that's the way his system works.

In the Chicago method, there's no such thing as a distinct offer of action. Scenes are a continually unfolding acting activity — acting without text — where the main rule is to not consciously attempt to deny the reality of the scene. Instead of active story progression, focus is mainly on the current thing that is happening in the scene. Sometimes choices must be made to choose a more active path, to prevent spontaneous crazy absurd choices or make choices which fit into a game — in the game of the scene sense — but aside from this, and assuming Napier is correct in his assessment of rules, you can do whatever you want and it is just part of the reality of the scene.

In both cases, the model has a trickle up effect. Advancing a scene with strong perceptible offers, will deliver a different style of scene to one where there aren't big perceptible offers. And as we saw with group mind, these effects are amplified over the course of a scene. But we're now starting to get ahead of ourselves.

So which model is correct, or which is best?

Obviously both are correct, or one of them would have been disproved and discarded by now. Their development on either side of the Atlantic has meant that each has had time to flourish and be refined into a working model for improvisation. As in other domains such as languages or sports, we're lucky to still have at least two distinct and working models that we can use for theatrical improvisation.

Arguing which is best is a fool's errand, because objectively each model has attributes which work better for certain circumstances. Each is better than the other at delivering certain styles of scenes for example, and often it can be as simple as just one method making better sense than the other for certain types of improvisors.[88]

The mental model that Johnstone improvisors have is not the same that Chicago method improvisors have. Blocking is not only not a term used in

---

[88] This was certainly the case for me. I learned one way, and it didn't work for my brain, so I switched to the other.

the Chicago method, but it makes no sense in that method because blocking is about advancing actions. The idea of a perceivable offer to advance action only exists in Johnstone's impro, so in the Chicago method it's like comparing apples to nervousness — it makes no sense.

Often practitioners try to resolve the differences between methods by using terms used by the opposing method. For example Chicago method improvisors are starting to use the term "offer", even though technically offers don't exist in the method. And Johnstone improvisors have started framing Chicago relationship scene techniques as active story advances, as a way of improvising more grounded or realistic long form scenes in the Johnstone method. But these kinds of techniques don't ever work as well as when used with the method for which they were developed.

The reason we've gone into such detail in this chapter, is to highlight the fact that these are two very distinct models. When we learn one of them, we internalise it. And when we perform with it, we — our conscious and unconscious — are performing within that internalised model.

Yes, and... and yes!

Theatre director William Ball wrote in his 1984 book *A Sense of Direction*, that the term "positation" describes the collaborative intuition of a theatre group. He says if we can "persuade all the individuals in this collaborative art to work within the same system [..] of respect for the intuition, the collective unconscious flourishes." His word positation has since lost this meaning, but the philosophy of it carries on. Ruth Zaporah's *Action Theater*, an improvisation technique for dance and movement, also embraces the idea of saying yes to the unconscious, or yes to what she calls the "arisings" from the unconscious.

It should be of no surprise that Ball was in San Francisco from 1967, and Zaporah from 1969. San Francisco at that time was becoming a melting pot of new ideas and experimentation in theatre, including the use of improvisation in various domains. Del Close was also in San Francisco at that time, working with *The Committee*, an improv theatre group that ran from 1963 to 1971. Ball also spent time in Chicago in 1966 when his *American Conservatory Theater* was just starting out, at the same time as *Second City* was reaching its seventh year. Whether it's called positation, arising, or "Yes, and...", the technique of saying yes and agreeing or accepting all ideas has now spread to many domains outside of improvised comedy, and is more a rallying cry for creative teamwork and collaboration.

The phrase "Yes, and..." specifically, comes from the Chicago method of improv. It's the technique of saying yes — agreeing —, then adding more — "anding". "Yes, and..." has no similar phrase in Keith Johnstone's impro. Offer and acceptance seems close, but as we saw above, the Chicago method has no notion of offers, as everything is part of the scene.

A more common phrase used by Johnstone's followers is "Advance and extend", where advances are made first and then detail is added later. For example "Mary was eating a banana. It was an almost fluorescent yellow, allowing her to see in the dark and stay healthy at the same time." An advance was made with Mary eating a banana, then the banana and eating are extended by adding detail.

While Johnstone's writings often refer to advancing, he doesn't explicitly mention advance and extend in either of his books. But there are implicit references and a few in other books regarding Johnstone[89]. In both of his books, he refers to advancing the story, advancing the narrative and advancing the action, and in *Impro for Storytellers* there is a short reference to extending platforms [90]. *The Book of Moose* — a newsletter written by Johnstone throughout the 1980s and early 1990s [91] — also discusses advancing[92].

"Yes, and..." refers to agreeing to something and then adding something more. *Truth in Comedy* states that "whenever two actors are on stage, they agree with each other to the Nth degree."

Agreeing is a continual process of accepting what is happening in the scene, which makes it similar to Johnstone's offer and acceptance. But in the

---

[89] The 1995 book *Something Like a Drug. An Unauthorized Oral History of Theatresports*, does define both advance and extend.
[90] We won't cover Johnstone's platforms and tilts in this book, but they're similar to the UCB base reality and game finding, but without the game finding. *Truth in comedy* also makes reference to Johnstone's platform ideas as breaking the routine.
[91] *The Book of Moose* newsletter was for the actors at the Loose Moose Theatre, and later for global licensees of Johnstone's various show formats. Much of it was also later reworked and included in his second book *Impro for Storytellers*.
[92] The Canadian Improv Games also have a game called Expand and Advance, where a director calls out either expand or advance and the players focus on the last called thing.

Chicago method, agreement is the most important rule, or as *Truth in Comedy* puts it "Agreement is the one rule that can never be broken: players must be in agreement to forward the action of the scene."

This harks back to our discussions on agreement and acceptance, but the origins of "Yes, and…" are more simplistic. *Truth in Comedy* says that "Yes, and…" is about characters literally responding in scenes with lines starting with "Yes, and…". Johnstone uses a similar technique in *Impro*, in that he also discusses literally saying "yes" for each line in a scene. Over time it became understood that it isn't about the *characters* literally saying "yes", it's about the *actors* saying "yes", as in listening and agreeing.

More recently "Yes, and…" has become even more problematic, and used as a kind of clunky mantra for living, meaning you should say yes to everything, "and" then… add to it. I don't know about you, but there's a lot of things in life I certainly wouldn't say yes to and then add to. And as a mantra, the point is probably more about the "anding" than the "yessing". As in go out do stuff, make stuff happen, and don't wait for something to come to you so you can say yes to it.

Now you could argue that the words themselves aren't too important, as when we improvise we're basically making offers and accepting them. But, the prevalence of "Yes, and…" in the Chicago community regarding agreement and advancing, shows us otherwise.

As shown in *Truth in Comedy*, the Chicago method focuses heavily on the "Yes" part of the phrase, with the "and" following it with slightly less importance. Even the way it is verbally spoken gives this impression, "Yes! And…" The emphasis is on an excited yes!

The Chicago method has, for this reason, a tendency to spend a significant amount of time agreeing to things, causing improvisors to focus on and explore the detail of offers. Improvisors will latch onto a statement or a word or a movement and become more and more detailed or focused on that last thing that happened. There is another common Chicago method phrase "deal with the last/current thing" which highlights this as well. You focus on the last thing because you're saying yes to it. And typically often Chicago method improvisors will use either dialogue or physicality to agree to "the last thing" and then explore it.

The following is an example initiation of a scene, as it might be performed by a Chicago method improvisor.

> MARK: Hi Frank. So this is your big new dog?
>
> FRANK: Yeah, this is Thug. He's a dalmatian guard dog.
>
> MARK: I'm not really into dogs, especially if they're called Thug.
>
> FRANKE: Do you have a problem with Thug, Mark?
>
> MARK: No. It's just that it's a pretty big dalmation.
>
> FRANK: All dalmations are big Mark.
>
> MARK: I think this one's a little too big.
>
> FRANK: Well I like them big. Thug's so big he just ate my other dog. … And he's still hungry, Mark.

Each line refers directly to the content of the previous line. As if each line is saying "Yes, yes, I know, and this too…"

The following is an example start of a scene as it might be performed in Johnstone's impro.

> MARK: Hi Frank. So this is your big new dog?
>
> FRANK: It's all about security, Mark. This is Thug, he's my killer guard dog.
>
> *Another player steps out and becomes the dog, which jumps on Mark licking him profusely.*
>
> MARK: Get him off me Frank! He can tell I'm a cat person!
>
> *Frank has an evil laugh.*
>
> FRANK: Ha ha ha! Now give me all your money Mark, or I'll have Thug and his friends…
>
> *More players step out and become dogs.*
>
> FRANK: …lick you to death!

In this case, each line is an offer of an idea, an advance in the story, and the following line accepts that offer by advancing the idea — the story — with a new offer.

In the example Chicago improv scene, there is a building tension about one character having a dog, whereas in the Johnstone impro scene there is an unfolding narrative made up of active story advances — new things keep happening.

If you analyse the Chicago scene with Johnstone's Advance and Extend, it works, but it isn't the larger narrative and action advances advocated by Johnstone. Conversely if you analyse the Johnstone scene with "Yes And", it's not quite right, there's no clear "Yes" bit in each line and there are missed offers or moves. It's mostly all the "and" part of "Yes, and", and the players could be accused of constantly ignoring "the last thing".

Either of these scenes could have been performed in either method, but they are examples of how the models generally apply to such scenes. As each method tends to build scenes in this manner, this helps contribute to why each seems slightly different when it is watched by an audience used to the other method.

These approaches to improvising aren't just on–stage techniques, they also tend to be used by improvisors when offstage in the way they typically riff off other players and non-players. Hang out with a bunch of Johnstone improvisors and the comedy will be more about riffing to advance a humorous idea into new jokes. Hang out with Chicago improvisors, and your joke will usually be drilled into, in a spiral of exploring an idea, pattern or game.

In Johnstone's impro, whether it be "Advance and Extend" or "Offer and Acceptance", the focus is always on making distinct advancing offers and moving forward first, then worrying about any supporting detail later. Ideas or offers which are not dealt with are "shelved" in case they come back later, such as the reference to licking in the above scene. This is then reinforced by the story requirements of Johnstone's system.

But Johnstone had also seen the Chicago method techniques used by *Second City* and Del Close at iO in the 1980s, and developed a technique to try to replicate what he thought was a kind of pausing of story, in his own method.

In *Impro for Storytellers*, he discusses "Advancing (And Not advancing)", a technique for drilling into the detail of the current action, by making it "more interesting". If I were to mime washing dishes, I might make that more interesting by focusing on my reflection in a plate, then I might use my breath to moisten a dirty spot and dry it off with a cloth, and then I might place it on the drying rack only to watch it slip off and smash onto the floor. Another example might be simply two people humorously discussing which colour socks are best, before the God of Smart Dressing appears and the scene begins in earnest. This is called not advancing the scene, and is unfortunately used most sparingly by improvisors using his method.[93] Some practitioners have said that this is still an advancing story according to Johnstone's method, but that's not what he's saying.

Johnstone's model is also most often used for scenes which are time compressed — long stories performed in a short scene. In such scenes it is important to move forward through the narrative, with improvisors only stopping to add detail when they feel they need to. Johnstone's method works extremely well for this kind of scene.

Even in scenic long–form improvisation — a longer series of scenes much like a more traditional play — using the Johnstone method will tend to time compress scenes without the audience or players realising it. Non-advancing lines of dialogue and action that you'd normally expect in a real-world scene or in the Chicago method are often simply left out.

The two methods, Chicago and Johnstone, have often been referred to as inward focused and outward focused respectively. While there are several reasons why these are appropriate terms, the main one is because "Yes, and…" leads to more inward focused scenes, dealing with the detail of the last thing, whereas "Offer/Acceptance" and "Advance/Extend" — as well as "Advancing (Not Advancing)", which by implication that it is an exception to the rule — lead to more outward focused scenes.

The phrase "Yes, and…" has been adopted by Keith Johnstone improvisors in recent years, but it isn't suited to Johnstone's methods, at least not in the

---

[93] *Impro for Storytellers* was published after Johnstone had visited *Second City* and Del Close at iO. It is certainly possible that he saw the types of scenes generated by the Chicago method, and integrated them into his system as Advancing (And Not advancing).

same way as it has been for the Chicago method.⁹⁴ If anything, in Johnstone's impro "Yes, and…" could possibly be phrased as "And… Yes!". Johnstone's method is all about making offers and active advances, so the focus is more on the "and" than the "yes". We're still "yessing", but not to the Nth degree before an advance.

Chicago scenes are highly focused vignettes connected by detours, where the players are working in synchrony to explore every detail as it arises. Johnstone scenes on the other hand are often actors independently and alternately making advances while the other players catch up and support them. Like a football team they move forward co-ordinated and supporting each other, but with individual control and artistic expression.

Considering the misinterpretation of "Yes, and…" as a literal line of dialogue, the differences in use between the methods, and the questionable use as a life rule, perhaps it's time to stop using the phrase as a catch all for everything in improvisation and life.

Scene attributes

Nothing stirs up arguments between the Johnstone and Chicago devotees more, than a discussion about story vs. relationship. Many believe that if there is a difference between the styles, then this is the main difference. But this ignores certain aspects of Johnstone's teachings, namely that he also believes that relationship is important. So why so much focus on story?

Scenes in the theatre, whether improvised or scripted, as well as scenes in real life, can be analysed by a number of different attributes which apply in various ways and to varying degrees. And while there are always exceptions in art and in life, for our purposes we're talking about the majority of scenes which always have them.

For example, all scenes have characters. Whether they be real or acted people, animals or objects, scenes have at least some kind of character who does the work of drawing the attention of the viewer. Scenes also have emotional content, and it is the emotional content which woos the audience into

---

[94] There is a Keith Johnstone exercise called "Yes, and", an exercise which is used for accepting offers, which reins in a tendency for Johnstone improvisors to make big advances, but it is not a literal philosophy of his method. He also has an exercise called "Yes let's!" which is all about commitment and agreement, but is out of context with what we're discussing.

empathising with or cheering either for or against the characters. Scenes also have a story, a running narrative of what happens throughout the scene. And they can also have an overarching game and individual games within the scene.

And then there are what could be called contributing attributes, such as the relationship between the characters, the backstory, the location in which the scene takes place — Spolin's Where — and the objectives and points of view of the characters. All of these affect the emotional content, the story and the characters.

And if we stretch this idea further, theatre games also have special attributes such as a goal to reach. For example, in an exercise like "Mirror" — where one player mirrors another — the goal is to mirror the other player. The leading and following are what drive the exercise — the scene — forward. Different games have different goals, but having a goal like this is another scene attribute.

With so many attributes available in the analysis of a scene, a common thought of beginning improvisors is to figure out — learn — how to progress a scene by contributing all of these attributes at once. Obviously some of the more structured or restrictive games or scenes are going to dictate focusing on certain attributes, but in open scenes where there are no or minimal restrictions, how can we possibly focus on everything at the same time? Especially if we're just a beginner.

Various teachers have different theories on which skills are required to generate these attributes in a scene. But the danger of this is that students will learn from multiple teachers, and then try to actively introduce once again emotion, relationship, story, backstory, location, game and all the other possible attributes, all at the same time, and then wonder why the scene lacks vibrancy, passion or comedy.

A common belief is that if all scenes contain all these attributes, then we need to make sure all this stuff is built into the scene by the improvisor. There is an almost infinite number of exercises that could teach players how to focus on all of these attributes individually, but that's not a particularly good idea considering how long it would take and how overloaded an improvisor's mind would be. The idea that we should experience all of these attributes in training is a good one, as understanding scene mechanics is certainly important. But focusing on all of them at the same time while improvising, simply doesn't work. What we find when players do this, is that even the most internalised skills and knowledge, can't compensate for all the conscious thinking involved with analysing a scene in progress. Let alone figuring out the right amount of each attribute which needs to be added to the scene. We just can't keep that many things in our conscious, or as active unconscious processes.

The reality however, is that many of these attributes affect each other, and by concentrating on only a few, the others will just naturally appear on their own. Different methods have their own techniques, which short circuit conscious awareness of many of these attributes.

A scene is a series of beats, which is driven forward by attention to specific scene attributes, whether it be story, relationship, game or whatever else a particular method would want to focus on. And this is what makes most improvisation methods different from each other.

This idea seems to have been lost in recent times and has contributed to the myth that all improvisation is the same. But even as early as 1967 this was understood as being the case, as John Hodgson's and Ernest Richards' book *Improvisation* states that there are different methods for improvising, and even lists a number or scene attributes for scene progression, including story, character, dialogue and theme.[95]

Let's look at story, one of the key differentiating scene attributes between Johnstone and Chicago. The Chicago method avoids any conscious development of story in a scene, because it is the relationship between the characters that makes the scene. This is true, but every scene still has a story. Regardless of what happens in a scene, a story will always be obvious by the end of the scene anyway, so why bother consciously writing one? Story is a retrospective artefact — scene attribute — of what happened after the scene ended. Focusing on story in the Chicago method simply detracts from what makes the scene work, the relationship between the characters — or more specifically, the emotion generated by the relationship between the characters.

---

[95] Actually, I thought I'd discovered this idea all on my own, until I came across their book. They don't mention scene attributes specifically, but reading between the lines it is in there. Likewise Robert Newton's 1937 book *Acting Improvised* describes a number of scene types which could also map to scene attributes.

In Johnstone's method however, it is assumed that the concentration on advancing story and status transactions, will automatically generate relationships between characters. And while he also says that relationships are important, it is the story structure that drives the scene forward, and it is the status transactions that drive the character interactions that form the relationship. Focus on the story and advancing offers, along with status transactions, and the relationship will then come as well.

Johnstone noticed that in real life we all play status games with the people we interact with without realising it, and he was able to codify a method for using these status transactions as a scene progression technique. We're not talking about relationship, career or character status, such as mother and daughter, boss and worker, or high status guard to a low status queen. We're talking about the status transactions that occur in everyday communications between people in the real world, constantly changing often every few seconds and with each line of dialogue.

By using status transactions, he felt he was able to do away with many of Stanislavsky's techniques for developing character and action from a script, such as "given circumstances" for finding character motivation and objective. However, Stanislavsky's work is for scripted theatre and rehearsed dialogue and action, and status transactions on the other hand are simply one of the attributes of a character and scene. So, while playing status transactions conveniently creates emotional responses and dynamics, it also makes sense that these are causing the actors to justify status — justification being a key technique for building scenes and creating comedy.

So what is story, and why would we want to focus on it?

A story is effectively a collection of events or actions which happen in sequence. Discoveries may happen along the way which change the reality or interpretation of earlier story points[96], but still, a story is a continually unfolding narrative.

Stories have a start and an end, however not all starts of stories are interesting. Jack and the Beanstalk for example, is pretty boring as a story, until his

---

[96] I like to think of story as what happened to the characters, whereas I think of plot as the way they're presented to the audience. For example, in the movie *The Sixth Sense*, up until near the end of the film, both the psychiatrist protagonist and the audience don't realise that he is dead. The story is about a dead psychiatrist, but the plot only makes that clear at the end.

mother scolds him about the beans and throws them out the window. If we were improvising this story for a short–form scene in order to simply reproduce Jack and the Beanstalk with a different genre or restriction, then it would be OK to simply play out the story in its entirety, less the boring bits. But if we were to perform only a part of the story, just one scene within the story of Jack and the Beanstalk, in real time, then the first scene we come across that's interesting is probably when his mother first sees the beans. And we wouldn't start the scene at Jack walking in the door, or even saying hello to his mother. The most exciting part, and therefore the best scene initiation, is possibly the mother saying "You swapped our cow for beans?!"

This is called "entering the story"[97], the idea that you don't start telling a story at the beginning, where time is wasted on exposition. You instead enter it at a key moment so that the scene is interesting from the moment the scene begins. This is particularly important in improvisation, as we'll find out later when we look at metapragmatics.

The story of Jack and the Beanstalk occurs in a real time of several days, so obviously we can't perform that story in a 3 minute improvised scene. And if we were to play just the key plot points, this would also take much longer than 3 minutes, yet short–form improvisors do this all the time. So how come?

Short–form and Johnstone method scenes often compress time. To replay the story of Jack and the Beanstalk, improvisors take the collection of plot points in the story, and play only the key seconds of those plot points. Not only that, but they also leave out any extraneous physical actions or dialogue which don't contribute to the main story — for example Jack's long walk from the bean merchant back to his house. The story is stripped to its bare bones. In improvisation this is a skeleton or time compressed story or scene.

If you're a Johnstone improvisor, you would generally play the skeleton story plot points, whereas if you're a Chicago method improvisor, then you would most likely play just one plot point, or at least you'd flesh out the detail within one or two plot points. With Johnstone, the fun is the transition from the cow to the giant, possibly with the odd moment along the way when more detail is required. But in the Chicago method, it is the emotional relationship

---

[97] Or "start in the middle", which is also the name of a section in the book *Truth in Comedy*.

or game between Jack and one of either the cow seller, his mother, or one of the talking collectibles from the giant.

Again this isn't a hard and fast thing, as Johnstone trained improvisors certainly do improvise real time emotional relationships as if scenes from a play, and often treat relationship as story in order to fit with his model. But his model works much better with time compressed scenes. In the Johnstone method for example, a scene at a table in a restaurant between two people, will typically escalate into absurdity or high drama, or progress through status transitions and emotional states at a higher pace than what would be the case in reality. Discussion between the characters would also be more likely to carry story advancing offers, giving the impression that the scene is about the relationship between the characters, but with larger story advances within that relationship. Whereas with the Chicago method, it would most likely be just a funny version of a scene you'd see in a dramatic play.

As we saw in the section on group mind, an improvised scene is a complex adaptive system, and one of the effects of such a system is the amplification of effects. When it comes to different styles, small changes in style tend to get amplified through emergence. In the case of Johnstone's impro, story tends to amplify throughout a scene, and in the case of the Chicago methods, relationship, and inward focus on the "last thing" tend to amplify, thus reinforcing these attributes of each method.

The two main models

Johnstone's scene progression begins with spontaneity, which generates offers of information that are perceptible nuggets of story that advance an unfolding scene, which are then accepted by corresponding offers, which acknowledge previous offers, and continue to advance the story. Detail is added — extended — as needed, and detours can drill into moments and detail from time to time — "not advancing". The progression of the scene can be blocked with certain offers which are out of context with the scene or story, causing it to pause or rewind, and the scene is often time compressed. Status transactions are used to create additional advances, emotion, and interesting character interplay, and characters are often caricatures or have exaggerated traits.

This is the mental model of many improvisors who learn and perform with the methods and techniques devised by Keith Johnstone, even though they may not realise it. This model has in the past been almost universally referred to by devotees as "impro", the title of Johnstone's first book, but in recent years this has begun to change to "improv". And while Johnstone's opinion and methods have changed in recent years[98], this is the model that he is known for today.

The Chicago model on the other hand begins with spontaneous acting without text, where a character is a thin veil over the actor, and which tends to be more realistic or less stereotyped than Johnstone's impro. Responses are played for truth, to the detail of what is currently happening, and with the focus on the emotional relationship between the characters and optionally the game of the scene. A scene is a story, but that's simply an after-effect.

Once you understand that the models are different — they focus on different scene attributes — other differences become more apparent as well. For example, as we'll see later when we look at short-form and long-form, Johnstone's impro has on average more laughs per minute — LPMs. His system allows improvisors to quickly skip from action to action, meaning the improvisors can optimise what is funny, which in turn causes the audience to laugh more than is average in the Chicago method, and is one of a number of reasons why Johnstone's method is more often used for short-form improvisation than the Chicago method.

Another difference is the amount of dialogue which is used. Because the audience is laughing more, they find it difficult to hear ongoing dialogue, so improvisors have two choices: either slow down and pause for laughter, or minimise dialogue in deference to physical comedy. This happens more often in Johnstone's system, and improvisors are more likely to mime physical objects, manipulate other improvisors and perform more physical comedy. The historical influence of clowning, mask, pantomime, and *commedia dell'arte* in Europe, also contributed to the physicality of impro. As such Johnstone based improvisors tend to train more in physicality and object work than do Chicago method improvisors, often leading to more "talking head" style scenes in the Chicago method.

---

[98] Theresa Robbins Dudeck's book *Keith Johnstone: A Critical Biography*, gives more detail on the origins of Johnstone's methods, and how his opinions have changed over the years up to today.

The increase in physicality also means that absurd physical comedy and the absurdity curve are also more likely with Johnstone based improvisors. The absurdity curve is the idea that in order to break the expectations of an audience, a minor step toward absurdity is required. And in order to break the expectation of minor absurdity, more absurdity is required, and so on and so on until maximum absurdity is reached[99]. This is called the absurdity curve, and is used a lot in comedy, particularly in theatre games where restrictions can often force improvisors into justifications which lead to absurd situations.

Coincidence, group mind and priming are more likely to happen in the Chicago method, due to the focus on specific detail and dealing with yessing the last thing. Whereas with Johnstone the focus is more on advancing the narrative, and so improvisors tend to draw more upon story over the course of a scene. With individuals advancing their own narrative more often with Johnstone's impro, this can create a degree of hierarchy amongst players in scenes, and according to complex systems theory, group mind isn't as obvious or effective in this situation. No wonder *Truth In Comedy* strongly discusses group mind, and Johnstone's writings do not.

At this point it's worth mentioning *Playback Theatre* again. Superficially it may look like they use a variation of Johnstone's impro in their longer scenes, because they focus on replaying stories. But take a closer look and that's not the case. *Playback Theatre* uses neither story nor relationship as a primary driver of scene work. The reason being that they're not improvising a new scene, but playing back an already described one. Techniques such as "Advance and extend" and "Yes, And" are for discovering a scene as it is created for the first time — for progressing a new as yet unknown scene. These are improvised scene progression skills, and when you're acting an already written story, there is no need for scene discovery. It is still improvisation — because there are other elements to discover such as characters, dialogue and emotion — but often many of the other scene attributes have also been locked in by the teller and conductor before the scene starts.

Playback Theatre's core short–forms — fluid sculptures and pairs — are short reflections on a theme or emotion, and thus also have no need for creating a

---

[99] There is a better and more detailed explanation of the absurdity curve in the book *The Improv Handbook: The Ultimate Guide to Improvising in Comedy, Theatre, and Beyond*, by Tom Salinsky and Deborah Frances-White.

scene with a story or relationship. Over the years many additional short–form improvisation games have been adapted for use in *Playback Theatre*, but they still all focus on the best possible matching of the improvisation with the teller's story, and thus have the same needs as longer scenes.

Playback Theatre uses neither the Johnstone nor Chicago methods because many of these techniques are redundant for the types of scenes they perform. But what about some of the other skills that a *Playback Theatre* actor needs? Where do they come from? Their style of play varies around the world, so my guess is that each *Playback Theatre* is influenced by the predominant improvisation method in their local area.[100]

Viola Spolin's theatre games on the other hand, progress scenes using a focus or goal, which sits on top of other pre–set scene attributes such as character or use of language. The focus for each game is what drives the game forward, and like the Chicago method, the story in such scenes will appear retrospectively.

Evolution of styles

We could go on and look at many more differences between the two main models, but it would become more of an academic exercise with diminishing returns. Whether any specific aspect of one model is significant enough to make an obvious difference in the style of play or how the brain works while improvising, doesn't matter that much.

The models are different, if only because certain aspects — such as driving story — are contradictory. They were developed independently on different sides of the planet, in a time when global communications such as the Internet did not exist. Yet the documenting of the methods in books, and even the meeting of Keith Johnstone and Del Close in 1982, hasn't been strong enough to merge the two models. They're different, and different enough that both have survived until today, with not much sign of compromise. This alone makes the differences between them significant.

---

[100] The Sydney *Playback Theatre* has been around for 36 years, so there has been much cross pollination between Johnstone and *Playback Theatre* over that time, especially considering that Australian acting schools still only teach Johnstone and not Chicago. Whether this is true with other cities around the world, I don't know.

Yet the idea that improvisation is the same the world over has perpetuated through books, and with travelling teachers who should probably know better. Each model frames improvisation in a different way, and while there are some core principles which are the same, such as utilising spontaneity, presence and agreement, things do begin to vary from then on. As far as scene progression goes, the techniques are very different, and on the whole generate different kinds of scenes.

When we learn and use a particular method, we're committing to its mental model, the world of improvisation as understood by that particular model. Over time as that model develops and improvisors discover new things about improvisation, they in turn get integrated into the model. As other communities meet each other, the models slowly evolve, with groups often making their own changes due to cultural or other reasons, creating new branches and variations of each model all over the world.

The model most often used in Sydney for example, is a variation of Keith Johnstone's model from the mid–1980s, when *Theatresports* was still developing in the early days of *Loose Moose Theatre Company*. This has since been adapted over the years to suit Australian culture and the types of people who were drawn to improvisation at the time, along with some of Johnstone's improvements to his method over later years. This is slightly different to what is currently taught at *Loose Moose*, yet still clearly built on the same core principles.

Variations in models often occur where one variation of a method moves closer in specific ways to another model. For example, the terms "platform" and "tilt" came about in 1994 because Johnstone saw that what made a story interesting, was the break from the normal reality of a scene. This may have been influenced by the Chicago method, because it is similar — but not identical — to the Chicago method's use of game and subsequently UCB's creation of a base reality and the first unusual thing.[101]

---

[101] Platforms and tilts were a late discovery by Keith Johnstone, announced for the first time in August 1994 issue of his *Theatresports and Life Game Newsletter*. *Truth in Comedy* was first published in April 1994 and was the first written work on Del Close's game of the scene and game move theories. Considering Johnstone's earlier visits to Chicago, it is possible he was influenced by Close's work on game. Moreno on the other hand had already discovered similar techniques back in 1922-1923.

A good analogy is LEGO vs. Meccano. They're both kits containing basic building blocks, designed to allow us to build stuff. In LEGO, the world is built up by simply adding blocks on top of one another, and higher level elements such as walls and general architecture elements are built upwards as we think ahead about what the end result will be when complete. Meccano on the other hand is more about structure, weight and balance. There is no concept of a wall in Meccano, but you can build a wall-like supporting structure, by connecting elements as you would in the real world with cross beams and reinforcement techniques.

When we build with each kit, we're buying into the mental model of how its world works. And when we buy kits to build bigger structures such as a bridge or a house, those projects look and are constructed uniquely for that particular set of LEGO or Meccano components. We don't see the same projects in both types of kits — for example an ocean liner in Meccano or a box girder bridge in LEGO — because each kit is designed to take advantage of the basic building blocks of either LEGO or Meccano.[102]

Improvisation is the same. We're buying into the mental model of a particular method, but also the types of scenes that are usually performed using that method, or which work better with that method.

It took Keith Johnstone decades to formalise his impro system, which is decades of research and experimentation in order to come up with what works for him. Likewise, the Chicago model of improvisation took almost 30 years to get from an acting technique into the standalone form that is the foundation of the structured *Harold* we see today.

Once the core improvisation techniques had been developed into a framework for progressing an improvised scene, later improvisors began to develop more higher level structures and show formats, as well as filling out more detail in the core of the two models. So more recently we've seen techniques such as TJ Jagodowski and David Pasquesi's heat and weight[103], David Razowsky's Jerry chart of emotional heightening, relationship scene

---

[102] And of course a child's interest in building a box girder bridge would most likely diminish somewhat when they get a LEGO tie fighter for their birthday!

[103] You can find more about heat and weight on the web or in TJ & Dave's book *Improvisation at the Speed of Life*.

mapping[104] and Miles Stroth's position play[105]. Improvisation theory is still developing, and the two models are still doing their best not to converge.

Show form differences

Theatresports integrates many of Keith Johnstone's theories on improvised acting, and is thus supposed to be performed using Johnstone's impro system. All of the structure, rules and guidelines for it have been tweaked over the years into the working format that we have today, and that is all based upon what his impro system does and doesn't do.

If Chicago method improvisors put on a *Theatresports* show, it would not be *Theatresports* and it wouldn't look like *Theatresports*. This is because the Chicago method doesn't have the same mental model that was used to build *Theatresports* in the first place. Likewise with *ComedySportz*, which is based on Keith Johnstone's method and has been adapted to focus on comedy rather than scenes.

Alternatively, the *Harold* is a show format primarily developed and optimised by Del Close over the course of about 15 years, possibly more depending on your definition of the modern *Harold*. It was built on top of the Chicago method of improvisation, which builds scenes that generally explore more of the emotional relationship in the current moment than Johnstone. This is an integral part of the Chicago model, and one of the main reasons the *Harold* works so well.

Harold is a meta version of a Chicago method scene. It is a collection of themes and topics which in turn have meta themes at various levels. Because a Johnstone scene is based on story, often more things happen in an impro scene than would be allowed in a Chicago method scene. In fact, when Johnstone method trained improvisors perform a *Harold*, the result tends to be a collection of stories and characters, and they tend not to include

---

[104] A type of relationship scene that is used as a template for another scene, usually with a high stakes scene mapped over a low stakes scene. e.g. A father talking to his daughter's date for the night, but treating it like a police interview, or a loving couple splitting up to go to different shops at the mall, but played like one of the high stakes scenes from William Shakespeare's play *Romeo and Juliet*.

[105] Miles Stroth, formerly of the Del Close troupe *The Family*, believes that every scene can be identified as one or a combination of four scene types: Realistic, Straight/Absurd, Character Driven and Alternate Reality. By identifying the scene type, you then know what your character should be doing for the scene. You can find more about Stroth and his scene types via the website for his *Pack Theatre*.

moments, themes, meta themes, or in the case of UCB's *Harold*, games of the scene.

A Johnstone *Harold* is actually a great example of where the two models can let you down. When Johnstone improvisors look to Chicago for show ideas and decide to perform a *Harold*, it more often falls flat and doesn't play very well to an audience. Sydney in particular has gone through several cycles of *Harold* performances by Johnstone trained improvisors over the last 30 years, and still it won't stick with audiences — roughly every 10 years, so in the mid–1990s, the mid–2000s and the mid–2010s.

This isn't to say that you can't perform *Theatresports* in the Chicago method or a *Harold* with Johnstone's impro system. But it does mean that these forms have been optimised for those styles, and so will on average provide much better results if performed in the relevant style.

When you start to look at other show formats, you begin to see other method influences and optimisations as well. A *La Ronde*[106] for example looks quite different when performed with the different methods. Being a character study, the story is not important, but considering each character performs two scenes in a row in the initial "round", the result is often that the scenes are a connected story, which then drifts into the scene work as well. This makes the Chicago method *La Ronde* more difficult to learn and perform, due to the tendency to introduce story, but ultimately more watchable considering it was designed as a character study with the Chicago method.

Any format which requires a long source scene or master scene also works better with the Chicago method, because Johnstone's story and potential absurdity curve tends to introduce more ideas in less detail than the Chicago method's less ideas in more detail. Master scenes can also be more difficult in a single location for Johnstone improvisors due to the want to actively advance story. However advanced Johnstone improvisors do have an easier time because they often end up using some Chicago method techniques in order to do so, whether they realise it or not. But longer scenes with multiple

---

[106] A character exercise where players alternate playing with each other until they're back at the original player. For example, the first scene might be players A and B, then A is tagged out by C and we see a scene between B and C, then D tags out B and we see a scene with C and D etc. We look at the La Ronde format in more detail in a later chapter.

locations and a strong story arc usually work better with the Johnstone method.

The differences become more obvious once you start watching shows in the different methods. For example, I once saw an improvised zombie show which started with 6 Johnstone method improvisors playing the roles of uninfected people in a zombie apocalypse. The audience would vote off a player to become a zombie every few minutes, until there was only one survivor left. As each improvisor died, they would sing an improvised song based on an audience suggestion and then get carried off by a supporting cast of zombies. That player would be made up backstage as a new zombie, and would join the other zombies when they next came out. This married Johnstone's faux competition and audience interaction with a themed show to great effect. The problem however, was that much of the improvised scene work consisted of the players interacting while hiding in their shelter from the zombies, still knowing full well that they would probably be dead in about 30 minutes. Even so, the characters just didn't seem to care about each other or even themselves. And worse, the audience didn't care about them either. This seemed to be because they were working through active story advances in their interactions. Had the Chicago method been used for the interaction scenes, it may have made for a much more engaging show about life, death, relationships and their emotional state in that moment, instead of being a theatrical zombie themed show with great audience interaction, zombie costume, makeup and set design.[107]

But Keith Johnstone's signature show formats are where his method really shines. *Theatresports*, *Micetro*, *Life Game* and *Gorilla Theatre* were all perfected over the years by Johnstone to fit a particular problem he had with players at the time. As such they are all custom designed for his method. Gorilla Theatre for example, relies on a small cast who rotate as director of each new scene. Because story is universally understood by audiences and is a core part of Johnstone's method, story is one of the key attributes that the directors use for scenes. When performed in the Chicago method however, directing players on story conflicts with their training, creating scenes that resist story advances. Different method, different kind of show. The same is

---

[107] It obviously depends on what the audience prefers to see, and what their expectations are going into a show. In this case, this is what I would have preferred to see. But the point is that the show would have been very different if it had used a different method.

true of Johnstone's *Life Game*. The form begins with an interview with an audience member or invited guest, and the improvisors then perform scenes from their life. These would be presented differently with Johnstone's method — narrating a story — or the Chicago method — focusing on moments.

So how did these two main styles end up so different?

Johnstone's background was as a writer, not an actor[108], but he did eventually become a theatre director and academic, in a domain where classical British theories of acting were dominant. In the writers group at the Royal Court Theatre, improvisation was used for a short period of time to act out variations for written scripts which Johnstone and others were reviewing. This background and experience, along with his accidental rejection of some of Stanislavsky's key work[109] — "given circumstances" in scene analysis — lead to his focus on story, status and other literary and European style acting elements.

The Chicago improvisors were on the other hand American actors in a community where Stanislavsky and his disciples had developed the predominant acting theories. Heavily influenced by Viola Spolin due to her son Paul's connection to David Sheppard's work on improvised acting, the Chicago method was built upon the theories of American acting and Spolin's developments in creativity, problem solving and group work.

The reason why we have two main models, and not one or three, is simply due to luck. Are there other models which could have been discovered and become popular as well? We don't know, but considering the number of relevant scene attributes, there could well have been. Just as interesting though, is that there was a decisive moment in Johnstone's development of impro, when his model could have moved either closer to that which was being developed in Chicago, or further away from it, as it eventually did. In his book *Impro: Improvisation and the Theatre*, Johnstone discusses this defining moment where he brings his extensive knowledge of story and

---

[108] Johnstone still isn't an actor, nor is he a regular improvisor. This makes him fairly unique, in that he has limited experience in performing improvisation, and his experience is primarily directorial.
[109] Johnstone now regrets this decision to reject Stanislavsky's work. However, without it his method would be a lot different, and possibly closer to the Chicago method.

writing to bear, and decides what his theory should and shouldn't include. He says:

> *Content lies in the structure, in what happens, not in what the characters say.*
>
> ...
>
> *My decision was that content should be ignored.*
>
> ...
>
> *Once you decide to ignore content it becomes possible to understand exactly what a narrative is, because you can concentrate on structure.*

This narrative structure idea lies at the core of Johnstone's teachings, with the understanding that the dialogue will follow the action as needed without having to consciously think about it. Focus on the story, and it will pull in everything else that's needed for the scene. This is the opposite of the Chicago method, where you ignore the story and structure and focus on the content, and it will automatically create story retrospectively.

Not only is Johnstone's model different to the Chicago model, but it is the way it is because Johnstone consciously made it so, not through some random selection or optimisation over the years. The Chicago method is an improvisation technique for acting in scenes, and Johnstone's style is an all-encompassing system for improvising active story based scenes which are often time compressed.

This isn't to say that story and relationship don't apply in both methods — Johnstone is very clear about the importance of relationship — it's just that they're not the primary focus when improvising with his system.

Cross training

With two main methods of scene progression, and new students often desperate to learn as much as possible, how difficult is it to retrain in a different improvisation method, or even cross train in two methods at the same time? They both use similar exercises, so why is it so hard?

Cross training would seem to be a great idea, because the more you know and can internalise about improvisation, the better you'll be. The problem is when you're internalising contradictory methods, or methods which have conflicting views on techniques, you end up plateauing because you're in a cycle of learning and unlearning that never matures.[110] We're not talking about learning facts or processes such as advanced mathematics or how to build a house, we're talking about training our unconscious and muscle memory, which are much more delicate and fickle beasts. And to complicate matters, learning contradictory skills requires removing old habits, which is difficult considering we're trying to remove well-travelled neural pathways.

A common misunderstanding of the brain is that we're born with it, it grows, and we're stuck with it. But the brain can and does physically change as we age, as we learn, practise and think. And drugs and other chemicals as well as environmental effects can also permanently physically change the brain. This is called neuroplasticity, the ability of the brain to change over a person's life.

The most common example of this is practising a skill to develop muscle memory. Our brains change and forge new neural pathways and connections as we change our understanding, ability and behaviour. But it also means that undoing old habits requires not only forging new pathways, but making them strong enough to override and remove old ones. As most addicts know, removing old habits is difficult. Old habits do indeed die hard.

Each of the main improvisation methods has different curves of learning and experience. Certain techniques are only applicable in one method or variations of methods, and some techniques are learned in different ways or in different orders to the other method or variations of it. Some techniques are also completely missing from one method or variation, yet are core principles in others.

Cross training can give you a wider range of techniques than those required for a particular style of improvisation, but cross training can also prevent

---

[110] I once knew a long form troupe that trained for about 5 years before imploding. The players were all trained in the core skills of one method and then tried to improve in a range of cross training skills, without realising that they were doing so. Because they didn't know there were different methods, they were caught in a continuous cycle of learning and unlearning. They would have guest coaches teach various skills from different models, and then when they found those skills conflicting, they simply brought someone else in with their own different style or background in a different model. After six months they would be back once again learning a skill they'd just unlearned and previously learned earlier in the year. When they eventually broke up, most of the players gave up improvising, with most of them still not knowing why they never improved.

some of this internalisation from happening, because time spent internalising one technique can often be cancelled out the next day while learning an opposing technique.

One aspect of this is something called interference theory — the idea that previously learned memories and behaviours can have a negative influence on understanding new ones. Learn one school of improvisation, with all its methods, techniques and motor skills, and this will affect our ability to learn other schools, and even the older techniques in the same method can become unlearned. It's not impossible to learn more than one school at a time, but it is more difficult, and it's unlikely we'll reach higher levels of achievement unless we're focused on only one school.

When we learn how to improvise, we also build up a knowledge base of techniques that we've discovered ourselves, both consciously and unconsciously. These techniques aren't taught or consciously learned, they're what we as individuals have extrapolated from the training we've been through, like the ongoing unconscious muscle movements and balance analysis that we perform while riding a bike. If we were to learn a different school of improvisation, then this knowledgebase is going to drive our core skills, and this won't be consciously corrected in class because they're ingrained, unconscious and not taught in the curriculum. This means we're trying to learn a skill while our unconscious underpinnings are wanting to do something different. And we see this in the play of improvisors who have been taught in one school and are now learning with a different school.

Short–form games vs long–form scenes work in a similar way, in that there are contradictory techniques between the two. Not so much as between say Johnstone and Chicago where there are big differences, but certainly the mindset that's required for short–form vs. long–form, and the need for more analytic focus in the case of short–form. But there are situations where cross training forms does work well, such as training in say musical theatrical improvisation and the *Harold* can be very beneficial, if both are using the same core model.

Warm ups also become more important while cross training. You can't just run into class hoping to be present. You're better off designing a warm up for the method and techniques you're about to learn, and when that becomes habitual, it will allow you to pull up the correct mental model that you require for that style.

Ultimately, be conscious of what works for you. The science says that the best way to improve is to become expert in one method before learning a new one. Good habits are as easy to learn as bad habits, and across methods a habit could be both good and bad. You don't want to internalise the good habits of one method, and then have them vanquished as bad habits in your very next class.

When I first figured out the differences between the methods, I consciously pushed away everything and everyone from the method that I'd been originally trained in, and focused solely on the method I wanted to be expert in. This meant no longer going to workshops, playing in shows, playing with friends, and anything else that would possibly undo the training I was doing for the new method. In the early days of this conversion, I'd often find myself in an unfortunate situation where I was playing with people trained in an opposing method. In those days it was very difficult to maintain the new method, and in fact I could feel it being undone as I played those scenes. I became more in my head, because I was trying to figure out how to play with these people, so I was in a much more conscious state, and I was playing in a way that contradicted my unconscious training. That's a big problem because it begins to reverse the internalisation process.

After playing with people of the opposing method, I would have to actively think through core principles and guidelines again to make sure they were correctly internalised. It was difficult no longer playing with friends, and avoiding international teachers' workshops was particularly hard, but looking back I can see that it was the right decision and has made me a much better improvisor.

Ultimately, we still don't know enough to say definitely whether cross training can achieve the same levels of ability as training in separate styles, but the research suggests not. Very experienced improvisors can play with players of other methods, but when it happens you can see the pull between the two methods. One player will want to advance ahead and the other will want to focus on the current thing. It doesn't necessarily make a bad scene, but when comedy comes from the method and depends on all the players using that method, mixed methods tend to not be as funny. Generally though, it would seem for most players it is much rarer if not impossible to reach those lofty heights of improvised brilliance by cross training.

1960s to 1970s

By the 1960s, theatrical improvisation as a craft and art had been proven by *The Compass Players*, *Second City* and the earlier work of Moreno, Spolin, Sills and Shepherd. Along with Keith Johnstone's *Theatre Machine* in the U.K., the 1960s was a decade of exploration of what else might be possible with improvisation.

Of most interest to us however, are Del Close beginning to explore the *Harold* at *The Committee* as a standalone show format, John Cassavetes and Mike Leigh showing that improvisation could be used to great effect in the development of films and plays, and Augusto Boal's use of improvisation as revolution, in South America.

John Cassavetes

John Cassavetes was an American actor, director and writer who was active from 1951 until his death in 1989 at the age of 59. He's often held up as an innovator in the use of improvisation and the cinéma vérité style of filmmaking — the use of camera, acting and direction techniques to create more realistic performances.

Most acting is a fake representation of reality. Actors have rehearsed their performance, their lines are usually already scripted and memorised, and their movements on stage have been locked in. While the best actors can approach realism in their characters and their emotions, they are still subservient to what is in the script, and they are no longer unconsciously surprised or inspired by the material. In popular films for example, nobody stumbles over their words, or says "umm" or "ahh", unless it's in the script and thus part of the plot. Actors don't look like they're searching for words, except in usually less than subtle forced facial movements. As humans we unconsciously read thousands of different facial micro–expressions, and can often sense when something is amiss in someone's behaviour, and an actor, according to our unconscious, is rarely acting like they would in real life. But we have trained ourselves to ignore this when watching traditional actors.

Cinéma vérité attempts to avoid this problem and allows actors to respond realistically and to appear unrehearsed. They're actually looking for what to say, or reacting a certain way, for the very first time.

In 1956, Cassavetes started running acting workshops in collaboration with acting coach Burt Lane — who would end up doing most of the work. When he was available to teach, Cassavetes worked a lot with improvisation and what could possibly be called shock techniques that would keep the students on their toes and away from rehearsed action, giving them a more naturalistic style of acting. Cassavetes was already familiar with Viola Spolin's work by then — almost a decade before her first book *Improvisation for the Theater* was published in 1963.

In 1957 — the same year as the St Louis *The Compass Players* — a chance dream occurred where Cassavetes created some characters that represented the people in his class. He had them running through various improvised scenarios, until one in particular "exploded with life"[111]. This was the foundation for his first film, *Shadows*, which was mostly improvised. Cassavetes describes this process in Ray Carney's 2001 book *Cassavetes on Cassavetes* as being all part of a dream, but it's unclear if it's literally a dream while sleeping, or an actual goal "dream" of his.

During shooting, a rough story outline was used to guide the scenes, but there was no script or detailed story arc, and the actors were given free rein to move and speak as they wished. For this reason, the film has an improvised feel, and there are moments which are funny but aren't supposed to be, due

---

[111] In Cassavetes' words, quoted from Ray Carney's 2001 book *Cassavetes on Cassavetes*.

to improvisation being used and those takes not being edited out — we'll look at why improvisation is always *potentially* funny in a later chapter.

After a generally bad reception, Cassavetes reshot more than half of the film and reordered many of the scenes, based instead on a written script. He considers this second 1959 version as the definitive version, and unfortunately his estate now won't allow the original 1957 version to be shown in public. The 1957 version was also lost for over 40 years until a print was discovered in an attic in 2003, so very few people have seen the original fully improvised film.

Shadows was the only completely improvised film Cassavetes directed, and all of his later films are strictly scripted. However, true to the cinéma vérité style, he regularly used camera and direction techniques that added realism and that often made the acting look naturalistic or improvised. Actors were free to deliver their lines however they liked, but he also used a range of techniques to put the actors under pressure, that created performances that looked like unrehearsed performances and that were more realistic. He would change the lines or blocking for characters, or give actors different directions at the last minute without telling their scene partner, allowing the camera to capture a real response to the change. He'd also often shoot several takes one after the other without pause, in the hope that the actor's emotions and inner critic would put them under pressure and affect their performance in some realistic way.

But there's another Cassavetes directed film that is much more interesting for improvisors than *Shadows*.[112] Released in 1977, *Opening Night* follows an aged film star in a stage play as it tours the U.S., with many of the scenes showing both the backstage and on stage action throughout various performances. As the ageing star descends into mental illness and breakdown, she begins adding improvised elements to the play at each performance, throwing off the other actors and forcing them to improvise and justify their responses.

For the scenes shot as part of an actual play, Cassavetes brought in members of the public as the audience, and gave them no instruction aside from saying

---

[112] Much of this factual detail comes from Ray Carney's *Cassavetes on Cassavetes*, but the analysis is mine.

they were free to respond as they wished. This gave the film even more of a feeling of being improvised or naturalistic.

In the final scene, Cassavetes' character and the ageing star — played by Cassavetes' real wife Gena Rowlands — improvise together past the end of the play to the amusement and acclaim of the audience. This was apparently shot three different times with a different emotion each time, giving him more options in a film which was effectively written during the editing process.

Cassavetes began work on *Opening Night* as early as 1968, and completed it in 1977. Coincidentally, in 1975 Cassavetes had starred in *Mikey and Nicky*, a film written and controversially directed [113] by Elaine May. It's not unrealistic to think that working with May, may have had some influence on *Opening Night*.

In *Opening Night*, the strength of Cassavetes' methods becomes clear when we consider that the dialogue for the film was scripted, yet they still seem — to an improvisor no less — that they really are improvising to camera. They're actors playing characters who are acting and improvising, and who must switch back and forth between a traditional acting style and a more naturalistic acting style, in a single shot. For improvisors, it's an extraordinary film.

Mike Leigh

Mike Leigh is a film and theatre director from the U.K. Born in 1943, he entered the Royal Academy of Dramatic Art (RADA) on a scholarship to train as an actor in 1960. He was disappointed in what he perceived as conservative and contrived acting techniques, focusing more on delivering academically trained actors who could competently interpret or inhabit the roles they were given. Leigh feels that the actor should be included in the creative process, exploring roles and relating them to real life or naturalism.

---

[113] May spent the original $1.8 million budget for *Mikey and Nicky* and it had blown out to $4.3 million before Paramount Pictures took it out of her control. May used up to 3 cameras per scene, and often left them rolling for hours at a time. She ended up shooting 1.4 million feet of film, which compared to the 10 thousand feet used in the resulting film is 140 times as much as the final product.

Two events triggered Leigh's move into improvised play and film making. First, he saw John Cassavetes' film *Shadows* in 1960[114], and felt that it might be possible to create full plays using improvisation as a rehearsal technique. Secondly, in director Peter Brook's version of the play *Marat/Sade* in 1965, Brook sent his actors to a mental hospital to develop their characters as part of their rehearsal process, and which was subsequently broadcast in part as a documentary segment on the BBC. Having seen both the play and the documentary, Leigh figured the next step would be to develop characters through rehearsal, and to then develop an entire play through improvisation. He used a similar process when he later moved into film.

Leigh's process begins with a rough idea of what the film might be about. He then uses improvisation with his actors to develop and explore a number of different characters for each actor, after which he selects which character each actor should play. Improvisation then continues to fully flesh out the characters, firstly alone with the director, but then much later with other actors — who usually don't know who else has been cast. After this intense rehearsal process, Leigh writes a rough scenario and begins shooting. On set, improvised scenes continue to refine the action and dialogue into the final, ready to shoot scene, at which point the camera finally begins to roll. Once much of the film has been shot, Leigh takes time out from shooting to improvise the final key scenes, which for most of the actors has been kept secret or was unknown until this point. Then these final scenes are in turn shot as well.

Like Cassavetes' techniques, this brings a naturalistic and improvisational feel to his work, as the characters in each scene are shot as if they were experiencing the scene for the first time.

The Committee

The Committee was an improvisational group based in San Francisco from 1963 to 1972, founded by ex–*Second City* director Alan Myerson. Mostly as a reaction against what he thought was *Second City*'s lack of strong political stance against the government of the time, *The Committee* used improvisation to develop satire similar to *Second City*, but with a stronger political focus.

---

[114] Quite possibly Cassevete's second version, which was partly scripted and released in 1959.

Del Close joined *The Committee* around 1966[115] where he began teaching and directing. At one point he was even running public workshops under the name of *The Sub-Committee*, where an audience could come along and improvise, as well as seasoned performers.

The Committee is well known these days due to a number of key events that happened there during those years: the early free form *Harold* format was invented there, before Close had arrived no less; Gary Austin started improvising there, and subsequently went on to found *The Groundlings* improvisation and sketch comedy group in 1974; and a lot of *The Committee*'s material ended up being shot to colour video, and this footage is now publicly available as reference material.

Theatre of the Oppressed

Augusto Boal was a Brazilian theatre practitioner and political activist, born in 1931 in Rio de Janeiro. Initially graduating as an industrial chemist in 1952, Boal moved to the U.S. to study chemistry and playwriting at Columbia University, including auditing[116] a number of classes at The Actors Studio. Upon returning in 1955, he was hired as a theatre director at the Teatro de Arena — Arena Theatre — in São Paulo, a theatre company focused on making theatre more accessible to the lower classes.

In 1970, Boal created *Newspaper Theatre*, a set of techniques for turning the current news into theatre content. *Newspaper Theatres* were set up all over Brazil, and Boal's *Nucleus Two* group would visit villages and towns to teach not only *Newspaper Theatre* techniques, but also the processes for making their own theatre. Boal refers to this as giving the working classes control of the means of production of theatre, a nod to Karl Marx's writings on workers controlling the means of production. In a country run by the military — after a U.S. supported coupe d'état in 1964 — theatre production empowered the population against the censorship and media control of the regime.

Boal was kidnapped and tortured by the regime in 1971 and exiled to Argentina for five years, where he wrote and published his most influential book, *Theatre of the Oppressed* in 1974 in Spanish, with an English translation first appearing in 1979. Originally to be published as two books, *Theatre of*

---

[115] Close left *Second City* in 1965, but it's unclear exactly when he ended up in San Francisco, as none of the key sources of information on Close specify a year.
[116] Sitting in to watch, without actually participating as part of the class.

the Oppressed is split roughly in half, with the first half a theoretical discourse on theatre and oppression, and the second documenting his practical work in Peru in 1973, along with several articles written in 1966 while at Teatro de Arena.

Theatre of the Oppressed discusses a number of theatre forms and techniques — including *Newspaper Theatre* — that use improvisation and Boal's idea of a "spect–actor" — a spectator who also interacts with a performance when necessary. Boal describes turning a spectator into an actor as a four-stage process, consisting of: warming up the body; preparing it physically through exercises and games; followed by several theatre forms for theatre as language, such as his *Forum Theatre* that allows participants to intervene and interact with actors; and finally, by using theatre forms for creating discourse amongst themselves, where the participants create original works, such as in Boal's *Newspaper Theatre*.

Forum Theatre begins with a Q&A with all the participants, highlighting a particular issue affecting the participants' community or region in regard to oppression. This is then either improvised or presented from previously prepared material, as a short ten to fifteen minute long play. The participants are then asked whether the issue was resolved, and if not, then the play is run a second time. This time the participants can replace any of the actors in the play at any time and change the action if they don't agree with it. All suggestions are accepted, and the play can be run many times so that every idea is explored by the participant who suggested it.

In *Theatre of the Oppressed*, Boal gives an example run through of a play, where workers in a factory attempt to rise up against their boss. Some of the participants want to blow up the factory, others try to organise a strike, and others want to form a union. Boal points out that while the theatre presented may not be that great, the result is that the participants are actively rehearsing actions they may consider taking later in real life. So, while a factory worker might not think that they could form a union on their own, the practice of doing so in Boal's *Forum Theatre* effectively becomes an empowering rehearsal for the real thing — yes, forming a union may now seem very possible, and the factory worker may now consider doing exactly that.

In Boal's theatre forms, scene progression of completely open ended improvised scenes is rare, and as such there is no — at least not documented — technique for doing so. So typically, Boal's improvisation is used to follow an already provided story or plot outline, or to enact a specific type of character. When spect–actors take on a role, they're also often acting out a consciously chosen story option or are improvising a specific character choice. In this way, *Theatre of the Oppressed* is thus once again similar to forms such as psychodrama — which Boal spent a short time with — and *Playback Theatre*. Whether *Forum Theatre* would change for the better if spect–actors had more specific improvisation and scene progression training — with scene attributes specific to the work — remains unclear.

Boal's *Theatre of the Oppressed* came about from specific events happening at a significant time in the history of South America, influenced — perhaps indirectly — by the work of Moreno and the Futurists, along with his experiences at The Actors Studio, and with Russian acting techniques such as Stanislavky's early work. Theatre forms such as *Forum Theatre* are a way of empowering people against their oppressors, but they also engage people with the arts, making them more creative, more confident, and more willing to look after themselves and their local community. Later, they may even take real life actions that they wouldn't normally consider.

The *Theatre of the Oppressed* sounds a lot like David Shepherd's failed dream of a workers' theatre back in 1952, but Shepherd was hoping to present completed works of theatre and for the workers to come up with the content and to then produce the work as well. Not to mention that South America in the 1960s and post–war Europe in the 1950s were very different from the mid–1950s industrial communities of America's Midwest. In Boal's terms, Shepherd's workers' theatre was still "spectacle theatre", where an audience watches a performance. Boal instead created a system where spectators do not need to prepare, yet are still able to contribute and participate. Boal puts it better when he says:

> *All the methods that I have discussed are forms of a rehearsal-theatre, and not a spectacle-theatre. One knows how these experiments will begin but not how they will end, because the spectator is freed from his chains, finally acts, and becomes a protagonist. Because they respond to the real needs of a popular audience they are practised with success and joy.*

Theatre, acting and empathy

From the mid–1950s onward, it was not unusual to find theatrical improvisation being used on stage in front of an audience, where a director no longer had the final say in what that performance must be. While a director can craft and polish an improvised work in rehearsal, they can't do that while the actor is improvising in front of an audience. Improvisors can play out a scene using spontaneity and scene progression, but this alone doesn't make improvisation watchable. It requires the actor to have specific skills for the theatre, in addition to those in spontaneity and scene progression. So which aspects or skills of theatrical improvisation are specifically related to entertaining an audience, and how does that work in practice?

Emotion

Emotions are the body's reaction to something which significantly affects it. They're psychological in the sense that they affect the way we think, and they're physical in the sense that we're preparing physically for an action in response to a particular emotion. Some say that emotion doesn't have to be conscious, that we can be angry for example without being consciously aware that we are. Feelings on the other hand, are our conscious and subjective recognition of emotions. Feelings are us sensing emotion, and thinking through the origins and consequences of the emotion.

Depending on which theory you prefer, there are between four and eight basic emotions, generally considered as variations on anger, disgust, fear, sadness, happiness, surprise and contempt, which are then combined to create other more complex emotions. Each of these corresponds with a number of specific facial expressions, body postures and types of breathing, which are trigged as the physical response to the emotion. It is these combinations of physical attributes that our brain uses to determine what emotional state another person is in, sometimes without that person even feeling that they have that emotion. This is why we often know more about someone else's emotional state than they do, and why conveying this to them can be a correspondingly emotional experience for the conveyer. For example, if a friend is anxious and we can see this from their physicality and actions, and they don't realise that they are, then we'll likely empathise with their emotion, and then delay telling them about it due to the increased anxiety or anger that it may cause for us as well.

This is why scene initiations in improvisation which convey an emotional state on a scene partner, give so much useful information to each player, because emotional empathy invokes emotions in our scene partner without them having to do anything. For example, a simple and vague line such as "It's OK, we'll push through it", is a strong emotional gift to a scene partner which immediately invokes emotional, physical and verbal responses, all of which convey intention and meaning for the audience. The whys and wherefores of the scene will follow as, and when, they need to.

In 1992, Psychologist Paul Ekman reported that mimicking the facial expressions of certain emotions, would cause the body to respond physically and adopt many of the other physical attributes related to that emotion[117], along with some of the subjective feelings of that emotion. This is because these muscular changes — called microexpressions — are wired into the central nervous system, and thus the emotion processing in the brain. Other studies have shown that vocalising sounds which involve the same muscle movements as emotion, also tend to cause the participants to feel those

---

[117] The participants were directed in how to perform the expression, so that the mirror system was not involved.

emotions. A great example of this is the theory that saying "cheese" when taking a photograph, forces the facial muscles to simulate a smile and therefore invoke a relaxed happiness. It doesn't just look like we're happier, it can also make us feel happier.

In 1983, Susana Bloch, Guy Santibañez and Pedro Orthous reported on their study of emotional effector patterns. Effector patterns are combinations of facial expressions, posture and breath, which together combine to reflect certain emotional states. Their research showed that by mimicking these effector patterns, actors could invoke both the subjective feeling and additional physiological traits of the corresponding emotion.

Bloch later developed an acting method based on this research, called "Alba Emoting", where actors are able to call upon specific emotions based on these physical attributes. Alba Emoting is similar to method acting and Stanislavsky's earlier work, where an actor uses a real memory they have which evokes emotions similar to those required by the character. Alba Emoting uses physiology to invoke the emotional feeling, and method acting uses personal memories to invoke the emotional feeling.

So far we've only discussed emotion through facial expressions, which are by far the most commonly researched due to them being the larger factor in invoking emotion. But there have been some studies into whether non-facial body positions can also convey or invoke emotion. A study by Harald G. Wallbott in 1998 showed that actors can use body movement and postures to simulate emotion which may be accurately interpreted — above the level of chance — without reference to a facial expression. Whether this also invokes emotion is unclear, although the mirror system should play some role and invoke at least some level of empathy in the viewer.

Emotion is important for actors, because it is through emotion that they evoke empathy from the audience. But this is a double edged sword, as the processes which evoke empathy in the audience, can also trigger those emotions in the actors.

How different actors evoke empathy from the audience, varies even more than there are differing schools and methods for doing so. And then there's just faking it, as many improvisors try to do, and which audiences often easily sense as faked, for the above reasons.

Theatre and empathy

We've done a lot of defining of terms so far, so thankfully no, we're not going to try and define theatre. The Internet is a big place and more than enough explanations exist. But some of the side effects of theatre do contribute to making improvisation what it is, and particularly what makes it funny.

Studies of theatre audiences have shown that there is no such thing as 100% suspension of disbelief while watching a theatre performance, at least not in the sense that we really believe that what we are watching is real. That's not why we enjoy theatre or what makes a good performance. Audiences don't believe that a performance is real, any more than they think movies or novels are real. Even when we think we're completely immersed in an engaging performance, our mind still flicks between the show content and the meta aspects of the performance. The phrase "suspension of disbelief" is the agreement we have with ourselves to treat the performance as real, and is not an actual belief that it is real. We are suspending the voice in our heads which keeps saying "this isn't real!"

For example, while watching a show, we often think about both the character and the actor throughout the performance. This is especially so with well-known leading movie actors such as say Michael Caine, George Clooney or Nicole Kidman for example, who are fairly constant from character to character. But this is also the case with actors who vary their roles — often called character actors — such as Harry Dean Stanton, Maggie Smith or more recently Ben Mendelsohn for example.

How often do we watch a film with Telly Savalas and when he appears for the first time we think to ourselves for a few seconds "oh, Kojak!", or with Carrie Fisher "look, it's Leia!"[118]. Yet they still get acting work, even though their most memorable roles should be a hindrance when it comes to suspension of disbelief.

Not only do we think about characters and actors, but we also think about where we are. With a theatre or cinema, we often look around us at the rest of the audience, the seat in front of us, the exit sign, or how the sets were

---

[118] I wrote this part of the book around 2010, but as I do my final review of the text Carrie Fisher has passed away. It was tempting to change this example to someone else because I thought it might look like I'd only chosen her because she was recently in the news. But it's a good example for me of how I feel when I watch one of my favourite films, *Drop Dead Fred*!

made. Movies have the ability to engage an audience more by getting right up in the actors' faces and with fast cutaways and edits. But with a stage performance, the audience has time to consider everything as actors move and speak in real time. Even the hollow and sometimes creaking sound of an actor's footsteps across the stage reminds us that the whole performance is a fake reality.

So, if we're not fully suspending our disbelief, and we know quite clearly that it's all fake, why do we still enjoy or engage with the experience? Why do we care about a character on stage, when we know it is really an actor pretending to be love struck and about to be killed by their ex-lover? We know full well that in about an hour they'll be in their comfortable dressing room being looked after by the crew, and receiving a pay cheque for doing exactly what they want to be doing with their lives. So why do we care about their character?

The main reason is empathy and the mirror system. The more believable a character is, and the more their ethics and morals align with ours, the more empathy we feel. Love, anger, jealousy, revenge, sadness, we feel it all because our mirror neurons are effectively putting ourselves in the place of the character who is displaying the physical attributes of the emotion that they and we should be feeling. We feel like we belong to the same group or family as them, which makes us support them and emote for them.

For example, if we're watching a film such as *Million Dollar Baby*, we're thinking of Clint Eastwood, any number of his previous roles, more particularly his man with no name character in the Sergio Leone spaghetti westerns, maybe his odd performance in the U.S. at the 2012 Republican National Convention, and how he keeps putting out movies at his age. Yet we still feel for his character Frank at the loss of Maggy as a proxy for the loss of his own daughter, which is ultimately all just made up and pretend. On stage, this effect can be pronounced because actors are often lesser known than on film, but then watching live action on an obvious stage tends to make up the difference.

Theatre is a neat mind trick. It doesn't make us think that something fake is real, it makes us think that we're thinking that something fake is real. We're being tricked by an evolutionary trait for learning new skills, which we've adapted into a method for entertaining ourselves. Theatre is all about emotion, inspiring empathy in an audience to experience or care about the emotions that the characters are feeling. The actor's main role therefore, is to represent the emotions of the performance, and to do so in a way which causes the audience to empathise with the character according to the wishes of the production. Theatrical improvisation is no different.

Acting

When an actor learns a scripted role, their early rehearsals often have a freshness and vibrancy to them, as they work with the emotions of the character. Rehearsals, which often involve improvisation, allow the actor to work through and refine their performance. Eventually their public performance is often just replaying the role, desensitised from the initial emotional stimulus or what it was that caused the initial freshness and vibrancy. Yet the actor's job is for each performance to seem like it is the very first time that it has been performed. This is often referred to as "the illusion of the first time"[119]. So how do they maintain that initial vibrancy on stage night after night?

Actors are affected by the audience, the space, their history, what they brought into the space on that day, their scene partner, their fellow cast members, the timing of the lighting and sound cues, and who knows what else. As such, every performance is new. They may know the lines, the blocking, the character's and actor's objectives, and how to imbue emotion into their character, but they are also influenced by everything else around them and inside them.

For example, an actor's line might be delivered a fraction of a second off, which in turn causes subtle changes in their scene partner's response, which may cause the lighting cues to ever so slightly change, which in turn may make the actor feel as though the scene is different to what was rehearsed. This then feeds back into the performance, with the actors constantly reading the audience, the other actors, the technical side of the production, and the scene, and with them adapting appropriately.

Scripted actors are constantly improvising throughout the rehearsal and performance process, but within heavily constrained limits compared to those of improvisors. They have also internalised this ability to improvise and read an audience, in order to make each performance feel fresh for that

---

[119] Named after the 1915 book *The Illusion of the First Time in Acting*, by William Gillette.

audience. But still, it is impossible for an actor to repeat a performance and to fully represent how their character would act if it was the very first time.

Improvisation on the other hand doesn't have this attribute. In most theatrical improvisation, everything which happens is actually new, with the freshness and vibrancy of being absolutely the first time it has been performed by the actors. The audience are partly reading the players as actors — in a theatre with an obvious theatre production around them — and partly reading the characters as real people with their first time actions and responses. As improvisors, we also know how to read and respond to an audience, and how to invoke emotion and evoke empathy. We may not have been explicitly taught this, but much like riding a bike, we've learned and internalised it through the experience of performance.

Why is improvisation funny?

Theatrical improvisation isn't drama or comedy without a script. If that were true, then we'd have improvised plays which feel like scripted plays. Writing a strong script takes time, working backwards and forwards through the work, polishing and refining. For this reason, improvised plays are never as good as high quality written plays.[120] So why do improvised scenes and plays still work so well for an audience?

Improvised scenes have a unique quality to them which makes them stand out as improvised, or as "possibly improvised". For improvisors who have internalised improvisation, Mike Leigh's films feel like they're improvised, the movie *Spinal Tap* feels improvised, and *TJ and Dave* at the top of their game still feel improvised. Improvisation feels different because it is improvised, because the facial and verbal responses play with the audience's understanding of what acting should look like.

Improvisation provides the actual first time, not the illusion of the first time. You can rehearse a facial micro-expression for example, but with the potential for up to 43 muscles involved in the process, it will never be as good

---

[120] In her book *Art By Committee*, Charna Halpern recalls a story by Del Close of a man named "Dario Foe" who won a Pulitzer Prize for a play he'd written, only to later announce that it was improvised. This is probably a reference to Dario Fo, an Italian theatre practitioner who won the 1997 Nobel Prize in Literature. The Pulitzer Prize is only given to American citizens and for a specific work, whereas the Nobel Prize in Literature is given to any person based on their entire body of work and the effect of that work on the world, which in Fo's case does include improvisation. He never won a Pulitzer Prize.

as a real microexpression. So when an improvisor is surprised, they are actually surprised, and when they're frustrated, they are actually frustrated. And the audience sees this as being more real than scripted acting — something that Cassevettes was always developing in his work.

And for us as improvisors, this is even more pronounced, because we recognise improvisation. Our unconscious is trained to listen and respond to improvised acting techniques. And because the style of a scene depends upon the method being used, we sense any similarities in the style of improvisation we're watching.

So what makes improvisation funny? First we need to look at laughter, why we laugh, and what makes us laugh.

Laughter is an inbuilt response to certain conditions within the conscious, which may or may not still be relevant to contemporary humans. There are a lot of theories on what causes laughter, but most converge on a single theory. That laughter is a response designed to reassure us when we've resolved a disconnect, between our perceived reality and an introduced reality. All jokes and comedy seem to conform to this pattern.

Let's use an example. "Why did the chicken cross the road? To get to the other side." is a classic joke, which has been used so much that it is now a mostly unfunny cliché. And yet while it is not laugh out loud funny, it is still amusing.

It's amusing because the initial question sets up a reality that the questioner is asking for a higher level reason for the chicken to cross the road, perhaps to return some late library books, or to reach its chicks that are playing in the opposite field. The expectation is that there is a high level reason for the chicken to need to cross the road, and that it has enough intelligence to know what this reason is.

The reply though is not a high level reason for crossing the road, it is the obvious mechanical task required for the chicken to get across the road. This requires no high level thinking on behalf of the chicken, and gives no information on why the chicken needed to actually cross. The reply is basically that this is just a chicken. There is thus a disconnect between the implication that the question is about high level reasons for an intelligent chicken to cross the road, and the reality that it was about a simple mechanical process for a stock standard chicken.

This cognitive conflict is then resolved once our brain figures out the actual meaning of "To get to the other side", and switches from the perceived reality of an intelligent anthropomorphic chicken, into what we should have really expected, just a normal chicken. Then laughter, or amusement ensues as a reassuring action.

Keep in mind that we never see an "actual reality", because reality is only what we perceive through our senses. We can never know whether the reality we perceive is the actual reality. Hence, we say there is a conflict between our current perceived reality, and a different reality, which may or may not be the actual reality.

There are other theories which break down different types of jokes into different sub-theories, however most of these are still a collision and resolving of alternative realities — our perceived reality and a different reality.

This resolving of two realities is an evolved fight or flight response. If we perceive that there may be two realities, then we begin to weigh up whether the confusion will be resolved or not, and thus whether fight or flight would be required if it cannot be resolved.

The classic example of this is a caveman seeing a rustle in some bushes, thinking it is a lion coming to eat him, when all of a sudden his caveman friend steps out of the bushes. Once the conflicting realities have been resolved, he laughs, which reassures him not so much that there is no longer any danger, but that he understands there was a conflict and it has been resolved.[121]

There is a limit though at which point the disconnect between realities is too great and is no longer funny. For example, if there is a rustle in the bushes,

---

[121] In the book *Inside Jokes, Using Humor to Reverse-Engineer the Mind*, Matthew M. Hurley says that "basic humor happens when you get a jolt of mirth because a belief that you, yourself, are committed to - without realizing it - becomes invalidated". Coincidentally, this book was co-written by Reginald Adams and Daniel Dennett, who we looked at in the chapter on how the mind works, so there is a lot of cognitive science behind their ideas. They also believe that laughter is a reward for recognising the conflict in the mental models, and not a reassurance of safety or a valid reality. But if this is the level of argument amongst scientists regarding laughter, then we can be confident that laughter is pretty much a resolution of conflict between two realities.

and then leaves blow out in the wind. In this case there's no conflict because nothing "makes a noise and steps out towards the caveman". The differences between a lion and wind are too great, and wind is an acceptable reason for the noise. Another example of this might be "Why did the chicken cross the road? Someone carried her."

Comedy, is material which is intended to, or accidentally triggers this disconnect or collision of contexts or realities.[122] What used to be a fight or flight response to danger, can be tricked into operating independently from actual danger, a trick of the mind that causes laughter in safe environments such as a theatre or in a social context. By looking at how this works and what triggers it, we can work out what makes improvised scenes funny, and how to make them funnier than they would normally be. Thankfully, the two main models of improvisation already focus on techniques which do this.

Comedy in improvisation comes about in a number of ways, including with standard comedy tropes — tried and true methods for constructing jokes — as used in written comedic works. Writing a good sketch or comedy scene can take time, often much longer than simply improvising a scene. So, while it is possible to perform improvised scenes as funny as written scenes, the reality is that improvisation also takes a lot of luck and other inputs, to generate a scene that is the quality of a polished written one. Luckily though, improvisation uniquely provides us with a number of other ways to generate comedy that written works do not. It is these attributes of improvisation that are more often used to make scenes funny, and often make them funnier than written works.

Most improvisational comedy happens due to discovery and justification of the unexpected. As a scene progresses, we're discovering which scene we are performing by just letting the scene go and seeing where it takes us. This discovery process uses the unconscious to find things that a consciously thinking writer may not find so easily.

I once saw a dinner table scene where an improvisor's hand movements, whether intended or not, lead their scene partner to see objects in the scene that they and the audience had not realised were there. This included a

---

[122] Note that we're not talking about the content of the material — for example a duck visiting the dentist — which is a technique often called a "clash of contexts", but a collision between the different and conflicting mental models which are constructed by the audience in their heads.

diamond necklace which they'd been dipping into their soup for the last minute or so. Discovering this made that audience think back over the last few minutes and rewrite their memories to make the scene fit with the dipping necklace. They experienced a collision of mentals models which was quickly resolved, and comedy ensued. "Do you like your soup with or without diamonds?"

The physicality and language used in scenes have this effect. What was a touching of the hair, could be a new hairdo or bad hair wax, an itching of the nose could be the beginnings of a fatal disease, or the openness of the guy serving you at the shop could be because he's your father.

Discovery naturally leads to the unexpected, a collision of contexts, because we keep discovering things that we didn't realise were there. As a scene progresses, there is missing information that the audience and other improvisors fill in without that information having been specifically added. For example, if the location of a scene hasn't been stated or physically shown, other aspects of the scene may give the impression that the scene is in a certain location. Then as new information comes into the scene, everyone — on stage and off — updates their understanding of the scene, often with the improvisors having to declare a location if they feel the scene and audience at that point needs to explicitly know.

For example, the dinner table scene above may end up being set on top of a mountain, and is only declared when the lady with the necklace says she's cold, like really cold. This might be interpreted as meaning they're outside in the cold and her scene partner declares that they are on top of a mountain, when she was really thinking that she was skimpily dressed. Collision of contexts is a natural by-product of this. In the case of a location, if we see a scene between two chefs, we may think by their physical actions that they are in a restaurant kitchen, but it may come out later that they are actually at a woodworking class, which due to the collision of contexts or realities, is funny, especially if everything they do to build a table is still chef like.

In the Chicago method, discovery happens a lot as a result of specificity — the drilling into detail which makes new discoveries. In the *TJ and Dave* film *Trust Us This Is All Made Up*, a bowl of individually wrapped sweets is discovered on the desk of a secretary, which leads to several physical games unwrapping and eating the sweets. The sweets have the very texture you'd expect, yet you'd rarely notice this if you came across a real bowl of sweets on a secretary's desk.

For Johnstone however, discovery is more about the unfolding action in the scene, what is going to happen next, and drawing upon whatever comes out of the unconscious to drive the scene forward. An example from Johnstone's first book *Impro* discusses a man rowing a boat to escape a bear, discovering an island, where he discovers a hut with a beautiful girl bathing in a tub, he then makes love to the girl, only to discover the bear rowing a boat to the island, taking off the bear suit to find he's an old man, who then makes love to the girl when the original man is hiding under the bed. In this case a stream of consciousness, along with the absurdity curve, and a collision of contexts with a bear rowing a boat and being a man, leads to the scene being funny. More particularly for Johnstone, it's not the kind of scene that a comedy writer would consider, and as a written sketch it wouldn't be nearly as funny. So why not?

When an audience watches an improvised performance, they are aware that it is improvised. There is a long running discussion about whether improvisors should ask for a suggestion to start a scene purely so that the audience knows that a show is improvised. But in practice if we say it is improvised, they will believe us. Even when an audience member comes up after a show and asks "Was that really improvised?", what they're really doing is questioning themselves, after having already given the improvisors the benefit of the doubt. Many improvised scenes would not work as a scripted piece, and the fact that they're laughing at it shows that they do accept the premise that it is all made up. These days however improvisation is much more well known, and it is not uncommon for audiences to be fully aware of improvisation as an art form.

As we've seen, suspension of disbelief isn't a 100% state of mind for an audience, it's only a rough agreement with the performers that they will pretend that the performance is real. Studies of theatre audiences show that people will shift their attentions throughout a performance, even with scripted works, where they will see and think about the character, their wants, desires and motivations, and then see and think about the actor, their history, their talents, their acting ability, and then back again to the character.

For improvised performance, this works well in our favour. The audience is already switching attention between the character and the actor, and it is only a small step to them caring about the outcome of something that's improvised by that actor, even if they don't consciously think that it is improvised. This gives the audience three levels of attention: the character and scene; the improvisor as an actor; and the empathy for the improvisor — because surely it's scary and difficult if you're improvising without a script. And when something is difficult, failure is possible, so the audience tends to feel for the players by laughing more than they may have if they'd known it was just written and rehearsed.

Improvised comedy taps into these three levels, and this doesn't happen in many other comedy forms. So yes, it is important for improvisation that the audience is aware that it is improvised. But most audiences already get it, because they're reading facial expressions of actors, and listening to dialogue of characters, that aren't exactly what is normally seen in acting. For this reason it may even seem to their unconscious as not being real actors, or not as optimised or rehearsed as real actors.

But audiences can also turn on a player if the player is not fully committed to at least trying to improvise a good scene, and this is one of the reasons why improvisors need to go on stage confidently and willing to excitedly launch into the unknown. The audience will empathise with the improvisor, support them and cheer for them, so long as the improvisor is seen to be committed and doing their best for the audience.

Mime is another good example of comedic specificity and the audience knowing a show is improvised. Detailed mime is funny because improvisors invest so much into miming something, when the audience knows that the improvisor knows that it is not real. A written sketch where a necklace is mimed being removed in great detail, would not be as funny as when done by an improvisor, because we don't believe that someone simply making up a scene, would mime a necklace in so much detail. This is especially true when taking off the necklace the wrong way and getting all tangled up in it. We find it funny because we're aware that they are actors, that the object doesn't exist, that they are not following the instructions of an offstage writer, they have full control of what they're doing, and yet they are treating it as if the object is the most important thing in the world for a character which doesn't really exist. This breaks our mental model and expectations. When a second improvisor also interacts with the same object, this often enhances the effect because now two improvisors are caring enough to pay so much attention to the detail of something that doesn't exist. The fact that the improvisors are seen to be having fun, also rubs off on the audience and they have more fun as a consequence.

Like most things in improvisation, the audience sees and hears more than anyone else, and this is especially the case with mime — because they are seeing all of the work on stage and how each improvisor is interacting with other improvisors. Mimed objects in particular can also look different depending on where players are located on stage. So if one player is looking across the stage at an invisible object — player on the left, object on the right — then they often have bad judgement on left to right placement on the stage. Likewise, if an upstage player is looking at an object downstage, they can be confused about how far downstage and what the object is lined up with from left to right. You can see this in practice by having players surround an invisible table, with one player placing an object from stage left, and another player picking it up again from upstage — they will usually be in different locations in 3D space.

While the audience has the best perception of what is in, and what is happening in, a scene, the next best perception of a scene is by the currently off-stage group members — they're part of the performance, but currently also effectively audience members. Next is the scene partner — they're interacting with the scene, but see more than the player who is performing the actions. And the least effective perception of a scene is by the person doing the actual miming or improvising.

It is for this reason, that meaning and intention in improvisation are mostly in the hands of the receivers — the audience — not the improvisor who is doing the acting.

We could break discovery and the unexpected down into a number of different contributors, but there are two main effects of the improvisation process which are unique to improvised comedy, and which contribute to the comedy generated from it: misunderstandings and misinterpretations between improvisors; and the bleeding of meta information into scenes. Neither of these exists in written works. They're unique to improvisation.

When two people improvise a scene, any misunderstandings are potentially comedy, and it's just the level of experience that determines whether it has a positive or negative effect on the scene. Even at the beginners' level, if two improvisors go on stage with conflicting scene initiations, then family and friends will find this funny, because they feel for the improvisors, but also due to the clash of contexts.

I was once in a scene which started with my scene partner making a bed and tucking in the sheets, so I joined in. We played the scene for about a minute while playing out the relationship, with the location not yet important enough to be mentioned. Then about a minute in, my scene partner declared that this was no time for such a discussion while we were preparing the boat for our fishing trip. The audience found this funny, because they were expecting the scene to be in a bedroom, but it turned out that it was on a boat ramp. Also, the emotional intensity in the scene suddenly seemed a lot different, because we were no longer together in a bedroom. There is a collision of contexts, and comedy ensues.

I've heard it argued that this is more an effect of bad mime skills, but unless an object or location is actually real, there's always going to be an element of interpretation by an audience of what they think improvisors are actually doing. Is pouring a drink located in a kitchen, a bar, or at an outside BBQ? Are we tucking in bed sheets in a bedroom in a house, or in a bedroom on a boat? Or is it just packing a row boat? It is up to the players to decide when this needs to be confirmed in the scene, before it ends up being too much of a difference between what the audience and the players are expecting. If the clarification of preparing the boat had been made at the end of the scene instead, then perhaps it wouldn't have been so funny, as there is a point at which a collision of contexts turns from misunderstanding to just plain wrong. Or maybe it would have been funnier, considering how much of the scene would need to change retrospectively in people's minds.

The same thing happens with dialogue — when a player says one thing, but really means another. This can come about many different ways using language, for example using certain homophones — words that sound the same but are different — or colloquial sayings which are literally interpreted. When this kind of dialogue is accepted in a way that is contrary to what is expected by the audience in the scene, a collision of contexts occurs and the audience laughs.

Here are a few examples of possible misunderstandings.

    WENDY: Get your hand off my heart.

This could be interpreted as "Get your hand off my art".

>PAUL: I will love you until the day that I die.

This could set up the literal expectation that the Paul won't have very long to live.

>HENRY: I'm going to visit them all.

This could be interpreted as "I'm going to visit the mall" along with its associated status, emotion and stakes changes.

>AMY: You don't love me anymore.

This is interpreted differently depending on whether the emphasis is "love" or "me". Either of which could be unintended.

If these examples were included in a written sketch, they wouldn't be as funny, because either it would be assumed that "misunderstanding" is the game of the sketch, or it would just seem a bit clunky or amateur to have misinterpreted dialogue when a writer could have used clearer phrasing. And when the improvisors justify the statement, that in itself causes additional collisions of context.

>WENDY: Get your hand off my heart.
>
>PETER: But it's so beautiful. I love Cubism!
>
>WENDY: So do I, but when we're just practising the burglary, can we just pretend to touch the paintings?

The other main contributor to improvised comedy, is the use of meta information. Meta information is information about the theatre space, the actors or the process being used to generate the scene. This will often bleed into the content of a scene. I was in a scene once where I was sitting in the driver's seat of a car, and my dad came up to the left side window to speak to me. For left side drive vehicles such as in the U.S., this wouldn't seem unusual, but in Australia where our cars are right side drive, there was an additional element to the scene. This lead to the scene being about why my dad thought it a good idea to import a 40 foot long Cadillac — the stereotype Australians have of U.S. cars — and where on earth I was going to park it in the inner city laneways where I live. Meta information regarding the size of the stage and the other player's physical position in the space, determined the content of the scene.

Meta bleed is often considered bad form in improvisation. But so long as it makes sense with the type of show, type of improvisation, and the expectations of the audience, then it's usually not a problem. After all, the audience are probably already distracted — throughout the show — by how small the space is that you booked for your new improvised show, so why not play to those concerns? Perhaps reassuring them at the same time that you feel the same way and that it's not an issue for you and so it shouldn't be an issue for them either.

Sydney *Theatresports* spent 20 years at the same theatre, performing seasons regularly on Sunday evenings on the set of whatever play was running that week, and the set was constantly being referred to and used in scenes. Once there was a set with real railway tracks, and the rest of the stage was entirely covered in large pebbles. I remember one particular scene where a player initiated by picking up a stone, tossing it between the rail sleepers, and saying "I can't come in for dinner Mum, I'm practising for the world hopscotch championships."

Dialogue can also contain meta information, such as the line "You don't listen to me anymore. You're not giving me anything to work with here!" which could be interpreted as being said by both the character as dialogue and the actor making a meta reference about their scene partner.

Short–form tends to take more advantage of misunderstandings and meta bleed than long–form. The frantic nature of some short–form performances, along with the restrictions of theatre games, throw up more obstacles to be justified than in a more grounded discovery based long–form. And one of the key things about justification, is that it realigns or changes context. Justification is by nature a comedic device.

Theatre games also tend to lock in language or physical restrictions which then conflict with a scene set up or initiation, so a conflict of contexts is already built into the scene before it even starts. Comedy ensues at the collision of contexts, and becomes even funnier when the conflicts are recognised and then justified. And often these misunderstandings are ignored in a scene anyway, meaning that often they appear much later in a scene where the collision of contexts may have an even greater effect.

It's not unusual in short–form to perform a scene where the audience has chosen a number of unrelated attributes which need to be justified and reconciled, say "finger painting" and "global trade agreement" for example. In fact, this could well be a possible definition of short–form: a restrictive framework with open ended discovery that automatically generates collisions of context, which then optimises LPMs — laughs per minute — through justification. Although "short theatre games" is still probably better.

The amount of mental model built upon a fallacy, contributes to the amount of humour. As we build a mental model in our head of what is happening in a scene, the more that we have wrong, the more we must reconcile the model when we realise that we have it wrong. If the improvisors think they are lovers in a laundry doing their washing after having a fight, and the audience thinks they're in a pinball arcade hitting on each other, then the audience members have a lot of reconciling to do when they realise what the improvisors think they're doing. Mental models are built when the unconscious believes in a certain reality, so it is important for comedy that a reality is built in a way that maximises recognition for the audience. The more the audience can see the reality that the scene is building, and the more detail there is to that reality, the bigger the laughs when it is revealed that the audience is wrong. Just don't be too wrong.

In the film *Trust Us This Is All Made Up*, TJ Jagodowski and David Pasquesi start their show with one guy consoling another guy after an outburst in the boss' office. A potential rebellion is building at the company based on what has happened. While the relationship between them is the engaging thing in the scene, it's not until a few minutes in that it is clarified that the scene is about the boss' coaching of the softball team and his selection of batting order. This is the first big laugh of the show, because it is not what was expected by the audience. They expected it to be a reason with much higher stakes and about their office work.

Because nothing is real until it comes out in a scene, softball could well have been decided just before it was spoken as a comedic choice, or it could have been felt well before it came out because the improvisors were in perfect sync and flow. As improvisors gain experience, choices like this become so second nature — internalised — that they start as a comedic choice in their early years but become an organic unconscious choice in their later years. This isn't because the scene is "always right there in front of them", but because their unconscious has been well trained in what makes a good comedic and seemingly grounded choice. They have internalised the progression of such scenes.

This broken mental model works just as well when an improvisor doesn't see the mental model built by their scene partner and the audience — such as in my bed vs. boat example. When they do realise that their mental model is wrong, not only does comedy ensue, but the audience typically feels for the improvisor — empathises — as they struggle through justifying their recent responses against what they've just realised is the truth.

When improvising on a blank stage, everything is open to interpretation, and that's where improvisation's specific comedy tropes begin to take advantage of the improvisation process. Here's a fish, here's a wedding, now justify the connection. But as a scene progresses, the facts and mental models get clarified and locked in, and the opportunity for misunderstandings is minimised — not completely removed, but reduced. And as misunderstandings are minimised, as there is less of the unexpected, and less justification required, there's also less opportunities for improvisation specific comedy.

In the case of short–form, some specific facts are usually pre-set at the beginning of a scene, but the rest of the scene is completely open to being discovered and justified against the pre-sets, usually with much hilarity. On the other hand, when pre-setting very detailed scene setups in both short–form and long–form — including attributes such as location, vocation, an actual set with actual props, a backstory, and character attributes — the opportunity for improvisation specific comedy is reduced. This doesn't mean it won't be funny, just that it won't be *as* funny because those improvisation specific effects are no longer being used as much as they typically would be.

This is how dramatic non-comedic improvisation is possible, by minimising misunderstandings — and thus justification — by pre–setting many of the attributes for a scene. Even an actual theatre set or real props can minimise misunderstandings, meaning that the more "theatrical play–like" that an improvised show is, the less funny it generally becomes.

And the converse is also true, in that when we focus on the open discovery side of improvisation, and not so much on pre–set information, there is more potential for comedy.

Improvisation can't not be funny, because you can't fully remove these comedy effects from the improvisation process. This doesn't mean you can't do a serious improvised drama, it's just that there will still be moments of comedy in the work, or at least the potential for comedy. But the more detail and specificity you pre-set for a dramatic work, the less improvisation specific comedy will be present.

Playback Theatre for example, improvises a very specific story given by the teller — the audience member telling their personal story. When acted out, the scenes are often funny, which is interesting considering that these are personal stories of audience members, and must be handled delicately. Even improvised dramatic plays, which are not designed to be funny, still have their funny moments.

The improvisation process compensates for the lack of time available to perfect a written comedy script, and the audience forgives the performers in a way that can make a less than perfect improvised scene funnier than a well-crafted scripted sketch. In fact, audiences will usually laugh more intensely at meta or what we call metapragmatic action and dialogue — so long as it doesn't wreck the scene — than non-meta action and dialogue for this very reason, whereas in a sketch or written comedic play this isn't the case.

When improvisation is used with standard comedy tropes — as it typically is — it's even funnier. But ultimately improvised comedy is already funny because it is improvised, and it is the existence of an audience and our scene partner which allows improvisation to be funny. And when we add callbacks and reincorporation, there's an additional layer of comedy — a collision of context — as the audience briefly considers whether it's actually improvised after all. This is also why solo scenes on average are more difficult to make as funny as scenes with more than one improvisor. In solo work, the improvisation specific comedy elements only come from the audience and improvisor, and not the other improvisors in the scene. Misunderstandings and justification have less of an impact, because a single improvisor is now in control of the entire mental model.

Theatrical improvisation is funny because it requires improvisors. And improvisors are unique, unpredictable, random and fallible human beings. We are continually trying to understand and justify the unexpected effects of a complex system in which we have no real control. When improvisation is used for open scenes — without pre-set information, sets, props or anything else — improvisation always has enormous potential for being funny. It won't *always* be funny, but so long as the improvisors are present and not in their heads, improvisation always has the *potential* to be funny. Whether intentional or not, unrestricted *theatrical improvisation can't not be funny.*

The rule of three

The reason the rule of three applies in comedy should by now be pretty obvious. The first instance of something is the initial presentation of the "thing". The second instance is the confirmation of repetition and sets up the expectation that there may be a third. The third instance is usually unlike the first and second, and this breaks the expectation, creating comedy from a collision of contexts.

The rule of three is used extensively throughout comedic improvisation, from listening and action, all the way up through scenework and up to show forms. And because humans are pattern matching machines, this means we're constantly looking for coincidences, which often turn out to only repeat once. Thus comedy often ensues when it repeats more than once and then breaks the expectation that it will repeat again.

1970s

The 1970s was a decade of consolidation, and the prelude to the modern era of improvisation. All the discoveries up until then had been about the core principles, and the basics of scene progression, allowing scenes to be improvised from scratch without scenarios. These discoveries were explored more throughout the 1970s, and we began to understand more about improvisation as it spread to other branches of the performing arts.

Contact Improvisation

Dancer Steve Paxton began developing *Contact Improvisation* in 1972. While experimenting with a combination of standing meditation, aikido — a martial art — and controlled falling and dance, Paxton developed *Magnesium*, a performance work and forerunner to *Contact Improvisation*. In *Magnesium*, dancers improvised collisions in the air in random body positions, and then landed safely again by positioning their limbs for support or for a roll, as in aikido.

After *Magnesium*, Paxton developed *Contact Improvisation*, replacing the air contact with slower grounded types of specific movements, and where the dancers are almost always in physical contact with each other at one or more points on their body. While the work is improvised, like most improvised domains there is a fixed language of movement and shape which dancers must learn, in order for them to be able to respond correctly to the movements offered by their dance partner.

While originally for two people, pretty quickly group improvisations began to appear all around the world, where large groups of dancers — often strangers — would improvise in contact for several hours at a time.

Action Theater

Ruth Zaporah was born in 1936, discovered Zen in 1953 when 17 years old, and by the late 1950s was improvising her own dance and movement by experimenting with combinations of elements she hadn't seen anyone else doing. In *Improvisation On the Edge: Notes from On and Off Stage*, Zaporah writes that she was "making dances out of oddly juxtaposed elements, such as reading a recipe while walking a tightrope, dancing while blowing up balloons, binding myself in infinite layers of corsets and then squirming to get out of them while reciting Emily Dickinson".

In 1967 she was hired as a movement expert at Towson State College in Maryland. Expecting to teach dance, she was surprised to find that her very first class was twenty acting students wanting to better embody their characters. Zaporah didn't know what "embody" or "character" meant, so instead she began to explore with them improvised movement and dance based on mindfulness and Zen practice.

Moving to the Bay Area of San Francisco in 1970, she continued experimenting by teaching and performing, finally developing *Action Theater* into a method for dance and movement.

Action Theater is described in Zaporah's 1995 book *Action Theater. The Improvisation of Presence*. Structured as a twenty day training programme, the book details many parallel concepts with theatrical improvisation. These include spontaneity, listening and creativity, along with the use of freeze and pause — a Viola Spolin concept — narrative, emotion and humour. *Action Theater* also includes built in techniques for contrasting and varying movement, something not always taught in theatrical improvisation.

Zaporah sees *Action Theater* as a meeting of two disciplines: body and movement, through which presence is the result.

Canadian Improv Games

David Shepherd and Howard Gerome started the *Improv Olympics* in New York in 1972. It was a competitive format for teams of improvisors, which Shepherd thought would be a great way to combine watching sport on TV with going out to the theatre. Co-incidentally, this was a similar idea as Keith Johnstone[123], who permanently moved from the U.K. to Calgary, Canada in 1974.

The audience would write scene suggestions on cards at the top of the show, and the teams would act out scenes from the cards. Like Moreno's *Theatre of Spontaneity*, the audience could jump up and direct the scenes if they wanted, and later in the show audience members were selected to come up and play various characters. *Improv Olympics* quickly spread to various high schools in the area.

In 1974 Toronto based *Homemade Theatre* invited Shepherd and Gerome to bring the format to their annual week long theatrical improvisation festival. *Homemade Theatre* added a more professional theatre look[124], and added elements that made it look more like a professional sporting event, including referees, rounds highlighting a particular type of improvisation skill, and names which reflected events in the real Olympics. They also created amateur and professional leagues. The show only ran at the festival, but then in 1976 *Homemade Theatre* started touring it and teaching it around Ontario.

Around 1977, Jamie "Willie" Wyllie was a student at one of the schools where *Homemade Theatre* ran a workshop. Along with Gerome, and with input from Shepherd and his protégé Michael Golding, they built *Improv Olympics* into what is now the Canadian wide *Canadian Improv Games*, which then went national in 1988. *Canadian Improv Games* now uses Keith

---

[123] While memories vary on exactly what Keith Johnstone contributed to the development of *Theatresports*, the consensus is that he had the idea for a pro wrestling version of improvised scenes while still in the U.K., along with improvisors competing in challenges for stage time. But many of the later developments in *Theatresports* are similar if not the same as the *Improv Olympics* and *Canadian Improv Games*. While Johnstone may not have been aware of *Improv Olympics* at the time, it is certainly possible that some of his actor and student cast may well have been. Considering that *Improv Olympics* used Viola Spolin's games for training and rehearsal, and that both Johnstone and Spolin were leaders in the field — Johnstone often claimed as much — it is pretty incredible that at that time Johnstone had never heard of Spolin or *Improv Olympics*.

[124] Although the surviving video footage does not give the impression of a professional looking theatre event.

Johnstone's impro method, which is more appropriate for the style of improvisation used and watched by teenagers — due to the use of story and active advances. Wyllie ended up as a lawyer and died in 2014 at the age of 56.

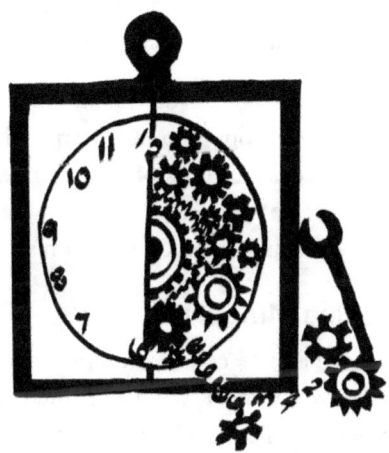

How scenes work

We now have all the theory in place for how to improvise, and have looked at the progress of that theory throughout the 20th century. We know what to do when we improvise, but how does an improvised scene actually work? We're not talking about techniques like game of the scene or platforms and tilts, we're talking about how an improvised scene works, regardless of the method.

We discussed some of what a scene is when we looked at scene progression — the attributes of a scene and which methods focus on which attributes. But what about the structure of a scene or its component parts? Whether it be short-form or long-form, or Johnstone or Chicago, breaking a scene down into component parts gives more detail about how scenes work and helps identify areas for improvement. But how can we do that in a generic way when the various methods and their variations are so different?

Most books on improvisation will tell us how the author thinks we should start a scene, but this will vary from author to author. Is it best to start a scene with a hard initiation, a strong offer to drive the scene forward, or is it better to soft initiate and just see what happens? Should we start with nothing, discovering everything from within the scene, or start with a premise, an already formed idea? Should we start with CROW — Character, Relationship, Objective and Where — a status choice, or with a quick build to a platform? Or should we start with something relating to the characters, like an emotion or an actual character?

Well it all depends on the method and style of improvisation we're using and what we're hoping to achieve from it. Different schools and show forms often require certain types of initiation, or at least work better with certain types. So how do we analyse an improvised scene when even the very beginning of the scene has so much variation?

Acting without text

The closest cousin to improvising a scene, which doesn't involve improvisation, is acting a scripted scene[125]. There's been a lot of analysis and theory applied to acting over the last hundred and fifty years that is extremely useful for improvisors. And as we saw in our history chapters, many of the core texts or books on improvisation are by actors, or those with a background in acting theory.

There are several ways to consider the structure of a play, but the most common is as a sequence of events through which a lead character or protagonist travels. This is often broken down into a setup followed by an inciting incident at the beginning, which is a call to action for the character, followed by escalating or rising action throughout the main part of the play, which then leads to climax and then resolution — also known as the dénouement — after which the character or their view has changed in some way.

This structure maps well to the beginning, middle and end of a play, which in itself is often referred to as a 3 act structure: an inciting incident, the rising action, and a resolution. More detailed theories on structure then break these down into further parts or stages, often descending into a mire of theory and logic which turns playwriting into more of a computer program than a piece of art. Robert McKee's popular book *Story: Substance, Structure, Style and the Principles of Screenwriting* arguably falls into this category[126].

---

[125] There are however schools of thought that say actors are always improvising regardless of the existence of pre-written text, which I also agree with.
[126] Often referred to as the screenwriter's bible, obviously its complexity doesn't preclude it from being useful.

Christopher Vogler published a more usable story structure in recent times with his 1992 book *The Writer's Journey*, which in itself is a 12 stage hero's journey adaptation of the 1949 book *The Hero with a Thousand Faces* by Joseph Campbell. Vogler's structure is detailed enough to be of practical use, but at the same time simple enough to grasp without requiring a course in playwriting.[127]

But McKee, Vogler and Campbell are only the most recent explorers of story structure. Russian theatre director Georgi Tovstonogov for example described a 5 part event structure. This consisted of: the initial event or given circumstance which happened before the play starts and which pervades the whole play; the primary event — the call to action — ; the central event which triggers the run to the end; the final event conclusion; and the principal event or dénouement which resolves the original given circumstances.

Heading then to England, E.M. Forster's book *Aspects of the Novel* summarises a series of lectures he gave on, obviously enough, aspects of the novel, where he describes amongst other things the structure of both story and plot. And Aristotle's *Poetics* written around 335 BCE examines the structure of poetry, including story, in tragedy and epics — historically a poem with an expansive story and with a hero. A second part to *Poetics* discussing comedy specifically, has unfortunately since been lost. But I'm guessing any useful insights beyond interest value, would have been already thoroughly explored by the huge number of comedy writing books that have been published in recent years.

In Johnstone's impro, story is a key scene attribute. And while often Johnstone method improvisors will lessen its priority in long–form improvisation, their scenes still tend to follow common story principles. In longer scenic improvisation, an understanding of story is also useful for Chicago method improvisors for connecting scenes together in certain circumstances, however it is often difficult to resist the temptation to focus

---

[127] Vogler was working as a story consultant for Disney Pictures in 1987, where he wrote a 7 page memo summarising how Campbell's book applied to movie writing. The memo was passed around and became extremely popular in Hollywood, leading to his writing of *The Writer's Journey*.

on story in scenes, simply because that's the way we think about and remember real life.[128]

Coming back to plays — our closest non-improvising medium — it was Stanislavsky who originally proposed a method of scene analysis for directors and actors, which has been adapted over the years but is still the basis for scene analysis used today.

According to Stanislavsky, the point of a play is called the super–objective or super–task, and is the objective which drives the entire play. It is the play's reason for being. The various story structures discussed above all serve as a structure to deliver the super–objective to the audience. For example, the super–objective of the play *Hamlet* might be considered "Revenge", "Revenge Hamlet's father" or more specifically perhaps Hamlet's need to "expose and kill Claudius". Super–objective is often equated with a character and what their service is to the point of the play, but is still the ultimate reason why the play exists.

Within the play, characters have their own objectives they wish to achieve — typically based on specific verbs — which serve both the structure or plot of the play as well as the super–objective. As the play progresses, the character's objectives change as the scenes change. In *Hamlet*, again, Hamlet's various objectives throughout the play include but are obviously not limited to: discovering the truth through his father's ghost; resolving whether to commit suicide; and getting Claudius to identify himself as the murderer of his father. These objectives are then broken down into smaller and smaller objectives, often as short as a few seconds or a few words, but also could be so long as several paragraphs. In Stanislavsky terms, these are called *units of action* or *beats*, and read like a step by step plan of action for a character through the play.

The journey from the beginning to the end of a play, via the super–objective, smaller objectives and sub-objectives, is called the through line. This doesn't mean the character has the same objective all the way through the play, just that the smaller sub-objectives together serve the plot and the play's super–objective.

---

[128] And once you start thinking about story, group mind and complexity theory kicks in and begins to amplify it.

This is becoming heady at this point, and if you're not already familiar with this kind of script analysis then you could be excused for wondering what this has to do with improvisation. Luckily this is where we begin to talk about the origins and uses of improvisation's point of view, game moves and heightening.

The word *beat* is believed to be the misheard and Americanised version of Stanislavsky's term *bit*[129], representing a unit of action. Units of action typically heighten the player's objective to a point where something changes in the action, which causes the objective to change, thus triggering a new unit of action. A heightened objective usually comes with heightened emotion, and as we know, it is the emotion that allows the audience to empathise with the character.

Second City alumnus David Razowsky teaches heightened units of action in his improv workshops, and uses an emotion heightening diagram he calls the Jerry Chart[130] to show how this works. While Razowsky often refers to this as emotional energy or emotional heightening, it is actually the heightening of a combined beat, objective and emotion over a unit of action, until something changes it into a new beat. This is a great example of over a century of theatre theory being newly applied to improvisation. But it is not the only example.

Point of view

In improvisation, we have a phrase similar to objective which means roughly the same thing, and that's "point of view". A character's point of view is a guiding emotion, belief or trait which the actor uses to filter and respond within a scene. A point of view might be as simple as jealousy or love for example, with jealousy or love then colouring the character's responses throughout the scene. Points of view can also be fairly complex, for example always wanting to take over whatever their scene partner says or does, or they can be meta–game based such as only ever giving one word responses. Often these are referred to as beliefs or statements of inspiration for a character, but these are also points of view.

---

[129] A bit can also refer to a part or section of a stand–up comedy routine, but that's not how we're using it here.
[130] Search the web for David Razowsky and Jerry Chart and you should find the video where he explains this concept.

Points of view are different from objectives because an objective or sub-objective is something which a character wants to tactically achieve in a beat, whereas a point of view is a guiding statement of how the character generally acts in a beat. Ultimately though they are the same thing, something that guides the character through the beat until something else does.

In their book *The Art of Directing*, John W. Kirk, Ralph Bellas and Christina Kirk refer to *pre–motive* as being the reason for a character having a particular objective, which also hooks into the idea of character point of view. So for example, Mary may feel anger towards her sister Jane for stealing her boyfriend Frank. This is her pre–motive. So she tries to get back at Jane by breaking up her relationship with Frank. This is her objective over a number of scenes or part of a scene. She may try giving Jane examples of when Frank couldn't be trusted in the past, as a way of her questioning her relationship. If this is successful, then Jane's objective and emotional state would most likely change in line with Razowsky's Jerry Chart.

Mary's sub–objectives may change every few lines based on the tactics she uses to try and break up Jane's relationship, which supports each of her higher level objectives. When we strip this back from a script into improvisation where there is no initial pre–set pre–motive, we could say that Mary's point of view is to "keep trying to break up Jane's new relationship", or to "convince Jane that Frank is untrustworthy", or that "you can't trust anyone".

Mick Napier was the first to document the need to keep points of view consistent throughout an entire scene. In his first book *Improvise: Scene from the Inside Out*, he says that even with an hour long scene, you should keep the same point of view throughout. This is certainly possible, and exploring the many facets of a single point of view can be an engaging way to improvise. But this is also a big departure from scripted acting.

But ironically for Napier, sticking with the same point of view limits the number of possible scenes you can perform. There may be a huge number of great scenes where the point of view does change and quite often, so why would you want to exclude the possibility of discovering those scenes? Character points of view do change in scripted plays, but they change when they need to and not when they're not working. This seems to be a better interpretation of what Napier is saying, that improvisors shouldn't change their point of view, because it's usually for the wrong reason.[131] And to cover those circumstances where a point of view change may be OK, he discusses a concept called "pull out/pull in", which reverses the point of view for a line or two before returning it to its original state.

Initially this seems similar to what Razowsky is saying in that point of view can and does change, but Razowsky has linked the technique with traditional script analysis, in that change happens when it needs to, and happens according to an emotional state and objective change, and not because it's intentional at a meta level. Once improvisors are trained to notice such a change, it is fairly easy for all the players in a scene to notice changes in individual players, as those changes approach and as they occur. The noticing of them allows us to better engage with how these changes transition and to be more aware of our point of view for the upcoming beat.

Point of view is often compared to the super-objective of a play, but this is an odd choice considering the super-objective does not directly match the low level objectives and sub-objectives. It could be argued that the point of view in improvisation continually influences the character at a higher level, much like a super-objective would across a play. But point of view is rarely played this way in improvised scenes. More often it is played as a consistent objective or sub-objective which influences every action by the character in the scene. This often takes away scene and relationship depth, the truth of the scene, and the truthful emotion that's needed for audience empathy. As well as limiting the number of possible scenes there are that we can play.

Improvisation is beyond our control, so we will change our point of view in scenes at some point in our life, either by accident, in response to something in a scene, or intentionally. There are even short–form performance games where the goal is for the characters to change or swap their points of view. So learn how to change point of view and be conscious of heightening units of action and objectives, regardless of whether you think doing so is a valid part of your method.

Metapragmatics

Jacob Moreno originally explored the idea of a specific language and structure of an improvised scene back in the 1921, and subsequently documented it in

---

[131] Napier gives a good description of all the different reasons you might change a character's point of view, in his book *Improvise: Scene from the Inside Out*.

his book *The Theatre of Spontaneity*. But real scientific analysis of theatrical improvisation didn't occur until R. Keith Sawyer[132], then studying for a doctorate in psychology, happened to fall into playing keyboards for the Chicago improv community from 1992 to 1994. He took notes and videos of his time there, and in 2003 released his research as *Improvised Dialogues: Emergence and Creativity in Conversation*, an unfortunately very much ignored book[133] on conversational analysis and improvisation.

The study of the way people communicate, dates back to the mid 20th century, with the main discoveries — for our purposes — made by Mikhail Bakhtin and Erving Goffman. In his 1975 book *The Dialogic Imagination: Four Essays*, Bakhtin found that spoken communication contains many more layers of meaning than the literal spoken words. He says that the interpretation of what is being said, depends on many factors, including the socio-economic and cultural backgrounds of the participants, as well as the subjective context in which each person finds themself in the conversation. Not only that but it is often possible to determine facts beyond the literal conversation, such as how people feel about themselves and others, whether they are channelling[134] other people, and how they communicate internally with themselves.

For example, the sentence "Can I talk to you Michael?" at face value is asking Michael whether the speaker can talk to him and by implication, now. He already is talking to him, so the question seems redundant. We talk to people all the time so the implication is that it is either: a long talk when Michael seems currently busy with something else; a more serious talk requiring privacy; or both. It could also indicate that the speaker is uncomfortable about what they wish to talk about — perhaps this situation hasn't come up before or it didn't go well last time it happened. And this is all before applying the personal subjective context of Michael and the speaker.

---

[132] Sawyer is one of the great accidents of improvisation theory. He was already formally studying creativity and the psychology of how people communicate, and yet found himself almost by accident in a position where he needed to know the theory and practice of Chicago method improv, as well as being required to watch improvisation for key musical cues. His early work on improvisation analysis would most likely not have happened but for these coincidences, and his later work on creativity may not have ultimately taken the direction it did.

[133] Sawyer dedicated his book to "the Chicago improvisational theater community", which makes it even more of a shame that his work has been ignored.

[134] In the non-new age sense of paraphrasing and carrying and reusing emotion and meaning from others.

A year before *The Dialogic Imagination*, Erving Goffman released his book *Frame Analysis*, in which he details how conversations may be analysed using what's called an interactional frame, a frame within which conversation occurs, like a theatre performance. The actions of each participant contributes to the frame of the conversation, and the conversation itself then influences the participants and their next contributions. As the participants and the conversation all interact, the conversation is discovered through the emergence that we looked at previously in complex systems. This works the same in improvisation. Scene partners build a scene together, which Goffman calls the interactional frame. The scene then influences each of the players' moves via emergence, just like group mind and priming do, with an effect called downward causation. Downward causation is the way the scene as a whole, influences the players' actions.

In normal conversations, the participants interact similar to actors working through units of action with objectives, super-objectives, pre-motives and tactics[135]. They have an awareness of an audience, whether it be the other participants or people in the periphery, in which to invoke empathy. Keith Johnstone's status work in his book *Impro: Improvisation and the Theatre* ties in nicely with this idea, that status is an always changing aspect of communication and drives the relationship between people.

Bakhtin's work on dialogical analysis and Erving's work on conversational framing and analysis, led Sawyer to analyse several years of improvised scenes in the early 1990s, which then allowed him to identify metapragmatic communication in improvisation. Metapragmatics is the underlying communication between actors about what is happening or needs to happen during a scene. This communication is going on all the time while a scene is in progress and often even the most experienced improvisors are completely unaware of it.

If you took a scene out of the middle of a scripted play and performed it to a new audience, there's a good chance the scene may not make sense outside the context of the play. This would seem initially to be just due to the difference between a scripted scene from a play and an improvised scene. Most improvisation is a scene or collection of scenes from a longer unseen

---

[135] My words, not Goffman's.

work, so they are often scenes which stand alone and don't require you to see the longer work.

For example, if we took Hamlet's "to be or not to be" soliloquy from the play *Hamlet*, and played that as an improvised scene, it would lack context and thus be confusing for the audience to understand fully. So from this it would seem that improvised scenes are a pretty small subset of all possible scenes, a subset which only includes scenes which require no context or explanation for the audience before they are performed. Surely improvisation isn't so limiting?

Written plays however have the same problem in their opening scenes, it's just that the dialogue and staging have been carefully designed so that all the necessary context and exposition is included in the scene, but without it being too obvious to the audience that this is being conveyed to them. We also do this in improvisation, often without realising it.

In short–form improvisation this is easy, the context is usually either explained to the audience up front, or the audience makes the decision themselves as part of an ask–for or audience suggestion. So what about long–form improvisation? As it turns out most improvisors in both short–form and long–form improvisation, have devised acting methods which do convey scene context to an audience, so that they can play isolated scenes without too much exposition.

When we perform an improvised scene, we're communicating all the time, not just with dialogue and physical actions, but with every single movement and sound we make. And with this we communicate with our scene partners on two levels: character to character and actor to actor. The character to character communication is simply the way the characters interact on stage, what they say, what they do, what is being acted out in the scene for the audience.

Actor to actor communication on the other hand, is where the actors are telling each other what they want the other character to do or what they think is happening in the scene. Actor to actor communication is mostly unseen by an untrained audience. So how does character to character and actor to actor communication happen at the same time, and without the audience realising it?

One common guideline for long-form improvisation is to name the characters at the top of the scene, or at least in the first few lines, and to repeat it several times. This allows both the actors and the audience to know which character is which, in case they need to return later.

In the Chicago method this is a fairly prominent guideline, because the work often contains multiple connected scenes with the same characters. In Johnstone's impro however, there is no such guideline regarding names, partly because the focus is on the narrative journey of generic character types, and characters that are less likely to return in a different scene. But regardless of the method, names in long-form are usually important.[136]

For example, if a character named Charlie was introduced in an early scene, and in a later scene an actor comes on and says "Charlie, you cooked me dinner for my birthday!", then we know that the character Charlie is in the scene, and depending on the actor saying the line and the character they bring on, we'll have a fairly good idea who they are and what the scene is about. Likewise, we know that unless duplicate naming is part of the point of the scene, there will be no other characters named Charlie, just the original Charlie. This isn't like real life of course, where names are random and you simply get what you get.

Communicating a name in this way is called "metapragmatic". It is communication about communication, and it is the actors telling each other about the scene.

In the above scene with Charlie, we're entering the story. We're starting the scene a little way into it, so we would assume if this were real life, the "Charlie" at the beginning of the line would not be needed, because the characters already know who each other are. So "Charlie" is metapragmatic. It is added so that actor A can tell actor B that they want the character Charlie who was used in an earlier scene, or they are specifically labelling the character so they can be referenced in a later scene. Likewise if this were real life, it would possibly have already been discussed that this was their birthday, so subsequently "for my birthday" is possibly also metapragmatic, depending on how such a scene would be presented, whether one of the characters entered

---

[136] When Johnstone method improvisors perform long-form, they begin to discover and use many of the techniques developed for Chicago method long form, such as in this case naming characters.

the scene during or after the initiation, or whether both characters started in the scene.

If we assume that earlier in the scene — the part of the scene we never saw because we started the scene in the middle of it — there would have been some exchange such as "Hi Charlie I'm home." "Oh hi May, happy birthday", then the full line of dialogue "Charlie, you cooked me dinner for my birthday!" with the metapragmatics removed would instead be "You cooked me dinner!" This is a much more realistic thing to say, but also may not have enough detail to drive the scene forward. So instead we say "Charlie, you cooked me dinner for my birthday!"

There are two types of metapragmatics: one that gives scene context, and one that's a back channel communication between actors as the scene plays out.

Scene context metapragmatics appear mostly at the beginning of a scene, within the initiation and first few seconds of the scene, and it gives the audience context and the other actors information on the initiation. Context metapragmatics are what we use to improvise a single scene, without having to see the whole play it came from in order to understand it. Over time as we begin to understand the context of the scene, context metapragmatics decreases, leaving the actors with just the scene itself to play with.

Back channel metapragmatics is where actors communicate mid-scene. The line of dialogue "Get out of my way Mary, I'm leaving and that's all there is to it!" is a character line. It possibly has scene context metapragmatics in the naming and relationship set up — depending on what was in the scene before it — but it is also a clear instruction to the other actor "Don't let me leave!" This kind of metapragmatics usually happens at the end of a beat or unit of action if you think back to Razowsky's Jerry Chart for example. A change in objective triggers a brief metapragmatic negotiation between the actors to confirm their points of view, and then it's back to the characters playing another unit of action.

Most of this happens without us realising it, as we've trained our unconscious to work this way by trial and error while improvising scenes in class or on stage. And while some improvisation training will make a point of the different types of initiations and their uses, as well as the use of names and a few other metapragmatic techniques, I've not come across any writing or practices aside from Sawyer's work which looks at metapragmatics as a whole.[137]

Sawyer states that improvisation metapragmatics creates the emergent effects in scenes. And because culture, language and improvisation training are all similar across players working together — most of which is controlled by the unconscious — improvised scenes can't help but converge on a single group agreement.

The use of metapragmatics is often difficult to spot in improvised scenes, because a lot of the time we don't know we're doing it. But where they are most obvious are in scene initiations. Hard initiations are heavy on context metapragmatics, they're loaded with information that you wouldn't include in a real life situation or even in a single scene where it is part of a longer play. While often clunky, the benefit of hard initiations is that they get the scene context out of the way fast so that the scene can begin in earnest. Hard initiations usually come from a premise, as it is easier to have an idea for a scene and hard initiate it, than to come in with nothing and instantly hard initiate at the top of the scene. This means that premise–based scenes are better at getting to the meat of a scene, because if you have an idea pulled from an opening, and your scene partner recognises it, then there's no negotiation required at the top of the scene.

Soft initiations don't include much information about the scene at all. The point is that the players will discover the scene together mostly from scratch. From this it would seem like soft initiations are a waste of time, if they just increase the amount of metapragmatics, and delay getting to the meat of the scene. Soft initiations however do have their benefits. The main one being open ended negotiation and discovery, which allows almost any scene to happen after the initiation. In soft initiations, the metapragmatics continues further into the scene than with a hard initiation, however it is not as obvious to the audience. Because the scene builds more over time, the audience doesn't feel like they're being beaten over the head with exposition compressed into one or two lines of a hard initiation.

---

[137] For a number of years now I've often included metapragmatics or at least observations and techniques based on it in my improvisation workshops, and have found that it greatly increases the understanding and flow of improvised scenes for the improvisors involved. When players understand how a scene is negotiated between actors, they begin to minimise metapragmatics and are more confident and better equipped to perform more dynamic and free flowing scenes.

Metapragmatics is generally a high percentage of the communication at the top of a scene compared to the end, and decreases as the scene begins to take shape, regardless of the type of initiation. Short–form improvisation specifically, tends to start and continue with a higher percentage of metapragmatics, due to the restrictions on what may be done in the scene. This often causes a *clunkiness* in scenes where disconnected ideas must be connected together or justification is required to keep the scene in check.

With Keith Johnstone's methods, the use of metapragmatics are also higher due to the way his method values active advances over yessing, leaving open more unknown or undealt with details within the scene, which may in turn lead to more need for justification and metapragmatics. But this in theory opens up more creative options in the scene, because the goal posts are continually changing.

On the other hand, long–form improvisation in general uses relatively less metapragmatics. Forms such as *Harold* and those which use game of the scene, still use a moderately high degree of metapragmatics relative to other long–form formats, whereas long–form scenic improvisation similar to *TJ and Dave* or *Dasariski*, use much less metapragmatics. This is particularly the case with the Chicago method which gives priority to focusing inward on the last thing, instead of active advances where there is a potential for misunderstanding early in a scene. This also means there is more opportunity for interaction between the characters in long–form, because more detail about the current moment has been contributed to the scene, and thus less need for metapragmatics.

Metapragmatics is necessary. It tells the actors and the audience what is happening, but it is also our job as improvisors to minimise it as much as possible. The fun stuff, the meat of the scene, what the scene is about, is mostly in the character to character communication, not the metapragmatics. This means minimising as much as possible the amount of metapragmatics and the work involved in negotiating beat changes. The less actor–to–actor or actor–to–audience communication we do, the more time we can spend on what the audience really loves to watch, the actual scene.

Metapragmatics isn't usually a primary focus in improvisation training, and aside from a few guidelines such as character naming and initiation types, is mostly learned through experience. This is often why we set up scenes for newer improvisors, because we're teaching them the character and scenework side of the work, and not so much the actor's additional responsibilities to the audience and their scene partners — metapragmatics — which is a different muscle.

All information on improvisation makes us a better improvisor, and the more we understand the craft, the better we will be. But aside from that, while interesting, how does the understanding of metapragmatics make us a better improvisor?

Once we begin to recognise metapragmatics, like anything else, it begins to stand out more. By recognising when this happens, we're training ourselves to improve the quality of communicating metapragmatics without making it so obvious to the audience.

For improvisation teachers in particular, they also start to better see the actor-to-actor communication in scenes and more clearly see the thinking processes of students. This in turn allows them to give better feedback, which makes them a better teacher, and both teacher and student become better improvisors.

Game

A *game* is an exercise with some rules and objectives. In the case of improvisation, this is either a scene or a skill exercise wrapped in a rule or two, with the goal being to do the best you can to get to the end of the game.

Short-form theatre games are the most obvious examples of this, with *Theatresports*, *ComedySportz*, the *Canadian Improv Games*, and *Whose Line Is It Anyway?* being just some of successful show formats which use acting exercises and parlour games to entertain a theatre audience.

As an example, "Accent Rollercoaster" is a short-form game where a scene is performed, with an offstage person calling out different accents which the players must switch to throughout the course of the scene. Another example is "Death in a minute", where a one-minute scene is performed and at some point in the scene someone must die. Both are also good training exercises, because improvisors are learning different accents, justification, and making more active choices.

Violin Spolin says in her book *Improvisation For The Theater*:

> *[..] the acceptance of all the imposed limitations creates the playing, out of which the game appears, or as in the theater, the scene [..]*

Spolin is saying that rules — whether they be short–form game rules or the core principles of improvisation — create limitations, and the limitations are what allow us to play. The game or scene then appears organically out of the playing. Supporting this, Spolin also says:

> *It is the energy released in solving the problem which forms the scene.*

A lot of Spolin's games are exactly this, a fun and spontaneous learning exercise with rules, an end goal, and a focus or main skill the exercise focuses on. The rules create the environment in which we can play, and from that the game appears, and playing the game forms a scene.

A game in long–form improvisation is slightly different. It is a pattern in a scene — something that happens more than once — and by repeating and heightening the pattern, we can derive humour from its repetition and escalation. Games can be played any number of times in a scene, for however long it seems necessary for the scene or fun for the audience. But it is still a tool of improvisation like any other — we don't need to actively play a game in a scene if we don't think it is the right choice. And because scenes have many attributes regardless of whether we focus on them or not, a lot of the time we may be playing a game without consciously realising it.

Written sketches take advantage of game playing, as games focus the point of a short scene into just a single comedic idea, which is defined and then played with. Most sketches are an exercise in defining and playing a single game, but that certainly doesn't mean all sketches must have one game. They may have multiple games or none.

Game of the scene on the other hand, is the idea that every scene has a single game, the game that is the scene, and everything in the scene is there to serve that game. In most schools based on the Chicago method, game of the scene is treated as just another attribute of a scene. You can pay attention to it if you wish, you can make the odd *game move* to push a scene towards a game or continue a game, but you don't have to actively make it your primary or even conscious focus.

The exception to this is UCB, where their method makes discovering and heightening the game of the scene mandatory, and the primary focus while improvising. This works in theory because individual scenes are relatively short with a single focus, in forms such as *Slacker*, *Montage* or *Harold* for example. But once you go beyond those types of forms into longer scenes, a single game of the scene begins to drag scenes down and shows its limits. In game of the scene, you can also *rest the game* for a while mid-scene, where you take a break from heightening the game. But again, the longer the scene, the more often you have to rest the game to keep it being engaging. And when you begin to rest the game more than play the game, you're really just using the core Chicago method and playing a game every so often, and no longer using UCB's game of the scene.

To trace the roots of game we need to go back to Stanislavsky's scene analysis. As actors play with and against the objectives in their units of action, they're playing a back and forth game as each beat progresses. Game in long-form improvisation tries to emulate this idea: in the absence of prewritten dialogue, higher level objectives or points of view are used as a game around which to improvise the dialogue.

The first to identify game in improvisation was Jacob Moreno, writing in 1948 about his experiments in the 1920s, where he gives detailed descriptions of players improvising around beats and objectives, and finding and playing a game within the scene. He then focused his actors on identifying a game to be played within the scene.

The influence of Moreno on improvisation isn't particularly well documented in popular books on improvisation, but Viola Spolin does acknowledge that she was influenced by the work of both Jacob Moreno and Neva Boyd. And this lead to her son Paul Sills and his influence in the Chicago improv community, which brings us back to Chicago's consideration of game.

The terms *game of the scene*, *game within the scene*, the *scene's deal*, or Close's original name *scenic game* are all interchangeable, and refer to a single all-encompassing game which develops within an improvised scene. For example, if a scene begins with an old couple sitting on a park bench discussing their life experiences, this may turn into them each trying to outdo each other with their experiences. This then becomes a game of one upmanship, which would be the game of the scene.

The initiation of a scene and the opening lines of dialogue, give hints to the potential for a game within the scene. This is used in the UCB model for premise–based scenes — scenes where one of the players already has an idea for the scene before it has started. UCB also uses organic initiations in their method, where the game is discovered organically as the scene evolves. But in both cases, the point is to discover and agree to the game as quickly as possible.

In game of the scene method play, scenes are segmented into two phases: an initial exploratory phase, followed by the game heightening phase. In the exploratory phase, the players set up what's called a base reality, a consistent universe for the scene to play in. They then look for the first unusual thing which happens in that base reality. They then use the unusual thing to find what else is true, which in turn identifies a game for the scene. So for example, if the scene organically begins with a couple in the kitchen doing the washing up, that's the base reality. Then one of them might pull an axe out of the sink, which may lead to a game where successive murder weapons are pulled out of the sink, all while the couple continue talking about who will take the kids to school the next day.

The game is heightened by considering the question "if this is true, what else is true", which ends up focusing and then amplifying the game throughout the remainder of the scene. Finding "what else is true" contributes to the collision of contexts, because it builds more of the mental model of the reality that is being created by the improvisors, which helps make it funnier because the audience's expectations keep being broken.

In the case of a premise–based initiation, the initiation tries to declare both the base reality and the game at the top of the scene, or at worst declare an unusual thing with an implied base reality. The exploratory phase in these cases is usually extremely short, often only a single line of dialogue which delivers the premise. But premises can be misunderstood or even missed completely, meaning that a premise–based initiation can be followed by more time in the base reality searching for the first unusual thing or a game to play. For the inexperienced, this can mean lots of exposition and metapragmatics, instead of an entertaining scene.

UCB's rationale for focusing on the game of the scene is that every improvised scene has some kind of game, whether it be character or relationship based, or something else. And so by finding the game, you will find the scene. This is like saying every scene has a story, so by finding the story we'll find the scene — which is effectively the core of Johnstone's method. Or similar to saying find the relationship between the characters and you'll find the scene.

But not all improvised scenes have a game. Using UCB's method, if the scene ends before the game is found, then obviously that's a scene without a game. It may not be a great scene, but it would still be a scene. Although one riposte is that when there is no game, having no game is the game, which makes it very difficult to argue with some game of the scene aficionados. But scenes may also have more than one game, or the game may only appear for a part of the scene, or there might be games within games etc. All of these are against the UCB method, but are still valid scenes. Again, it's often said that because they don't clearly fit the game of the scene mould, their meta–games are the game of the scene. e.g. when there are two games in a scene, the game of the scene is two games in a scene.

One of the reasons often given for game of the scene being an all–encompassing technique, is that "all movies and TV series have a game". Movies and theatre do have overarching super–objectives, and the characters have various motives and objectives, but these aren't games. Any games which are played, are between the characters in a scene, and even then, there's not always a game. And there is also other material which serves the movie or TV series story arc, the characters and the audience's empathetic responses, which clearly aren't part of a game. So when game of the scene players say that every form of comedy or story has a game, they're not being entirely accurate.

Game of the scene is often accused of being a mechanical method for improvising funny scenes. But this is because often the examples are mechanical scenes where a clear game is defined in the first 10 seconds, followed by another 1 minute and 50 seconds of heightening the game to its conclusion. Real life isn't like that, and neither is comedy. Yes, comedy is all about patterns, and games are the rules we discover and apply to those patterns, but in between is the acting and the art, and one without the other can get stale pretty quickly.

Game of the scene is now considered a technique for generating improvised sketches, either for use in an improvised show, or for transcribing into written or rehearsed sketches. UCB players have internalised the ability to start a scene with a strong game, and to be able to quickly identify and play out that game. Thus we have a strong sketch, premeditated from an idea, without the need to write it ahead of time, while leveraging the inherent funniness that is built into the improvisation process. No wonder the UCB method is as popular as it is. It's a great process for writing comedy.

Published before UCB existed, the book *Truth in Comedy* also talks about the *game within the scene*, and suggests that improvisors should look for *game moves* which indicate that a game within a scene is to be played:

> *When an improviser finds the game within a scene, he's found the scene, and that's why it's so important to pick up on any possible game moves.*

Interestingly enough, this states that the game of the scene *is* the scene, which is what UCB says as well. Most of the current four UCB members worked closely with Del Close around that time, so this isn't unexpected, and they often say that their method is simply what Close was originally proposing. But the Chicago based schools, including *iO Chicago* — founded by two of the authors of *Truth in Comedy*[138] — do not teach this. Instead they teach that games may be discovered and played throughout a scene, but that there is not always a game played to the nth degree.

Which brings us to Keith Johnstone. While Johnstone's impro can include some traditional game playing in his exercises and show forms, he has no comparable technique to Chicago or UCB's game of the scene, in either name or practice. With Johnstone's method, improvisors build a *platform*[139] — a normal reality at the start of the scene — and either wait for or initiate a *tilt* — an action that is out of the ordinary for the normal reality — which then pushes the scene toward the interesting or extraordinary. This compares well with UCB's game of the scene, which specifies the playing of a base reality at the beginning of the scene, before discovering the first unusual thing, which leads to the game.

While these platform/tilt and base reality/game theories seem similar at first, they're not. With Johnstone, the focus is on building a solid platform, and

---

[138] Charna Halpern and Del Close.
[139] Platforms and tilts were a late discovery for Johnstone, only appearing in print in 1994. It is possible that he was influenced by game moves in *Truth in Comedy*, which coincidentally was published in 1994.

once the platform has tilted anything can and will happen, often with the absurdity curve coming into play. With UCB, the whole point is to look for the first unusual thing, and due to the inward looking nature of the Chicago method, the game is a singular idea that is drilled into, heightened and played as hard as possible until the end of the scene, give or take the odd break if the game is rested. In Johnstone however, a continuing story with advancing actions simply shows the impact of the tilt over the course of the scene, and is not a focus on or amplification of the tilt itself.

While it is possible to play game of the scene with Johnstone's impro, it can cause scenes to stall if the scene focuses on a verbal or even non-verbal game which can't actively advance. And playing a game throughout a heavily advancing long–form scene can sometimes seem more like a distraction from the unfolding story.

Units of action can be seen quite clearly in styles of improvisation which focus on game moves and game of the scene. Players identify a game either of the scene or within the scene, and then more often than not play the character's objective to satisfy the game. iO and *The Family*[140] alumnus Miles Stroth's position play technique is similar. In position play, Stroth identifies 4 basic scene types, and says that once you recognise the type of scene, it is easy to then play out the objectives of those characters in that type of scene. In the "straight/absurd" scene type — one character is the absurd person that has an unusual belief or trait that is heightened, while the other is the straight normal person that reacts to the straight person's musings — and "character driven" scene types, these can often be played as games of the scene.

Resting the game is also like a change in the unit of action, which is a change in sub-objective, and which is a new beat within the scene. In scripted plays, the actors and the director work through the script identifying these elements, so they may be perfected in rehearsal. But in improvisation we're doing it on the fly.

Game of the scene isn't the all-encompassing technique it is often claimed to be. It is a technical method for generating funny scenes very quickly, but like Napier's rules argument, does not include all the funny scenes which potentially exist. And similar to switching between Johnstone and Chicago,

---

[140] *The Family* was a well known house team at iO Chicago in the early to mid-1990s, which trained and experimented under the direction of Del Close.

switching between the often fast and frantic UCB game style and other non-game Chicago methods can be difficult, because we're unlearning the "base reality" and "game finding and playing" that's already been internalised as improvisation. Not to mention in order to play a game of the scene, all the improvisors in the scene need to know that this is what is happening, otherwise the game most likely won't be found and heightened.

Whether game of the scene is significant or not, recognising it and playing it is still a very useful technique to learn.

General topics

Being in the arts, improvisors tend to not ask questions of science, but instead follow tradition and the advice of experienced improvisors — who are often just following tradition themselves. Traditions, while often helpful, aren't always guaranteed to be the best approach, as we well know from many of the great traditions such as hazing and wearing ties. And when it comes to experienced improvisors or improvisation schools, often they're just continuing many of the same old improvisation traditions.

There are some great questions we could be asking of improvisation that would help us better understand the craft and make us better improvisors. For example: can anyone improvise; in what ways do different audiences affect an improvisor; what is the real effect of drugs and alcohol on improvisation and does having a drink before a show have any negative effect; and does the freedom to fail really make that much sense?

This chapter is a collection of general improvisation topics, and an attempt to answer or explore them from a scientific perspective, now that we understand how improvisation works.

Short–form and long–form?

At first look it would seem that the definitions of short–form and long–form are pretty obvious: short scenes vs. long scenes. Mick Napier in his book

Improvise: Scene from the Inside Out uses this rough definition when he argues we don't need these terms because scene length shouldn't matter. This all sounds pretty obvious when you think about it, so why do we need such terms at all?

The problem with this argument is that Napier is using a certain definition of short–form and long–form that's not universally agreed, and this leads to his decision that we don't need these terms. [141] Like many things in improvisation, the real answer is more complex.

If we assume that short–form and long–form are really about short scenes and long scenes, then we have a dilemma — we have no definitions for short and long, aside from not long and not short. So, what is the number of minutes that makes a short scene become a long scene?

In Johnstone's classic short–form *Theatresports* show format, a scene can be roughly the same length as a scene in a *Harold*, the classic long–form format. In fact, some *Harold* scenes, particularly in the UCB style, can be much shorter than an average length scene in *Theatresports*. So the definition of short–form and long–form can't be the length of the scene, or even the show.

Another definition of short–form and long–form states that short–form has breaks between scenes where no improvisation takes place, and long–form is a continuing series of scenes without a break. But there are shows that have breaks between scenes, and are still considered long–form. For example, show forms with a monologist who tells real life stories based on suggestions from the audience, that is then followed by several inspired scenes before returning again to the monologist. The most well-known of these is *The Armando Diaz Theatrical Experience and Hootenanny*, a long running show at *iO Chicago*, that gives its name to shows of this format. UCB's popular show *Asssscat* also uses what we now call the *Armando* form.

Yet another definition states that short–form is theatre games with rules, whereas long–form is scenes without rules. Once again *Theatresports* contradicts this idea, because *Theatresports* as Johnstone intended it, doesn't use that many theatre games — they were only intended to break up the mainly open scenes of a show. On the other hand, some long–form shows do

---

[141] Napier continues using the terms short–form and long–form in his second book *Behind the scenes. improvising long form* 10 years later, so perhaps he's now changed his mind?

start with a game such as freeze tag or some other training exercise to warm up the audience.

And finally, there's the issue of LPMs, the argument that short–form has a high number of LPMs, and long–form is allowed a lower number of LPMs. This is often an audience expectation as well. Audiences expect high LPMs in a show billed as short–form, and they're more accepting of a slow build and low LPMs in a show billed as long–form. Obviously this isn't a particularly good definition, because I've seen many shows billed as short–form contain virtually no laughs at all, and shows billed as long–form with very high LPMs. Although this is usually more to do with the skill of the performers than anything else.

By the above definitions, an *Armando* or *Harold* could arguably be called short–form, and Johnstone's *Gorilla Theatre* or *Life Game* could be called long–form. So in this sense, Napier is right that the terms aren't useful at all.

According to Michael Gellman, the terms short–form and long–form came about almost by accident. In Chicago in the 1970s, at Del Close's insistence, Gellman began figuring out how to improvise a full-length play[142], and then started teaching what he'd discovered alongside Close's regular *Harold* classes. To distinguish the two streams, Gellman's class was titled "Long–form", and when the classes ended two years later, Close decided to appropriate the term for his own classes, presumably to distinguish them from the short scenes and sketches performed at *Second City*.

Assuming Gellman's story is correct, then the terms were chosen almost by accident, with no actual definition of what they really mean. This explains why arguments continue, because there's no exact definition that will categorise everything as either long–form or short–form.

At some point, someone in the Chicago community invented the term short–form to cover anything that wasn't related to Close's work, and it stuck. Likewise, the Johnstone community looked at some of the more scenic shows in the Chicago method, and then adopted the term long–form to mean "not

---

[142] Mary Scruggs and Michael Gellman wrote a book titled *Process – An Improviser's Journey* in 2008, describing Gellman's techniques for improvising a play. Interestingly, the book was written as a first person fictional diary of a student improvisor, similar to Konstantin Stanislavsky's diary of an acting student in *An Actor's Work* — in English known as the abridged *An Actor Prepares*.

one of the theatre game show formats". Thus, the terms short–form and long–form are actually defined differently between the two methods. And even within each method, you can find different definitions.

If you're a Johnstone method improvisor, then you will most likely think that short–form is games with breaks in between or theatre games, and long–form is where scenes connect together in a longer story without a break. Not that these are two clearly distinct definitions, because there are scenes and shows that could by this definition be both. Johnstone's *Life Game* format is a good example of this, because it could be short–form or long–form by most definitions.

However, if your background is the Chicago method, then you'll most likely think that all Chicago method improvisation is long–form, except theatre games formats such as *ComedySportz* and *Theatresports* which are short–form. Some Johnstone improvisors have even suggested that *Harold* is a short–form format, because it contains short scenes usually not connected by an obvious narrative.

And then there's *Playback Theatre*, that uses the terms short–form and long–form completely differently. *Playback Theatre* gradually increases audience participation over the course of a show. The audience is asked for simple ideas or concepts at the top of the show, and then once they gain confidence, audience members are asked to come on stage and tell more detailed true personal stories. The terms short–form and long–form are used to categorise the types of scenes used throughout the show, and not used to describe the show itself. Short–form scenes highlight an emotion, an idea or other concepts from a story, and are played in the beginning third of the show as the audience is being warmed up. These could be anything such as a simple tableau, a sound sculpture or short fragments of dialogue. Long–form scenes on the other hand generally replay a story or part of a story told by an audience member.

Basically, your exact definition of short–form and long–form will vary depending on your model of improvisation, and even then, there will be shows and scenes which fall into both of your definitions.

What this means is that the long running arguments about which is better, short–form or long–form, can never be resolved, because each method has its own slightly different definition. And even within those methods the definitions can be different and not exactly exclusive of each other. It is like asking which is better, *dogs* or *excitedly*.

The term short–form must still be useful however, because we still use it to fairly accurately explain what a show might be like, regardless of which method of improvisation we use. So there must be something about the terms that makes sense to us.

As a general rule, perhaps the difference is mostly about audience expectation, whether there will be high LPM theatre games and possibly Johnstone's story compression and the absurdity curve, or whether there will be comparatively lower LPMs with thematic or scenic exploration. Classifying them as such usually gives us and possibly audience members a much better idea of what a show might be like. For this reason, it is useful to keep using these terms, even though there really is no precise definition.

Freedom to fail

The word *failure* is fairly specific in its negativity — it means the opposite of success, with success being something we should be striving for. Other definitions are similarly negative and include being unsuccessful, and being in a not functioning state. In fact you'd have a difficult time finding a positive definition of the word failure, and yet we teach failure as a good thing to beginning improvisors who are often scared of failing before their first class has even started.

Instead of teaching that we always succeed at improvisation, we've redefined the meaning of failure. No improvisor I've met has ever said "I'm here to fail at improv". And lying to new improvisors during their first few levels — that failure is good thing — is going to hold them back from achieving greater things. Especially when after a few levels, they realise that failure isn't what they were told it was. We want new improvisors to succeed, so why do we tell it is OK not to?

We've taken the embracing of failure too far, too literally, and often out of context.

The freedom to fail has moved into the mainstream. Life coaches — an odd concept to begin with — encourage us to have and push through failures and to become better and more experienced people because of them. Business also now embraces the freedom to fail, recognising that risk and failure can help innovate as well as train staff in creative problem solving. In fact the first 10 Google search results for "freedom to fail" as at the time of writing, are all business related.

But businesses usually have clearly defined criteria for success and failure, as well as having an aversion to any failure linked with profit. So they've started adapting the phrase to be more conservative and risk averse, such as *freedom to fail in small ways*. And then there's the even more amusing and contradictory *freedom to fail forward*, which has also now found its way into life coaching.

The word failure only makes sense if there is a goal that can be achieved, and by implication, that there is success and failure at achieving that goal. In improvisation, the freedom to fail gives the impression that there is an end goal, and then confuses the issue by saying that failing to achieve this goal is OK. Saying that there is success and failure — a right way and a wrong way — and then saying that both are OK, is confusing for newer improvisors, and instils the idea that there is success and failure, good and bad, positive and negative, but doesn't explain the difference. It also personalises the failure, making the improvisor feel that they are failing, when there are countless other external influences which may have contributed to the perceived failure.

In *Impro for Storytellers*, Keith Johnstone uses the term failure to mean actual failure in the negative sense and that it is something to be ultimately avoided[143], just like it is outside of the improvisation community. As does Viola Spolin in *Improvisation for the Theater*, and so do Close, Halpern and Johnson in *Truth in Comedy*. It is true that you can't learn everything without failing, but that doesn't make failure an integral part of learning how to improvise.

But Johnstone goes further, saying that players should not even be thinking in terms of success and failure. This is because the process of improvisation is imperfect and random. There's no goal in the process of improvisation. As soon as you're improvising, at whatever level of skill, you can't say you're failing at improvising. You are improvising at the level of ability that you've been trained. Improvisation begins with the enacting of an internalised

---

[143] Although he also talks about players being able to fail gracefully while learning, and to not be negatively affected by it.

trained skill, which is then affected by so many things outside of the improvisor, that failure can really only be defined as not actually enacting the process of improvisation.

The tech start up world provides us with a good example. They use short iterations of innovation and review, using what's called a "spike", to develop incomplete or unknown technology ideas ahead of time. This allows them to test which ones may or may not work, or may not be achievable in the allocated time or budget. They are then able to "pivot" their business from one focus to a completely different focus if things don't work out as planned. If you took each test step, out of context, you could see what would traditionally be called failure. But in the big scheme of things, it is all just part and parcel of the process of building a product.

The same thing happens when businesses use failure to teach creative problem solving. They set up situations where failure occurs, so that their people can recognise it and develop tools for specifically dealing with it. No business lets their people fail at random tasks that are associated with the actual running of the business. Imagine if I failed at letting my manager know about a client who was potentially about to leave the business. I certainly wouldn't be applauded for using failure to learn what I should have done in the first place.

The main argument for embracing failure in improvisation, is that by failing we both recognise our limits and explore outside the bounds of our current thinking and knowledge. We learn by failing. This is a worthy goal, but it's not failure. In improvisation we learn by extending ourselves beyond what we think is possible or we are capable of. We often find ourselves in situations we've not been in before, and often we make choices that we think are great but the audience does not. This is not failure. This is learning. This is refactoring our internalised improvisation model, to consider our new insight.

Parachutists don't use failure, to learn. Neither do rocket scientists, surgeons, stunt people, most students, or even actors — rehearsal isn't about success and failure. Ask a rocket scientist if they're glad their rocket blew up so they could learn a thing or two, and they'll most likely grimace and walk away. Governments don't intentionally use failure to learn and improve, or they'd get voted out. And artists don't fail at art — although they may fail at making art a sustainable business, which at least has boundaries and fixed goals which they can measure against.

There is no failure in improvisation, and therefore there is no freedom to fail. Everything we do in improvisation is helpful, everything we do is OK, it's all part of the process of learning and enacting improvisation. Can we fail at say telling a conducted story for example, if we set success criteria or rules and then ignore the conductor? Yes. But that's not failing at improvisation, that's just not following the rules of a game. And in a performance situation that's usually OK anyway, because the audience is most likely still going to laugh and enjoy the show. There is no freedom to fail at improvisation, and we shouldn't be encouraging students that they will fail, and that failure is OK.

And then there's "failing spectacularly", which is just another way of saying "succeeding". We've invented the concept of failing spectacularly as a way of saying succeeding but using the word failing. We've once again changed the meaning of the word failure to mean something else.

The word failure was the wrong word to begin with, but for some reason we just don't have the heart to admit that we got it wrong in the first place — we'd much rather keep redefining failure to have positive meanings.

Improvisation is a continual process of improvement in what is a random creative process with much outside influence that is beyond the individual's control. Failure is not personal. You are enough, and everything you do is correct and part of the learning process. Whenever you improvise, you can't fail, because you're improvising. Or to adapt a popular Yoda quote: In improvisation there is no try. To try is to do, so either do or do not. And always succeed spectacularly!

Big and small audiences

Is improvisation performed in front of 3 people the same as improvisation performed in front of 100 or 1000 people? And do improvisors benefit from continually experiencing both?

I've seen very experienced improvisors who are used to playing to full houses in 1000 seat theatres, play miserably in an almost empty 300 seat theatre. They'll get in their heads and descend into meta improvisation, often calling out in scenes that the audience isn't laughing or that nothing they're doing seems to work. On the other hand, I've also seen improvisors used to smaller spaces, struggle to do a decent scene in bigger venues because they can't get a word in over all the laughter and it throws off their pacing.

What makes an audience laugh? People are different, and what makes a person laugh has a lot to do with them, their history, their popular knowledge, their intelligence, their mood at the time, their social standing, their experience of improvised comedy, etc. In comedy, one size certainly doesn't fit all. And when we put 300 different people into a room together, with the varying expectations they have of what they are about to experience, we find that every audience is different.

There is a ripple effect to laughter in an audience. By making one person laugh, it's more likely that a second, then a third, then more will laugh. And the bigger the audience, the more likely that one person will find a show funny, and the more likely that a ripple will gain traction. So what causes this initial ripple to occur?

There are several reasons why people will laugh only when someone else is already laughing. The most obvious is mirror neurons, which we've already covered so we won't look at them again. Another is to do with what's called group conformity.

In 1951, psychologist Solomon Asch ran a series of experiments to see under what conditions people in a group would agree with decisions made by the rest of the group, even if they didn't agree with the decision. His original test presented a group of participants with two cards, one with a single line on it, and one with three lines of different lengths. Each participant was then asked — in front of the rest of the group — which line out of the three, was the same length as the single line. This wasn't an optical illusion, and the correct line length was easy to identify. The trick was that only one of the people in the group was an actual participant, and the rest of the group were confederates secretly in on the experiment.

Each participant was tested a number of times in different tests to see which conditions would affect their answer. When the confederates all identified the correct line, the participant also identified the correct line. But when the confederates all identified the same incorrect line, in 37% of the tests the participant also identified the same incorrect line. Looking at the individual participants to see if some were skewing the results for the rest, it was found that 75% of the participants over the course of the experiments, identified an incorrect line at least once when the confederates also identified the wrong long line.

Why do people go along with a group decision as if it were their own, when they know it is clearly the wrong decision?

Through follow up interviews, Asch discovered two main reasons why: normative influence — because they wanted to fit in with the group — and informal influence — because they thought the group was better informed than them. He also found three main reactions that drove those reasons: distortion of perception, where the participant didn't realise the decision was wrong, they assumed it was correct; distortion of judgement, where the participants thought their perceptions were wrong and chose what they assumed would be correct; and distortion of action, where the participants went along with the group decision, so they didn't look stupid to the other members of the group.[144]

This happens when an audience laughs. Some don't think it's funny, yet laugh to fit in. And some laugh because they assume they should, but they don't yet understand why. This contributes to the number of people laughing and triggers others to take the same actions. Even if the audience member knows it's funny but not enough to be the only person laughing, then conformity and mirror neurons can make them laugh if enough other people are already laughing.

We can see this in action when sitting in the audience and triggering laughter ripples ourselves.[145] I've also had a few directors over the years say that when cast members aren't in that evening's show, they should still come to the show, sit in the audience and laugh so the rest of the audience laughs too. And in *Theatresports* it's common for cast members to laugh at the other teams when they are performing, to trigger laughter in the audience, and for audience mirror neurons to reflect that the players are having a good time.

Often experienced improvisors don't laugh as much as ordinary people watching comedic improvisation, because it's a bit like watching the digital matrix in the film *The Matrix* — it's all meta and comedy mechanics. But

---

[144] Asch's results have been questioned over the years about whether the participants — white men in America during the 1950s — could have skewed the result. Follow up experiments in the 1990s have shown that 3-5 confederates is the sweet spot that fits Asch's results, and that a bigger group tends to have less effect and begins to raise suspicions in the participant that it is rigged. Either way, the benefit of the doubt is still firmly in Asch's court.

[145] If you haven't tried starting a ripple of laughter in an audience, you should. Laugh at something that nobody else laughs at, but which might make people wonder if it's funny. In many cases they will begin laughing with you, even if it's not funny.

when I'm watching not so experienced improvisors, I do try to laugh more than I normally would, in order to trigger audience laughter and to give them a better experience on stage.

But the laughter ripple has both pros and cons. Usually when there is a ripple, either the comedy isn't as good as what would immediately cause the whole audience to erupt with laughter, or the funny line of dialogue simply wasn't heard in that part of the audience. As the ripple expands over the audience, it can become difficult for improvisors to continue speaking on stage, because they can't be heard. So improvisors with bigger audiences learn to leave gaps in the dialogue, and do more physical or mime work instead until the audience quietens down. As we've seen already, this can be a bigger problem in short-form due to the higher LPMs than long-form, but is less of a problem in Johnstone's impro where improvisors generally have more training in mime and object work.

From this we can determine that the bigger the audience, the easier it is to get a laugh. And if we can make a dozen people laugh, then we can more easily make a bigger audience laugh. But there are a few exceptions.

Where the small audience is in a big theatre with lots of empty seats, it can make the audience think that the show isn't very good — even if it is— and often an audience might be embarrassed to laugh if they perceive that this is this case. A smaller audience can void the group conformity and cause less of a ripple. This means that it's easier to get laughs from say a dozen people in a small venue, than a dozen people in a large venue, because the audience senses that full equals quality. I've seen a lot of shows that were hysterically funny, yet very few were laughing out loud.

The other exception is where the improvisors play to a larger audience than they are used to. They often find that they need to project more so that they are heard, and they need to slow down and leave more space for the audience to laugh. If they're not used to this style of play, then they could be thrown off more in their performance, potentially becoming more conscious and in their head as they work through an environment they're not used to.

Improvisors should spend time with both small and big audiences — if they are lucky enough to have the opportunity to — so that they know how to play to different audience sizes. And if they only play to bigger audiences, it is easy for them to be deluded into thinking that they are better than they really are.[146]

Can anyone improvise?

Michael Gellman says that improvisation is acting without text, so he's implying that improvisors are actors. One of my early mentors also once told me "Only actors should be allowed to improvise." This discouraged me and put me in my head for about a year as I wrestled with the idea that I didn't belong. I wasn't a trained actor, so why should I be performing on stage in front of a paying audience?[147]

Improvisors without formal actor training end up with acting skills as part of the learning process, and many end up taking separate acting classes as well, so being an improvisor also makes us an actor. There's an awful lot of great improvisors who can act, but have no formal acting training, but there's even more actors who can't improvise.

Viola Spolin certainly has another view of it, with the very first line of her book *Improvisation for the Theater* being "Everyone can act. Everyone can improvise." But in reality, can they?

Of course they can, but that's not really the question. The real question is: can anyone become good at it? By good I don't necessarily mean expert, but good enough for an audience to enjoy.

Jacob Moreno in his book *The Theatre of Spontaneity* said that there seems to be a "spontaneity talent" — a talent for improvisation that some actors have more than others. In his experiments, he noticed that some actors had a natural all–round ability to improvise in situations that are strange to them, and others either did not have that ability or had it to a lesser degree. He attempted to quantify this ability with what he called a "spontaneity quotient". But Moreno was writing this after only a few years of

---

[146] Peter Lead and I once spent 5 years in a weekly two–prov show in a small venue of 5-30 audience members. It was great training, as two improvisors making 5 people laugh makes you really work on your craft. On the other hand, playing to a large audience can at times be confusing, because they'll often just laugh at anything.

[147] There is an element of truth to what she said, because you need acting skills in order to improvise. But you can also learn to act to a certain degree in improvisation classes. Taking a couple of acting workshops doesn't hurt either. Keith Johnstone however says that "When *Theatresports* is captured by actors, they almost always isolate it from the community, but I prefer it when there's a mix of actors and 'real people'".

experimenting with improvisation, and he only used trained actors who at the time were also new to improvisation.

In any domain, there are a number of contributing factors that are required in order to be expert at something. For some domains, physical make up is the key determinant, such as height in basketball, or strength in weightlifting, but this doesn't apply for acting and improvisation. Sure, physiology may limit the roles we play, but it doesn't prevent us from being a good improvisor.

Another contributor to being expert at something is actually having an interest in the domain we wish to be an expert in — or more specifically not having a disinterest in it — and being willing to focus and do the hard work to improve. This is particularly poignant in improvisation, where there is an initial fear factor at play which people need to work through. If we can push through the fear, then the amazing world of improvisation is there for us to explore. After that, expertise comes through theory, training and practise, building muscle memory and internalising the domain.

Improvisation isn't difficult to learn, and it's not unusual for students to be entertaining on stage after only 24 hours of training[148]. Even the worst improvisor can still become acceptable, if not good, over time, so long as they have the drive to do so.

Improvisation is a great leveller. Shy people become less shy, people who can't act, learn to act, and people who aren't funny become funnier. Improvisation builds confidence, creativity and wit, and removes the "adult" filters that prevent us from being better peers for our children. This makes them more creative, makes them more confident, and turns them into more balanced adults. And this is already at a quite basic level of improvisation training.

So, can anyone learn to improvise well? Given the right training and circumstances, yes they can, in life, in their career, and on stage. In fact, I'd go further and say that everyone should learn improvisation, certainly for life skills at least, and it should be a standard part of any junior school curriculum, giving children the skills they'll need later in life in order to be better adults.

---

[148] Assuming an 8 week level 1 course of roughly 3 hours per week.

Forms

"Form" is short for format, usually a show format. It is the structure upon which the show hangs, and within which the players improvise. Common forms include *Harold*, *Theatresports*, *Armando*, *La Ronde* and dozens and dozens of others. At a certain point in an improvisor's learning curve, there is usually a focus on form, the feeling that they now know how to improvise and that different forms are the next exciting and shiny thing to play with.

Considering the difference between Keith Johnstone's impro and Chicago improv, scenes in a Johnstone method *Harold* are much different to those in a Chicago method *Harold*. Due to the priority given to story and active advances, connections and patterns tend to be more story based in impro. And because they're less inclined to focus on the last thing and drilling into the detail, this makes it more difficult to identify and heighten ideas, themes and games used in a Chicago method *Harold*.

Forms tend to work best with the skills they're built from, thus a *Harold* works better with the Chicago method. Likewise with *Theatresports*, the narrative, active advances and more time compressed scenes work better with Johnstone, whereas a Chicago method *Theatresports* tends not to have the same excitement, dynamism or LPMs.

Although forms work best with the method they were invented with, this doesn't mean you can't perform a *Harold* with Johnstone's impro, but you will produce a better *Harold* if you do it with the Chicago method, and vice versa. I've seen many Johnstone method groups being taught and trying to perform a *Harold*, with the result usually being a disconnected mess of story lines.[149]

Creativity

Until recently it was assumed that creativity was a magical process by which innovation occurs, when a talented individual has a light bulb moment, and something is invented out of thin air. We now know that this is not the case, and that creativity is a time consuming and mostly collaborative exercise.

---

[149] Due to the now global notoriety of *Harold*, some schools which teach the Johnstone method also teach *Harold*, because it's yet another way to bring students through classes. Although in the last few years there's been a vague acknowledgement that this doesn't work very well, and schools have replaced it with other Johnstone related techniques and forms.

And while it does involve some unconscious input, creativity mostly consists of a lot of conscious hard work.

We still don't know a lot about creativity, but we do have at least a rough definition: a process through which something new and useful or worthwhile is formed. So by this definition, is improvisation a creative exercise? And if it is, what can we learn from creativity research that may help us be better improvisors?

Creativity is a whole brain process, utilising both left and right hemispheres, and all of the functions that have been often incorrectly attributed to each. And because creativity is mostly a time consuming exercise, different brain functions are used at different times throughout the creative process.

The first staged model of creativity was published by Graham Wallas, in his 1926 book *The Art of Thought*, where he documented what he referred to as four distinct stages of a single achievement of thought. He called these the "stages of control", before the term creativity was coined a few years later. The four stages are: preparation; incubation; insight and verification.

The preparation stage is where information is researched and collected, giving you the knowledge needed to do the work. This is the internalisation stage, where you're gathering as much information as possible in order understand the domain you're working in. Reading this book is part of a preparation stage, as is an improvisation workshop, and also the early discovery parts of some improvised scenes. This is mostly a conscious thinking activity.

The second stage of creativity is incubation, where the information we've collected is continually explored and reorganised in the unconscious. This is a mostly unconscious activity, which leads to that "aha" moment, called the illumination stage or the moment of insight, or what Wallas called the "appearance of the happy idea".

Finally this is followed by the fourth stage, the verification of this insight, which is again a mostly conscious thinking activity.

Creativity is thus mostly a conscious thinking process. Improvisation itself is therefore not typically a creative exercise, at least by definition. But creativity can be used to explore new ideas in improvisation, and improvisation can certainly be used to help the creative process outside of improvisation.

Improvisation as a craft is more a tool or enabler of creativity than a product of it.

An interesting aside regarding creativity, is that problem finding is the more critical part of the process than problem solving, and that problem finding people are generally more creative and successful than problem solving people. This equally applies to theatrical improvisation where much of an improvised scene is about finding problems.

Personality types

The populist view up until a few years ago, was that an individual was either an introvert or an extravert[150]. Introverts being defined as either more inner focused or obtaining their energy from solo activities, and extraverts being more outside or externally focused or obtaining their energy from other people. But as we know, life is never that black and white. In fact both introverts and extraverts have degrees of focus on the inner self and the external. This is particularly the case for improvisors who are very often considered introverts, yet are able to seem extraverted in life or on stage.

Carl Jung popularised introversion and extraversion in 1923, saying that extraversion is a scale, with introversion and extraversion being defined by which end of the scale more often dominates in a person. In fact it's more like a continuum from introversion to extraversion, with most people having traits of both.

More recently the term ambiversion has become popular, commonly understood to be people who are in the middle of the introversion–extraversion continuum, or having equal traits of both. In fact ambiversion originated with Edmund Smith Conklin in his 1923 — ironically the same year as Jung — paper *The definition of introversion, extroversion and allied concepts*, where he suggested that the terms introversion and extraversion were coined in psychiatry while working with abnormal extremes, and not necessarily applying them to what he calls "normal people". For normal

---

[150] Science spells the word "extravert" with an "a", and this originates from Carl Jung who first introduced the term. It is also the correct Latin form. "extrovert" with an "o" was introduced later, and is now the popular spelling outside of scientific circles, although both spellings are still considered correct in U.S. and British English. It is believed that the spelling most likely changed when Phyllis Blanchard published her 1918 paper *A Psycho–Analytic Study of August Comte*, where she not only changed the spelling to an "o", but also changed or misinterpreted Jung's definition.

people, lying somewhere on the continuum, he called this ambiversion. So ambiversion was originally defined as whatever a normal balance might be. Only more recently has it been redefined in the popular press as being in the middle, with equal amounts of each.

So what does this mean for improvisation? Well, for most people, it means nothing. Most people have both introvert and extravert attributes, but may seem one or the other under certain conditions. And when people who are more introverted learn to improvise, more often than not they find extraversion as well.

What's more interesting, is that studies have found that extraverts — still considered normal and somewhere on our continuum — are more often happier than introverts. One reason cited for this is that social interaction has been proven to have a positive affect on people, and therefore it makes sense that extraverts would have more of this effect. However other studies have shown that this doesn't account for all the difference.

In 2012, Zelenski, Santoro and Whelan published a paper titled *Would Introverts Be Better Off if They Acted More Like Extraverts? Exploring Emotional and Cognitive Consequences of Counterdispositional Behavior*, to which their answer was yes. They found that introverts acting like extraverts increased their positivity and therefore their happiness. Whereas the opposite was not the case, and extraverts acting like introverts did not change their positivity — however they did suffer a decrease in cognitive ability. This could contribute to why improvisors are often more positive and happier than the general population, however there are many positive aspects of theatrical improvisation which also contribute, so it's not clear by how much.

Alcohol, drugs and stimulants

Improvisation and drugs traditionally go hand in hand, more particularly so with alcohol. Although marijuana, heroin and cocaine have been associated with improvisation at one time or another. And while we're at it, how about more available stimulants such as caffeine, nicotine and energy drinks? As far as I know, nobody has done any hard research or even theorised on whether drugs help or hinder improvisation. Let's have a look at how a number of different drugs affect the way we improvise.

The argument for drugs begins with alcohol. It is argued that having an alcoholic drink before performing, removes the filters and allows us to be more in the moment, as well as calming us down to reduce our fear. Just one drink before going on stage is a common mantra, because seriously, one beer isn't going to adversely affect our play is it? We can still operate heavy equipment with that blood alcohol level, so what's the big deal? While this points more to a lack of training in dealing with fear than anything else, the question remains, what is the effect of drugs and alcohol on an improvised performance, and are there drugs that will improve our ability to improvise?

The use of drugs is common throughout the history of art, particularly with writers and artists. I used to think that great poetry or novels which were written under the influence of drugs, shouldn't be considered great works, as it was the drugs that did the work, not the writer. And not every artist has access to the same drugs, meaning it's an unfair comparison with other art. In fact, studies show that rarely is great art made under the influence of drugs, and if they are used, they're usually not comparable to the best works, or are only used in the initial inspiration stage. As we've seen, creativity requires a lot of time with a clean and active mind in order to fully complete a work. Improvising is not like this, because the inspiration stage of a scene actually happens at the same time as the active creative stage, so using drugs for just the inspiration part isn't going to work like other artistic mediums.[151]

Like many first time improvisors, I started playing in shows in pubs and bars, surrounded by alcohol and intoxicated behaviour. I wasn't part of a drinking community, so I didn't partake before I went on stage, however after a few years, I eventually started having a drink before I went on stage. Not drunk, just relaxed. I felt more alive, more in control, and funnier while I was intoxicated, even with just one drink. That was until I started noticing how others would behave on stage after having only one drink. While alcohol reduces fear, it also takes off that creative edge and sharp intellect that are required to perform at a high level. Some improvisors don't care about performing at their best, and that's fine, but for most of us, we want to be the best we can.

In a general sense, no drug is going to make our brains better than they are already, otherwise everyone would be using them. Drugs don't improve our brains, or keep them normal. Drugs change the operation of various functions in our brains and bodies, and then change our perception of how

---

[151] This may however work for writing sketch.

we've been changed. They don't add capability to our brains, they take away ability and then disable our perception of what is normal behaviour. Even though the use of hallucinogens for example may seem to expand the mind in useful ways, they also inhibit the brain's ability to organise and control those experiences. And the impact of this on the rest of our brain is still going to leave us unable to improvise at a useful level.

Alcohol in particular is a depressant, which means it disables many brain functions that we need to operate as normal human beings. For starters, it depresses parts of our brain which inhibit certain behaviours, thus making us feel more outgoing and less fearful in social situations. Alcohol doesn't make us more confident. Alcohol disables the part of our brain that tells us not to be confident when there is something to be concerned about. This sounds like a good thing, because improvisors don't want to be inhibiting behaviours so let's turn all that off. But alcohol also inhibits many of the functions we need in order to actually improvise, as well as preventing other brain functions from working altogether.

Alcohol reduces the ability of nerves in the senses and muscles from correctly sending messages to the brain. It also blocks reasoning, learning, and access to our memory. By doing so, it prevents our brain from correctly analysing the state of our bodies, and so we think we are capable of more than we actually are. We feel happy and don't sense any of the real impairment. Alcohol also causes an initial increase in blood sugar, but also causes levels to fall later on, meaning there's an initial sugar hit and then a following come down.

Alcohol also makes us need to urinate more often, our skin go red, and induces countless other issues with body organs, luckily very few of which have too much of an effect on improvising. One additional side effect for improvisors though, is that as your body gets used to alcohol, it requires more alcohol per session to get the same affect. This means it's a slippery slope from not being able to improvise without a drink, to not being able to improvise unless drunk.

The second most popular illicit drug for improvisors is probably marijuana, which can cause euphoria, pain relief, creative thinking, relaxation and sensory awareness, but can also cause anxiety, clumsiness, forgetfulness, hunger, panic attacks, racing heart, mouth dryness, bloodshot eyes, paranoia, tiredness, poor coordination, inability to think clearly, memory loss, inability to learn, and uncontrollable laughter. I can improvise while hungry, with a dry mouth and bloodshot eyes, but the rest will all adversely affect my ability to improvise. The kicker though is that the effects are random, it depends on the person, it depends on the dose, and it can even depend upon our current emotional and mental state and our expectations of what may happen while high. Basically, we have no idea how marijuana will affect us until it has, and by then it has already disabled many of the brain functions we need to improvise well.

One of the most addictive recreational drugs is cocaine. Normally when we feel pleasure, our brain releases dopamine into our synapses, and from there the dopamine signals our neurons to tell us that we feel good. Cocaine prevents the dopamine from being released back to our brain for reuse, meaning that not only do we constantly feel the effects of dopamine, but it also prevents those neurons from handling other important messages, such as those to and from our senses and muscles. And when there's no more free dopamine available, we have a feeling of needing even more dopamine to replace the not yet released dopamine.

Cocaine's dopamine flood gives the user more confidence and more energy, but also increases blood pressure, decreases appetite, dilates pupils, and disables several brain functions that maintain mood — talk about method acting.

Heroin on the other hand is more of a no brainer than other drugs, as the immediate negative effects include sleepiness, nausea, vomiting and itching. It can also cause constipation and spontaneous abortion, but that's not going to affect most of us. On the positive side, it does loosen inhibitions and gives a general feeling of wellbeing. However, I'm not sure how useful we'd be in a scene when we can't actually stay awake.

Which brings us to caffeine. Surely caffeine is a good drug for improvisors? We know that caffeine keeps us awake, and so does the buzz of improvisation. So, it's an unfortunate coincidence that using both in the evening makes it more difficult to get to sleep. More specifically, caffeine is believed to increase vigilance, memory response, attention, and to decrease weariness. And the results of intellectual performances, such as reading, maths and some verbal tests, may also be restored when we're weary or bored — restored to normal capacity, not better than normal ability.

Interestingly caffeine has been shown to have different effects between introverts and extraverts. A 1980 study *The Interactive Effect of Introversion–Extraversion with Caffeine Induced Arousal on Verbal Performance*, by Kirby Gilliland, confirmed that for verbal tasks, introverts perform better than extraverts. And once caffeine is ingested — roughly between 1-2 cups of coffee — performance for both increases, however for introverts it increases more dramatically. But with higher doses — roughly 3-4 cups of coffee— the performance of introverts decreases back to normal, and that of extraverts increases.

Caffeine also increases the vigilance of auditory listening — for the equivalent of 1-2 cups of coffee — but only in extraverts. And large quantities of caffeine can cause anxiety and nervousness. So while improvisors should certainly benefit from the use of caffeine, this should be limited to the equivalent of roughly 1-2 cups of coffee for introverts, and 3-4 cups for extraverts.

But the important question is probably whether caffeine improves or hinders our ability to be present. Do the heightened attention and increased abilities make becoming present easier or more difficult, and does it make us more or less present? There's no known research on this, so we don't really know for sure. But there is a 2011 paper *Relationships between tea and other beverage consumption to work performance and mood* which looks at how various drinks affect work performance. They found that caffeine can reduce our level of presence if consumed during recovery or relaxing outside of work. So for example drinking caffeinated beverage after work, can often make it more difficult to become present the following day.

For more information on caffeine and its effects, the 1992 paper *Caffeine and the central nervous system: mechanisms of action, biochemical, metabolic and psychostimulant effects* by Nehlig, Daval and Debry is an excellent and quite thorough starting point.

Which brings us to energy drinks, which are similar to caffeine, but more specific. Energy drinks can contain a range of different ingredients that are supposed to help the brain and body. Guarana for example — extracted from an Amazonian plant of the same name — has been shown to be useful for weight loss, and is a good stimulant. However the main chemical that comes from Guarana is actually caffeine. Another common additive in energy drinks is taurine, which was named because it was originally extracted from ox bile, hence the name Red Bull, amongst others. Now artificially manufactured, taurine also has positive effects including weight loss and helps with a range of illnesses related to the heart, brain, respiration, blood pressure, hypertension and even epilepsy.

The evidence of whether these additional ingredients actually have an effect is contradictory. A recent review of the science behind energy drinks found that the common doses of these chemicals and extracts in drinks were so minimal, that the only real active ingredient was caffeine. But an earlier study did find that some energy drinks with taurine and glucuronolactone — a chemical that naturally occurs in the body and some plants — could slightly improve blood flow and physical performance. But the study was unclear about which chemical was the cause.

By far the most significant ingredients in energy drinks, which affect our brains and bodies, are caffeine and sugar. We've already looked at caffeine, but surely sugar can't have any noticeable effect on improvisation? Surprisingly, sugar has been found to have a negative effect on spatial learning and memory in rats[152]. And while this finding can't be directly tied to humans, and the actual quantities needed haven't been tested, some studies have suggested that this may be the case for us as well. If so, then coffee with sugar may well have the same effects as an energy or cola drink.

These days the secrecy of the tobacco companies is mostly over, and we now know most of the effects that smoking has on our health. Cigarette smoke contains around 4000 toxic chemicals, including carbon monoxide, ammonia, hydrogen cyanide, arsenic and lead, and it eventually kills you, usually painfully. And then for our purposes, there's nicotine.

Nicotine is also poisonous to the body — something that's not often pointed out when considering newer and purer nicotine delivery systems such as vaping. Nicotine in cigarette smoke reaches the brain within 10 seconds of inhaling, and then the effects disappear again after only a few minutes, making you want to inhale once again. Nicotine mimics adrenaline and can make you feel more alert, which sounds useful for improvisors. It also makes you feel more calm and relaxed, and releases dopamine to make smoking feel

---

[152] Researchers use tests such as the *Morris Water Maze* and *Barnes Maze*, to see if rats and mice are able to learn and retain the memory of how to exit a flooded pond or a pitted table top. You can find videos of each on YouTube if you're interested in that kind of thing.

pleasurable. These all sound like positive effects until you look at what happens a few minutes into an improvised performance — nicotine withdrawal.

Nicotine withdrawal can invoke feelings such as anxiety, irritability and depression, all of which are pretty bad for an improvisor. If you're performing short scenes and head off for a quick smoke between sets, then that may work for you. But perform for longer and smokers begin to feel the effects of withdrawal, and their play begins to change.

The advantages of nicotine for improvisation — being more alert, calm and pleasurable — can all be obtained in other ways than smoking. And thankfully, none of those will lead to our eventual death.

Ultimately, the best state to be in when we improvise, is completely sober. The brain functions best, the body functions best, we learn faster, we remember more in scenes, we become more focused, and we're more present, when our body, brain and training are all working normally. Often the need for alcohol or drugs before improvising is due to an inability to deal with the anxiety of performing or the pressure to deliver, and this usually then becomes a habit. A better option is to quit the intoxicants and learn to deal with the underlying issue — fear and anxiety.

If you wish to be a good improvisor, don't mix improvisation with alcohol and drugs. Unless of course that's the whole point of your show.

Sleep

I've rarely gotten enough sleep throughout my life, working long hours, doing all-nighters, and using stimulants to keep me awake. I was always tired.

When I first started improvising, I found that my fear would decrease and my mindfulness or ability to be in the moment would increase, the more sleep deprived that I was. I would look forward to improvising while sleep deprived! But this would increase up to a point where fear, analysis and self questioning would suddenly kick in, and the mindfulness would be gone. There seemed to be a line where sleep deprivation stopped being useful and started being detrimental to improvisation.

This increase in mindfulness is mostly due to sleep deprivation reducing the ability of the Default Mode Network to activate. With the DMN not fully active, we can't enter that resting thinking and self analysis state. Sleep deprivation has also been shown to reduce the ability to control emotional responses. So as sleep deprivation increases, so does the deactivation of other regions of the brain which we require in order to maintain a state of mindfulness, and then emotion, anxiety and the fight or flight response kicks in as we notice that we're not improvising as well as we have in the past.

With experience, we automatically activate and deactivate the various brain functions we need to improvise, and the problem becomes less of an issue. But obviously there's a point where we are so sleep deprived that we simply don't have the brain functions required to improvise, or even live. I'd certainly recommend against experimenting with anything that is guaranteed to kill us, especially if we wish to continue improvising.

Sleep deprivation has also been shown to reduce the speed of cognitive functions. We all know the feeling of when we're tired it takes longer to maintain focus and attention on what we're doing or thinking. It's the same with improvising. Interestingly, studies have also shown that meditation can decrease the need for sleep, as well as improving reaction times, meaning that meditation counteracts the negatives brought on by sleep deprivation.

In 2006, a number of different studies began to appear that linked short naps of around one hour, with memory consolidation. When we go to sleep at night, our brains begin to transfer the day's working memory to long term memory.[153] This process seems to be triggered by the beginning of the sleep process. These studies found that a short sleep — what is often called a power nap — can also trigger this process. This means that after learning something you wish to keep in long term memory, a power nap can actually help you consolidate your working memory. Experiments have shown that this includes both procedural memory — for procedure skills like muscle memory — and declarative memory — for remembering facts and events including spatial memory. I guess we'll see if improvisation schools begin providing a separate nap room for students to sleep after class!

---

[153] One study, *The Role of Sleep in Declarative Memory Consolidation — Direct Evidence by Intracranial EEG*, by Nikolai Axmacher, Sven Haupt, Guillén Fernándex, Christian E. Elger and Juergen Fell, found that the period after sleep is better able to transfer memories, and that it isn't specifically the sleep which causes this to happen. Either way, it is the link with sleep that is important.

In summary, sleep deprivation should be avoided by improvisors. A reduction of DMN activation is beneficial, but that is also easily controlled by being in a state of mindfulness and being in the moment. When we improvise, we want our brains to be 100% fit, and any lack of sleep will begin a gradual decline in brain function, through a period which may be partially beneficial, but ultimately is always going to be a less than optimal functioning brain. And when learning improvisation, or anything really, a power nap after class may well help with long term memory retention.

BMI and obesity

A 2016 paper titled *Effects of Body Mass Index and Body Fat Percent on Default Mode, Executive Control, and Salience Network Structure and Function*, showed that obesity may reduce cognitive performance, reward processing and make you more impulsive. BMI is the calculation of how obese a person is, and the study showed that BMI is correlated with the reduction in physical size of the brain, particularly in brain networks such as the DMN. The reduction in DMN capability doesn't sound too bad for an improvisor, however remember that when the DMN deactivates, it still maintains some limited activity for the task positive network.

Whether this means that being overweight will negatively impact the ability to improvise, is unclear. But it's research that is certainly worth following.

Your perception is your perception

> *It's hard enough being in your own head, let alone someone elses.*
>
> *– Jimmy Carrane and Liz Allen, in Improvising Better, A Guide for the Working Improviser*

Your perception is yours and yours alone. If a scene had a great relationship between characters, with believable characters with strong points of view, then that is your perception of the scene. It doesn't mean that your scene partner had the same perception, or that this is exactly what happened. Your scene partner may have been confused about the point of the scene, and may have misinterpreted the interaction between the characters as just chit chat, and not important to the scene. Neither player is wrong or right, it's just their perception of what happened, reflected through the mental models they have of the reality of the scene, and everything else they brought into the space before they began to improvise.

A few years ago I was playing in a two player team where throughout our set we would swap characters a number of times, with each improvisor taking over the character that the other had created. The effect was that each swap would cause the characters to be heightened or accentuated. This was because we each thought the characters of our scene partner were stronger than they actually were — remembering that we interpret actions such as a pinch as stronger than they actually are. And when we tagged back to our original characters, they would heighten as well. Videoing the entire set would show that the characters often heightened so much that they were almost different characters, or at least more rounded with a more focused point of view, mannerisms and accent.

So if the perception of each player is different, what does this mean for the director or coach?

It is usually easier for someone not performing in a scene, to see what is happening in that scene. This is the outside eye. As players we're present and listening to our scene partner, we aren't always listening to ourselves or the scene. We often have a picture of the scene in our head which hasn't yet been divulged in the scene, and we often have our own ideas of what the scene is about. So we're often not interpreting the scene in exactly the same way as our scene partner.

Outside the scene however, it is easier to see all the players in the scene, as well as the actual scene that neither of the players gets to see in its entirety. And it's easier to see what each player is actually contributing to the scene relative to each other. When teaching students a new structure, such as an opening or show form, pulling some players out as an audience to watch the rest of the group can be really beneficial. They'll often be quite surprised at how much they see, now that they're not performing.

Players should therefore not focus too much on retrospective analysis of a scene, unless asked by another player or when done by a coach or director as an outside eye. And certainly with no laying of blame, because player perceptions will often be very different. This is also why videoing a scene is a great way of analysing our own play, as it provides the outside eye that we don't get while in the scene.

Clothing and connotative colours

Sydney is predominantly a beach and sun sports culture, and as such we tend not to dress — indoors or outdoors — as formally as do landlocked or colder cities around the world. Our improvisation dress code on stage is like most other cities, but if anything, just a touch more dressed down. T-shirts are the norm for performing in pubs and bars, and the dress code generally goes up to smart but not over the top, in the much larger venues. We often have more shows where a random group comes together to play a single show than regular troupes, so it's common for individual players to be all dressed differently in the same show. I've never seen an improvised show in Sydney where the cast are all wearing suits, unless that's their actual costumes. Although there has been the odd black smart casual — usually ill-fitting, out of style, and still dusty after years at the bottom of the suitcase of old clothes that's hidden under the bed.

Improvisors should care more, because the clothes an improvisor wears on stage, does have an effect on them, their scene partners and the audience.

When I first started playing *Theatresports*, we were playing in a bar to about 100-150 people each week. It was a training show, so most of the players had just finished a couple of levels of impro training and were dying to entertain an audience. There was no dress code, and so people would often play in whatever they grabbed out of their wardrobe that day, which was mostly t-shirts and jeans — including the women.

During those shows, usually any t-shirt with a picture or writing would end up influencing a scene during the show. A picture of a puppy? Puppies or dogs would come up in a scene. The name of city? That city would come up in a scene. Even audience suggestions would be often be words directly taken from one of the player's t-shirts. It didn't happen all the time, but more often than chance would allow. We were priming the audience.

This is a bit like bringing a script into a scene, or an already rehearsed character, especially if they wore the same t-shirt another week as well. In fact it was quite common to remember t-shirts that stood out in this way, and to associate them with the individual players. This also reinforces the influence of the words or pictures. And I was as big an offender as anyone.

A 2015 paper titled *The Cognitive Consequences of Formal Clothing*, looked at the difference between cognitive tasks performed by people with casual or formal clothing. They found that wearing formal clothing enhanced abstract processing, which is what we want in improvisation.

But I was also regularly dying my hair different colours. Before learning to improvise, I would usually dye my hair either red or blue — I'd chop and change as I felt like it. My natural colour is brown, but if I had corporate work with clients, then I could simply dye over the red or blue with black. When I had blue hair, I was a bit of an audience favourite — they seemed to have a soft spot for me no matter what I did, and they were more likely to come up and say something nice to me after the show, such as "I loved that scene where…". On the other hand, whenever I had red hair, I had more trouble getting the audience on my side than when I was black or blue. I'd heard of connotative colours, I think most people have, but I didn't realise how much of an impact it had on stage until I got involved with scripted theatre production.

Every colour has certain connotations that effect our thoughts and emotions, often unconsciously. There are differences in meaning between cultures, but in many cases these tend to still be thematically linked or differently selected for reasons other than the effect of the colour on the brain. In Western culture, red is associated with anger, danger, energy, strength and violence. It draws attention to itself — possibly because fire, blood and lava are all red in colour. Phrases like "red with anger" and "red devil", and traffic lights and stops signs, all utilise red. It can also be associated with strong emotions, especially passion, desire and love, hence the phrase "red hot lover".

Blue on the other hand, is associated with calmness, loyalty, truth, stability and sincerity. IBM is often referred to as "Big Blue" because in the 1960s they were perceived to have many of these attributes.[154]

Green is often associated with nature, freshness, safety, growth, healing and wealth. Traffic lights and "on" buttons use green for this reason. Mint flavoured foods often use green for spearmint — or blue for peppermint. Purple is the colour of royalty, compassion, ambition, magic and mystery, and has the energy of red and the stability of blue.

---

[154] And their logo was blue, but that's not the only reason or every blue logoed company would also have the name.

These aren't hard and fast associations, because it also depends on the shade of colour, the other colours around it, and the subject of the colouration — whether it's a dress colour for a particular person, or the colour of their car for example. And there are contrary associations with the base colours as well, as blue can also be associated with clinical, stark, coldness or night.

Theatre uses connotative colours all the time, in the use of lighting, sets and costumes — it's an integral part of the production design process. In improvised comedy shows we don't have the luxury of knowing what's going to happen, so often an improvising lighting operator will use variously coloured lights to indicate many of these associations as they occur on stage. But this also depends on the experience and knowledge of the operator, and whether they come from a theatre background or are simply an improvisor flicking a white light on and off to bookend scenes.

The power pose

In 2010 a scientific paper appeared titled *Power Posing: Brief Nonverbal Displays Affect Neuroendocrine Levels and Risk Tolerance*. The authors discovered that a person holding two different "power poses" of one minute each, would amongst other things "embody power and instantly become more powerful", and that they would take higher financial risks. One of the authors, Amy Cuddy, then appeared at a 2012 TEDGlobal Talk where she explained power posing and the paper's findings — the video of which is apparently one of the most watched TED Talks ever.

However, a number of later papers have since disproved many of the effects of power posing, having discovered flaws in the methods used in the original paper, and having been unable to reproduce those results. Dana Carney, another author of the original paper, now also discredits the original findings and says "I do not believe that 'power pose' effects are real." This would seem to be the end of it — time to stop power posing in improvisation. But is it?

When Amy Cuddy's TED Talk video appeared, the power pose technique was quickly adopted by many disciplines, including theatrical and applied improvisation[155]. Cuddy then published a book in 2015 titled *Presence:*

---

[155] When the original power pose paper appeared, I integrated power poses into my workshops — with a few new exercises based on the technique — and I've seen other teachers and students use their own version of it in workshops and warm ups. I've also used it in the corporate environment, but it needs to be integrated in a way that doesn't seem like it's a trick.

Bringing Your Boldest Self to Your Biggest Challenges, which discusses the power of being present, and covers many of the ideas we've already discussed regarding presence — it gives you confidence, removes anxiety and promotes unconscious thinking.

One of the few consistently reproduced findings from the original power pose paper is that power posing gives the poser a greater feeling of power. This should be no surprise to improvisors, because we've been successfully using similar techniques in warm ups for decades. Exercises such as "Musical Hot Spot" and "I am a Tree" can induce a feeling of power, which can induce confidence and remove anxiety, because it induces presence. In fact any exercise which induces presence in some way will do the same thing as power posing, just without the initial power step.

So should we stop power posing in improvisation? If power posing is your key to presence, then absolutely keep doing it. However there are lots of exercises and games which do the same thing but don't involve holding a frozen pose for minutes at a time. So perhaps look at what might work for you instead of power posing.

Side coaching

Side coaching is the directing of improvisors in the middle of a scene. Some teachers side coach and others do not, and that often depends on their understanding of what happens in the players' heads while being side coached, and whether the benefits outweigh the negatives. Considering what we now know about the science behind improvisation, let's have a look at what actually happens during side coaching, and see whether the pros do outweigh the cons.

A common argument against side coaching is that it interrupts the progress of both the scene, and the improvisors' thought processes. Another is that there is no side coaching when performing, so why have it in rehearsal where external interruption, thinking in scenes and relying on director input might be internalised.

The phrase side coaching covers two main techniques. The most common is where an offstage director calls out instructions for the players to hear and act upon as they are playing. For example, while a scene is progressing, the director may call out "heighten your emotions" — which is a general note for individual players — or "Colin, stop talking" — which is a more personal note to maybe stop one of the players relying too much on dialogue.

This type of side coaching initially invokes divided attention, as the players divide attention between the scene and a sudden offstage voice. Divided attention isn't such a bad thing though, because as we know it helps with being present in the moment. But once the players recognise the voice of the director and figure out that they're being given a direction, their focus turns away from the scene, toward the director, where they comprehend the direction, who it was directed at, and then focus on how to apply it. When this happens, the scene will usually initially suffer, so this type of side coaching is best used for big changes in play, where the current moment of the scene is less important than the overarching structure of the scene or technique used by the players.

Examples of this would be refocusing players on the physical or the verbal, introducing a game such as only speaking with touching another player, or an instruction to keep looking for something as the scene progresses — such as an unusual thing, tilt or relationship.

The other type of side coaching is on–stage side coaching, which is used for tightly focused direction on what is happening in a scene at that moment. Examples include heightening something like an emotion, game, or character trait, or for more closely leading a player when an offstage direction hasn't worked.

When on–stage side coaching, the director stands slightly up or down stage from the player who is to be side coached, and slightly back from the direction of the player's focus. Shadowing the player, the player can see them standing close, but slightly further back from the action. The director is almost in line with the player's ear.

Directions of this type are given in first person, as if the director is the player, and they are given slightly before the player can respond. The player's mirror neurons and empathy kick in and they begin to mimic the attributes highlighted by the director. For example, consider the following scene:

> FRANK: Please don't leave, we can make this work.
>
> WENDY: No. We can't.

FRANK: I can change my ways, I can be a better husband.

WENDY: Too late Frank, you should have thought of that before I fell in love with Karen.

FRANK: I can't believe this. Why does this keep happening to me?

If the player playing Frank didn't seem to care too much about the situation compared to the dialogue he was giving, then an offstage direction of "more emotion" might be given. If this didn't work, then the director might get up and on–stage side coach as the scene progresses. For example in the above dialogue, after Wendy's "No. We can't.", the director may greatly heighten their emotion and excitedly say "please, oh please, please stay. Please!" and almost begin to break down and cry. The player cannot help but mimic the director. They usually won't mimic to the same degree, but it will typically be more than what they had been doing after the offstage direction. After Frank's "I can't believe this", the director might then jump in and say "why, why, why" while attempting to cry, or even turn to the player they're coaching and say "Oh my god, can we believe this?!!".

The key to this type of side coaching is not to give instruction, but to shadow and extend what the player is doing, and together the director and player are able to achieve more than just the player alone.

It is important to remember that side coaching should not stop a scene. Once a scene has stopped, it is difficult to restart, with the players having lost the moment and switched to analytic focus to consider the director's feedback. If there are benefits to continuing the scene after stopping it — perhaps it is the first time that player has ventured so far into a character, and we want to keep the scene that caused it — then consider using the word "pause" in conjunction with Viola Spolin's "No Motion" technique. "No Motion" is not a freezing of the players[156], but a resting period while keeping the current moment, actions and thoughts active.

While in no motion, clarifications or comments which are obvious to the players tend to work better than direction on what to change. So for example if a scene is meandering but it is clear to all but the players that the scene is about unrequited love, it may be worth pausing the scene, asking what the players think the scene is about, and then pointing out that "it seems as

---

[156] Which has its own negative connotations.

though player A is in love with player B, but player B doesn't realise it, so let's see what might happen with that, continue".

Side coaching is an extremely useful and effective technique. When a player can be positively changed while a scene progresses, they are able to actually experience both the change, the difference between the before and after, and the result of the change. This then becomes internalised because they are performing it at that moment, often finding that they can extend way past the limits that they'd previously placed on themselves.

Side coaching is an embodiment of experiential learning, and allows improvisors to improve much more quickly than they would have if only given notes after the scene had ended — and thus have the potential to be misunderstood.

La Ronde

In theatrical improvisation, *La Ronde* is a character based training exercise. It begins with two players in a two character scene, heightening character attributes. After a few minutes, once we have some fairly solid characters with points of view and objectives, a third player tags out one of the players. A new unrelated scene begins between the new player's character and the character for the player who stayed from the previous scene.[157] The new player now develops their own character, but the remaining player from the previous scene shows the same character in a different light or set of circumstances. This continues on through the cast, with each player developing a character for two scenes in a row. Eventually the player who was tagged out after the first scene, returns and plays the final scene with the last remaining character.

While primarily a character study, *La Ronde* has also been used in different ways as the basis of a show form. Either with just the "round" as described above, or with the addition of a more open montage style of play once the round has been completed. The important thing however is that the players

---

[157] I once failed an audition for a La Ronde team because apparently the characters in my two scenes were too similar, and I was only focusing on the current moment and not advancing the story. Several other players tried to point out to the selectors how a *La Ronde* works, which only worsened my chances. I no longer assume to know a show format when it is only mentioned by name, as different groups often misunderstand the original intention or interpret them differently.

always play the same character throughout the show, although they may also play support characters for other scenes.

La Ronde is a good character exercise for improvisation, but as a show form it limits the flexibility and stage time of the performers, who play a single character in only two scenes, and have no influence over the rest of the performance. And because each scene is usually about the interaction between characters, the Chicago method typically delivers a better series of scenes.

The name *La Ronde* comes from the French title of an Austrian play titled *Reigen*, which in English translates as *Round Dance*. The initial version was written by Arthur Schnitzler in Vienna around 1897, with copies given to his friends for private use in 1900.[158] The play takes a similar form to the improvised *La Ronde* — a series of a characters alternating until the original character returns at the end — however this is where the similarity ends.

In *Reigen*, each scene is about the sexual relations between characters, either through kissing, fondling or actual sexual intercourse. The resulting sex acts aren't included in the play, but the action leading up to them is. The first public performance of the play was in Berlin in 1920, and then in Vienna in 1921. The Vienna performance caused such a scandal that there were charges of immorality, which were later dismissed in court.[159]

Schnitzler was a writer and playwright. He lived in Vienna and was part of the Herrenhof Café group of expressionist writers and intellectuals during World War I, which led to the creation of a publishing house to bring the rights of Austrian works back to Austria. Jacob Moreno was living near Vienna at the same time, stationed at the Mitterndorf refugee camp, and also joined the group. Both men had originally trained as doctors and had become interested in the new field of psychology, and each had had at one time or another, personal contact with Sigmund Freud. Moreno even ended up editing the *Daimon* journal[160] created by the group in 1918, for which Schnitzler was one of the contributing writers. This was at the end of

---

[158] Different sources have different dates, including 1896, 1897 and 1900. Most likely he completed the initial version in 1897, and printed copies for his friends in 1900.
[159] This wasn't Schnitzler's first scandal. His 1900 story titled *Lieutenant Gustl* made fun of a — most likely fictional — army officer, and he was demoted from officer rank in the army reserve.
[160] *Daimon* became *Der Neue Daimon* in 1919 and then a few months later renamed again as *Die Gefährten*. By 1922 it had ceased publication.

Moreno's university training, and only three years before Moreno began his spontaneity theatre in 1921 — the year after *Reigen* first played in Berlin. Surprisingly, there is no evidence that they actively influenced each other's work, although Schniztler was known to have attended some of Moreno's *Theatre of Spontaneity*.

Most likely influenced by his interest in psychology, Schnitzler wrote the play not as individual characters, but as general character types. Consisting of a prostitute, soldier, chambermaid, young master, young wife, husband, sweet maid, poet, actress and count, *Reigen* explores the interaction of types and class, with minimal backstory or individual character attributes. There are no clear character objectives aside from each wanting to bed their scene partner as their character type. This makes the improvised *La Ronde* format very different to the original play.

After the scandal, Schnitzler prevented the play from being performed in German speaking countries, or for it to be adapted for film. Fortunately, the rights to a French version were given upon his death to his French interpreter, which lead to the name we use today and what is commonly recognised as the definitive film version — Max Ophüls' 1950 film, *La Ronde*.

Ophül's *La Ronde* is different again to the improvisation exercise. His biggest change is the addition of a narrator character, a proxy for Ophüls himself, who introduces each character and scene directly to the audience, interacts with the characters in different roles, and even directs them in their behaviour. The narrator is a meta character, seen symbolically cutting out sections of film where a sex scene is supposed to be, and repairing a broken carousel after a character can't perform sex when he needs to.

La Ronde as a play has been studied in dama schools for years, and was well known to many early improvisors. The *Playwrights Theater Club* for example, did two runs of *La Ronde* in the mid–1950s as *Rounddance*, with the second coinciding with the club's demise — the building was closed by the Chicago Fire Department. The club was the forerunner to *The Compass Players* in Chicago, that included many of the same players, including Paul Sills, David Shepherd, Mike Nichols and Barbara Harris. Whether *La Ronde* was ever turned into an exercise at the time however, isn't clear, but the first documented use specifically in improvisation, is when Craig Cackowski was working with the iO Chicago team *Frank Booth*. Remembering the play from college, he developed the exercise for their rehearsals, and as many of the members of *Frank Booth* were also teachers and coaches, it spread very quickly across the Chicago improv community.[161]

In summary, *La Ronde* is a good character exercise, but less of a show form without additional adaptation. Interestingly, the 1950 film also includes references to directing actors, symbolism, meta characters, breaking the fourth wall, and interacting with an audience, all of which also exist in some form in improvisation. *La Ronde* has been performed by improvisation groups the world over, however there is still much more to explore.

Foveal load

Humans have a fairly wide field of view. Each eyeball has 180° of vision from left to right, and by moving our eyes we can see roughly up to 270° around us without moving our heads. But this isn't all usable at the one time. The eye can only completely focus on a 1° field of view in the centre of the eye and the rest is seen in low resolution — what we refer to as our peripheral vision. In order to see in higher resolution away from right in front of us, the eye has to move so that it is directed at the object or point we wish to view.

Our eyes are moving around most of the time, even though we may not realise it, scanning our field of view in order to build up a high resolution picture of what we can see, and studies have shown that the more change there is in our field of view, the more our eyes move around to see it. This is called foveal load, and the more foveal load there is, the less peripheral vision we have and the smaller the eye movements tend to become. Basically the more there is to look at, the more we lose resolution in our periphery, and the less ability we have to focus on points in the wider field of view. This ability also reduces with age, with degradation beginning in the 20s and it decreasing into old age. But once we've seen something in our field of view,

---

[161] Cackowski remembers bringing it directly from studying the play in college, not from having seen it used in improvisation. He may have done that in isolation, but he also may not have been the first. In Rob Kozlowski's *The Art of Chicago Improv - Shortcuts to Long-Form Improvisation*, Kevin Mullaney says that Del Close was using it in classes and that it spread from there. According to Cackowski however, he wasn't aware of Close or anyone else using it until he did, so if Close had been using it, it wasn't common knowledge. Considering Kevin Mullaney was also on *Frank Booth*, and there is no earlier documented use of *La Ronde* from that era, it is likely that Cackowski was the first, and that it spread quickly from there, and to Close.

it is less likely to cause us to look at it again, unless it changes in some way, in which case it is again something new.

When the brain analyses vision, it is not looking at a continual stream of information, it actually samples images whenever the eye is not moving, like looking at still images from a still camera. This is because sampling an image while the eye is between two points, could sample something out of context with what the brain is interested in, something we never intended to look at. So, in order not to confuse us, our brain makes it look like a continual stream of video by averaging out the samples between the still images. This also allows us to compensate for other body and eye movements such as when we're focused on a single point while the head is moving.

The problem with averaging still images in this way, is that information can be missed. These eye movements are called saccades, and are some of the fastest muscle movements in human beings, taking between 20 and 200 milliseconds — a fifth of a second — to move from point to point. The brain also takes around 200 milliseconds to plan and begin moving the eye, making decisions on the importance of the movement and whether the eyes really do need to move, meaning that the entire process can take up to 400 milliseconds — almost half a second.

Visual attention switching — looking at different things as they draw our attention — still occurs independently of saccades, and we can switch attention to whatever we wish at any time before, during or after a saccade. But attention is what causes the saccade to begin. When we notice something in our peripheral vision, or we sense it with other non-visual means — we hear, smell or feel something — we switch visual attention to it and the brain begins planning a saccade to move the eyes to look at it. Once this planning has begun, we can still switch our attentions elsewhere if we wish, which cancels the planning of the movement, but once the physical movement of the eye has begun, it cannot be cancelled, even if our attention switches in the middle of it. This means that there is a 20 to 200 millisecond period where the eyes could be moving to a point which is no longer relevant, and then the same time again for it to move back again, all while the brain is no longer sampling the image.

But the news isn't all bad, because people can be trained so that foveal load does not reduce peripheral vision. Athletes at the higher levels of sports such as soccer and basketball for example, learn to maximise their peripheral vision, they prevent their eyes from moving so that the saccades don't occur, meaning there is less chance that they'll miss important visual information. Jugglers also for example, learn to focus on a single point so that their peripheral vision is optimised, and so that their eye movement doesn't blind them for up to half a second.

Saccades have also been shown to contain short term memory, which allows them to move the eyes up to 30 milliseconds faster to a point that has already been recently moved to. So if you're continually monitoring something you can see, it is faster to look back to it if you're also looking at other things.

What all this means for improvisation, hasn't been studied by scientists, but may be useful in better understanding how players focus on the visual. An interesting question might also be if when miming, we keep the images in our head, what does that mean for our ability to focus on the imaginary vs. the real?

Blink and blindness

Visual attention is the ability of our brains to analyse and filter visual images and to focus attention on what it thinks is important. If I throw you a ball, then your brain will analyse the image it has of me, what's behind me, the grass on the ground, the blue of the sky, and will then focus its attention on the ball, filtering out everything else. But it's not as simple as just filtering out static images. If you're driving a car in traffic, amongst all of the other moving vehicles, if one comes too close then your focus will be pulled towards that particular vehicle.

Inattentional blindness is when the brain does not draw your attention to something in your vision that it ordinarily should. A famous 1998 study by Christopher Chabris and Daniel Simons highlights a version of this called change blindness, where they asked participants to watch a video of a basketball game with players in both white and black shirts. Asking them to count the number of passes between players of one specific colour, roughly half the participants never saw a man in a gorilla suit join the game, look at the camera, and then walk off. They suggested that this is because we are often blind to exceptions in situations which we assume fit a normal pattern of expected behaviour.

A 2006 study by Daniel Memmert further showed that expertise in basketball increased the ability of participants to see the gorilla, most likely because the gorilla is outside the mental model used to process a game of basketball. More interesting though is his discovery through eye movement tracking that participants who saw the gorilla, spent the same amount of time on average looking at it, as those who did not report seeing it. They were looking right at it, but never saw it.

Another form of visual blindness is called attentional blink, and is where a second image shown quickly after another image, can cause the brain to not process or see the second image. You can see the result of this on the web, where there are countless videos which demonstrate the problem. These types of blindness are often caused by conditions related to cognitive overload. The eyes do notice the change and move to view it, however the time to process and analyse the meaning of the image isn't fast enough to actually process it before it changes again.

Emotion can also play a role in attentional blindness, as emotionally charged images and words draw more attention and cognitive processing than more routine images do.

There are a number of reasons why these types of blindness occur, some we understand and others we do not, but many of these problems can be averted through training, such as through improvements in the detail and processing of mental models as in the gorilla test. We'll talk about improving attention processing while improvising, in a later chapter.

Scripts and event segmentation

Memory scripts are mental models of processes or activities that we memorise as part of our daily life. For example brushing our teeth in the morning, travelling by train, or having a shower, are routine processes which we could write down in step by step order for someone else to follow. We remember hundreds of these memory scripts which help in our day to day life.

The term script was introduced in 1975 in a paper titled *Scripts, Plans, and Knowledge* by Roger C. Schank and Robert P. Abelson, where they described a script as a series of action steps for a task. The use of the term was based on its similar use in computer processing and of course from theatre use as a script for a play. They explored this idea further in 1977 with the release of their book *Scripts, plans, goals, and understanding*.

In 1979, Gordon Bower, John Black and Terrence Turner's paper *Scripts in Memory for Text* laid out a theory for mental models of scripts. They found that these scripts were not only memorised but had unconscious effects on our recollection and decision making. One of their discoveries was that a standard memorised script for something can introduce false recollections into a story which matches the script. For example if a story is recounted about visiting a restaurant to eat a meal, then it is often possible that the teller includes parts of the typical "visiting a restaurant" script, even though those events didn't happen in the original story.

Event segmentation is the mechanism by which our memories are split up into a series of events. For example, a trip to the supermarket for the week's shopping would be a fairly mundane memory, to the point that it would probably not be remembered for very long and would blur into other similar trips. But, if you met an old friend while in the fruit section, or you knocked over a stand full of on sale items, then you would most likely remember this. And you would remember this as an event.

There are still several theories for what causes event segmentation, however the most common at this point is that the brain is constantly monitoring our behaviour and actions and making predictions, and then automatically creates events for us when they don't fit with or they break a standard memory script. This idea was originally proposed in the 2007 paper *Event Percepton: A Mind-Brain Perspective* by Jeffrey Zacks, Nicole Speer, Khena Swallow, Todd Braver and Jeremy Reynolds.

A 2015 paper *Episodes, events, and models*, by Sangeet S. Khemlani, Anthony M. Harrison and J. Gregory Trafton looked at how we segment memory events, and theorised that different types of triggers have different weightings and priorities. A goal oriented task for example has the highest priority, and will tend not to be segmented by other triggers, so we would remember the task as a single memory. Location changes can also trigger segmentation, but often not at the expense of a goal oriented task. So cleaning the house would segment at the house level for cleaning, but would segment at the room level when remembering the steps in the cleaning process. Changes in characters and objects have the lowest priority in segmentation, and therefore are less inclined to be remembered when involved with goal and location changes.

This is highlighted in experiments by Gabriel Radvansky and David Copeland, documented in their 2006 paper *Walking through doorways causes forgetting: Situation models and experienced space*, which showed that carrying an object between two different rooms would cause less memory retention of the object than staying in the same room. Khemlani, Harrison and Trafton's theory is that the two rooms cause segmentation at the room level that supersedes the object as an event, meaning that the object is less inclined to be remembered over carrying the object in a particular room.

Research into event segmentation has accelerated in the 2000s, and has now seen use in practical domains as diverse as artificial intelligence and film editing. Movies can contain hundreds of cuts between different frames, for example we might see a train in the distance, we then cut to our hero in profile standing on top of the train, and then cut to directly in front of the hero's face so that it takes up the whole frame. These cuts are jarring on their own, but film editors have perfected ways to prevent this, mostly through trial and error.

In a nod to theatre, film is often presented along a left to right line of action, as if it were being shown on a stage. As the camera cuts to different frames, the camera must not cross this left to right line that in a theatre would be the back of the stage, which would mean having to look at the backs of the actors. This keeps people and objects on the same left to right side of the frame, regardless of where the camera is. This limits the amount of cognitive processing required by an audience to figure out why two actors have switched sides after the camera moves behind them. By sticking to this 180 degree rule, the audience can focus on the content and not the mechanics of film making. Although obviously not all films strictly follow this rule.

But the 180 degree rule isn't the only technique film editors use to minimise cognitive load at the same time as adding interest. Breaks in music, sound effects, colour, and continuity of frames will jar an audience out of their passive watching. For example, if we shoot a constant video of a person being interviewed by an interviewer, and then we remove the frames where they are listening to the interviewer talk, we'd end up with another cognitive distraction in what's called jump cuts. Jump cuts are where a moving image suddenly changes yet the camera angle and zoom does not. A person may have their head slightly angled with a smile, and then magically they're straight up and down with a frown. Film editors work around this by cutting to a shot of the interviewer, or by zooming out to show them both in frame, or a slightly less zoomed in head shot, before cutting back to the new zoomed in shot. Sometimes you can see these cuts because the resolution reduces as they zoom past the resolution of the original video recording.

Due to the way events segment, film editors often hide their cuts under a flow of action, so no particular cut stands out from the image. This can often be supported by carefully directed saccades. For example, if a point in the frame pulls the audience's focus — an explosion for example — then another point in the frame pulls focus — the hero running away — then the viewer is blinded while the eyes move — the saccade. While this is happening, the editor can cut to a different frame between the two events and the viewer won't notice the cut. This means action can continue without the audience being distracted by film cuts.

In all of this the opposite is also the case. Editors can use quicker cuts and zooms to pull focus, 180 degree angle changes, jump cuts and other techniques to create memory events and cognitive effects. So, for example, an important event in a hero's life might appear in the middle of a period of slower and quieter action, causing the audience to better remember the event.

For example, the reveal scene in the film *The Sixth Sense* uses the 180 degree rule with a line through the two characters, and cuts back and forth between three different frames: a close up of Dr Crowe; a close up of Anna; and a shot with both Crowe and Anna. In all three frames, the camera never moves and the focus point is always a third of the way down from the top and in from the right. The music also fades out and you can hear the creases in Crowe's shirt. This gives the audience a highly focused and unchanging visual and auditory viewpoint. When the ring finally drops to the floor, it makes a loud sound and the camera immediately starts moving, without a cut, to follow the ring and even continues in a spiral movement as the ring circles the floor, to drive the change home. This and Crowe's sudden confusion, all jar the viewer and create a memory event, and the reveal over the next 10-30 seconds drives it home.

Films which trick you into thinking you're in one reality, whereas at the end you find you're in a completely different reality, play well with audiences. This is one of the things that improvisation uses for comedic purposes as well, as we've already seen.

So why all the focus on visual attention and blindness?

These techniques are adaptable for use in theatre, although there's obviously no frames to edit, and there's less control over the viewer's focus. What directors find however is that for a physical change to be noted by an audience, as in the case of a character or prop movement, a clear lighting or sound cue and less movement elsewhere on stage is required to focus the audience's attention and to notice the change.

When an improvisor wishes to have attention drawn to them, they would do better to be the only movement at that moment. With the less than ideal attentiveness of live audiences, and the emotion and empathy that drives theatre, this becomes even more important.

Considering that improvisors are discovering in the moment, and listening is absolutely critical for improvisors on stage, these techniques can also be useful for controlling the attention of both the audience and our scene partners. I've seen countless scenes over the years where one improvisor does or says something important that is missed by their scene partner, but which could possibly have been avoided if they were aware of these techniques.

Goal oriented tasks are also more likely to cause memory event segmentation, and perhaps this is what makes games of the scene more memorable than other scene attributes. This may contribute to[162] the method's popularity with some improvisors. This may also contribute to non–improvisor audiences remembering short–form game based improvisation more than long–form, because games are clearly goal oriented tasks, stand out from the rest of a show, and are usually described as such to the audience.

We'll look at some more practical examples of using these techniques in a later section.

Dance marking

When dancers rehearse the choreography of a new work, they often perform it without the full physical movement required, and instead use specific gestures or subtle movements in place of the full performance level movements. Traditionally this has been understood as saving energy when it is not actually required, however more recent studies have suggested that there are more interesting reasons related to the unconscious.

---

[162] Contribute to. Not being the only reason.

By reducing the intensity of physical movements, the thought processes required to keep the full movement at a high enough level is greatly reduced. This in turn reduces the cognitive load, reduces the need for divided attention, and allows more processing power to be allocated to remembering or internalising the actual choreography. Dancers are offloading to their unconscious, a minimal version of their memory of the performance of a dance, leaving them with much more brain capacity for other tasks, like learning new choreography and self–coaching.

Whether there is an equivalent in improvisation I don't know, but it's an interesting concept nonetheless. We often want cognitive overload in order to suppress conscious rumination and filtering, but in training we want to be less in performance mode, and more in conscious analytic mode.

Lateralisation of brain function

The brain is physically separated into two hemispheres, giving us distinct right and left hemispheres, which are connected by a collection of neural fibres underneath the brain called the corpus collosum. While understanding the physical biology of the brain is not important in order to understand improvisation, some of the misconceptions that have arisen from it arguably are, such as left or right brain dominance.

Studies into brain function have shown that while the hemispheres are symmetrical and brain function mostly resides bilaterally — in both hemispheres — some brain functions can reside in one distinct hemisphere. For example, some language functions such as recognising grammar occur roughly in the left hemisphere, and some memory and spatial functions occur roughly in the right hemisphere. We say roughly, because high level brain functions are generally spread throughout both hemispheres, and often certain functions are in different hemispheres for different people — common with left vs. right handed people, but also occurs when comparing similarly handed people.

A common misconception is that people are either left brained or right brained, with left brained people being generally more logical or analytical, and right brained people being more intuitive, creative and artistic. The origin of this was when neurobiologist Roger Sperry published his work with split–brain epilepsy patients in the 1960s and his results were misinterpreted in popular culture.

Sperry's research lead to the discovery that cutting the corpus collosum — the neural fibres which connect the hemispheres — provides relief from seizures which jump between brain hemispheres. By comparing these patients to people with an intact corpus collosum, he was able to explore various brain functions by analysing the communication, or absence of it, between the hemispheres.

What we know now is that there is a lot of communication between the two hemispheres, and that any logic or artistic function is made up of a range of other functions which span both hemispheres. Damage to the connection — the corpus collosum — simply disconnects the various processes involved with a particular function, it doesn't disconnect or isolate the function itself.

People aren't left or right brained, or even left or right brain dominant, and neither do they switch between dominant hemispheres when thinking vs. feeling.[163] They can feel more creative or logical, but that has no relevance to hemisphere dominance. Recent research has also shown that people aren't genetically or biologically creative or logical, and that education and experience often lead a person in either direction.

There's been a lot of research into creativity and brain function lateralisation in the last 15 years, with many early experiments identifying the differences between left and right brain function. This can be seen in the huge number of popular self help books based on left and right hemispheric differences. But the science is now pointing to creativity and divergent thinking being more of a whole brain process. And while the right hemisphere does play a significant role, both the left hemisphere and the inter-communication between them is also very important.

Touch

Touching another person communicates a lot of information. A 1985 paper by Stanley E. Jones and A. Elaine Yarbrough titled *A naturalistic study of the meanings of touch*, identified 18 different meanings for touching a person. They categorised these into 6 similar types: positive affect, playful, control, ritualistic, task related and accidental touches. The positive affect type

---

[163] Keith Johnstone mentions lateralisation of brain function — by inference, not by name — several times in his second book *Improv for Storytellers*. When discussing emotional sounds, he suggests that they enact both hemispheres of the brain, and proposes that conflict between the hemispheres is one of the symptoms of stage fright.

includes meanings such as being supportive, appreciation, inclusion, affection and sexual attraction. The playful type also includes affectionate and sexual play, as well as play with aggression.

How often do we see these kinds of touches between players on stage? Touching another person isn't that common in real life, although there are the obvious common ones such as shaking hands, holding hands, hugging and kissing. Mirroring real life, many improvised scenes don't offer an opportunity for players to physically touch. But this may also be to do with improvisors not being experienced in doing so.

Beginner improvisors who are still learning acting skills, often haven't learned to distinguish the subtleties of the actor vs. the character relationship. The improvisor's fear can often be seen in the character on stage, as well as an inability to touch or get physically close to a scene partner. For example, it's not uncommon to see new improvisors playing characters who are supposed to be in love, yet refuse to touch and are leaning back away from each other as if they're strangers.

Studies show that touch can communicate emotions, or at least fear, disgust, sadness, sympathy, gratitude, happiness and love, to similar levels of success as both facial and verbal communications. If this is the case, then it is important that emotive touching is acted correctly, equally as much as facial and verbal expressions of emotion. Considering the body's mirror system, and the audience's need for empathy in suspension of disbelief, actors need to be careful not to convey the wrong kind of touching. For example, the leaning back away from each other when they're supposed to be attracted to each other, could negatively affect the audience's engagement with the scene and characters, even if they don't know exactly why.

One particularly appropriate paper by Brenda Major and Richard Heslin in 1982 looked at what audiences perceived from watching characters touch on stage, where one character initiates and the other does not touch back in response. Titled *Perceptions of Cross–Sex and Same–Sex Nonreciprocal touch: It Is Better To Give Than To Receive*, they found that the actors that initiated a touch were rated by the audience, higher than the actor receiving the touch, on criteria such as status/dominance, assertiveness and warmth/expressiveness. They also found that female audiences found male actors who initiated touch as more attractive, whereas male audiences found female actors who initiated touch as less attractive. In conclusion they found that initiating touch is generally more beneficial than receiving, and that touching between different sexes was seen as having more warmth and expressiveness.

But touch isn't just about playing characters on stage and communicating emotion to an audience. Some studies have shown that players touching each other while offstage can have an effect on their performance. In a 2010 study titled *Tactile Communication, Cooperation, and Performance: An Ethological Study of the NBA*, the authors Michael W. Kraus, Cassy Huang and Dacher Keltner look at the effects of touch on teammates in the U.S. National Basketball Association. They found that physical touch can promote cooperation, relief from stress, and can infer warmth and trust. Obviously, these are all attributes you'd want in a cast of improvisors who are working together in a troupe or team.

Other studies have also shown that touch can be used to influence social behaviours, such as a handshake or kiss making people more trusting or more willing to comply with instructions or intentions. As well as the strengthening of different kinds of relationships — not just romantically. How these effects work with improvisors who touch each other regularly is certainly something to think about, and possibly better explored by your own group.

Becoming a better improvisor

Understanding how improvisation works helps us become better improvisors. It provides us with more information on how we currently improvise, and on what we're not yet doing but possibly should be. It also shows us how to work with other improvisors, some of whom may not even be aware that there are other methods.

But what else does the science offer us that will help us improve even more?

Warming up

Why do we warm up? We're well trained, so why can't we just be present and ready to improvise at our best?

Warm ups do three things: warm up our creative instrument — our body and voice; make us present and attentive; and kick start the stream of ideas. I refer to it as IPS, for Instrument, Presence and Stream of ideas.

In his experiments, Jacob Moreno noticed that actors took time to get to a point of "crescendo" when they were really present, and plotted scenarios to take advantage of this predicted point within the performance. He didn't use improvisation warm up exercises to do this, he timed his shows so that he knew how long it roughly took for the actors to warm up as the show progressed. Modern improvisors know this feeling of "crescendo" too, but we try to reach it in warm up so that we can hit the stage already at that point of presence and with the potential for flow.

Most warm up exercises contribute to one or more aspects of IPS in various ways and to varying degrees.

The creative instrument

Stanislavsky discovered that muscular tension limits the ability to not only move, but also to feel. As such, a body totally free from tension is required for actors to be fully creative, emotionally reactive and physically flexible on stage.

Improvisation tends to be a more physical domain than scripted acting, due to the more surreal and absurdist scenes that tend to be found in fully improvised shows like *Theatresports* or *Harold*. Not only that, but you never know what physical state you might find yourself in during an improvised show, whereas a scripted work will have the physicality already blocked. Johnstone's system in particular tends to be very physical due to the narrative advances which require faster transitions of body shape, and the influences of clowning, mask and pantomime.

Control of breath is also an important technique to master as an actor or improvisor, for many reasons. The obvious one is for projection, so that all the audience can hear what the actors are saying. When two people are standing a metre apart, they do not need to use very loud voices. But when there is an audience extending 30 rows of seats back into a theatre, projection becomes much more important. To newer improvisors and those without voice training, this can be a difficult skill to master, because we're effectively speaking more loudly than is expected if standing that close to someone in real life. To them it would sound like shouting from only a few paces away. There are exercises specifically for projection that don't include breathing — such as taking repeating steps away from your scene partner while repeating lines of dialogue for example — but control of breath is going to have the biggest effect, or at least should be the first step. Yet rarely is this taught in improvisation schools, or at least consciously acknowledged.

Control of breathing is also useful for presence, shown by the fact that many meditation and mindfulness methods use breathing to focus and relax. But the same techniques can also be used to reduce anxiety and fear. Studies have shown that shallow breathing — only breathing in so far as the upper chest area — can exacerbate anxiety, whereas slower deep breathing into the gut — called diaphragmatic breathing — can reduce anxiety and fear, relax the body, and induce presence when used in conjunction with focused attention.

Exercises for body and voice warm up can be found in many artistic domains including acting, dance and singing, so we won't detail them here. Suffice to say that a good warm should start with physical and muscular exercises, as well as a vocal warm up, and should be built on good breath control.

Presence

Presence is a learned state, but experienced improvisors develop processes that allow them to become present fairly quickly. This is why experienced improvisors need minimal if any warm up in order to be present on stage. For beginners however, there are a number of tools that can help learn how to be present.

Meditation is a mind control technique which puts you into a state of mindfulness. But meditation is also a great life tool, as it grounds you and releases tension and negative emotions such as fear and anger, and enables some of the stages of creativity in improvisors.

There are numerous meditation techniques, but the simplest is called a breathing meditation. You focus on your breathing alone, which causes you to let go of your conscious thoughts and allows unconscious or repressed thoughts to bubble up into your conscious. At this point you simply acknowledge them and let them go. There are thousands of meditation websites with instructions on various techniques, or you can try a local meditation trainer to get you started. But the important thing when starting out, is knowing what it feels like to be present, as once you know that, it immediately becomes easier to find that state again.

Because presence is letting go of conscious thinking and the ability to switch attentions, meditation is the best tool there is for beginners to learn how to be present. It's a very freeing experience the first few times, and will begin to add new dimensions to a beginner's play. Over time they'll be able to go to a place of presence almost instantaneously, and will be able to arrive at a theatre ready to perform.

Exercises which prevent you from thinking or planning ahead, can also put you into a state of presence without realising it. "Pass The Clap" for example, specifically when it is used randomly across a circle of players, usually puts the players into a state where they are unable to think ahead. Word association is the same, you can't plan ahead, you can't think at all until you're given a word to associate with, and even then a response is required so quickly that only a present mind will be able to respond appropriately.

Divided attention is also a great way to become present, and many of Viola Spolin's exercises can be helpful for this. By focusing on a single goal within an exercise with additional rules, actors forget about where they are, the audience, or other concerns that exist outside that focus. This helps enable divided attention in order to be more present, which in turn helps internalise game rules and consciously reinforce the focus.

Divided attention causes cognitive load, which as a result forces presence. By splitting a player's focus between two or more things, the player becomes more attentive, more experiential, and more present. This is why many warm up games involve either divided attention or combine contrary game rules.

But divided attention is also a skill, and the more time we spend with divided attention between two things, the better we become at being able to focus on each, to a point where the divided attention no longer contributes as much to cognitive load and thus presence.

Take for example the "Alphabet" game, where each line of dialogue must start with the next letter of the alphabet:

> Bob: About time we got married Mary, I've been wanting to ask you for quite some time.
>
> Mary: Bob I really like you.
>
> Bob: Could you please give me a straight answer Mary, because really liking me doesn't sound particularly like a yes.
>
> Mary: Don't push me Bob…

Like most games of this type, this is a divided attention game, because we're reciting the alphabet at the same time as trying to make the dialogue work and perform a scene. As improvisors get better at the game, there's less cognitive load and divided attention, and thus less presence as a result. What this means for warm ups, is that groups should change their warm up routines from time to time if they include exercises that specifically use divided attention in order to cause an effect such as presence.

Stream of ideas

Once our body and voice are warmed up, and we are present, the final step is to start the stream of ideas. The word "idea" itself gives the impression of invention and thinking, but that's not what it is. It's letting the body express the images and feelings that are being generated by the unconscious, which we can now access because we are present. Keith Johnstone refers to this as a state of trance, and uses mask and trance exercises to induce such a state.

We've already discussed flow from a scientific perspective, and this is similar, it's a state where actions and responses simply flow out of our unconscious without much thought. This is the state we use on stage, our play state, and when in this state we still consciously think and notice things, sometimes unrelated to the scene, and our trained unconscious performs the scene for us.

This kind of flow or trance is fairly easy to induce once we've been trained to improvise and are completely present. Simply by being present and actively performing a short scene or improvised exercise, the internalised mental models for improvising become active and the unconscious simply begins the improvisation process.

The ultimate warm up

The warm up exercises commonly used to warm up before going on stage, are effective in various ways, and the exercises we need to be ready to perform will depend on us, our current state of mind, and to a lesser degree who we're warming up with.

Experienced improvisors can switch on in almost an instant and do not need much of a warm up, aside from physically warming up their instrument. This is possible when an improvisor learns how to turn on presence and the stream of ideas on call. This doesn't mean they don't need a warm up, just that they know how to more quickly switch on the things that a warm up typically does.

Warming up as a group has pros and cons. The biggest advantage is the bonding of a group before a performance, the visiting of shared in-jokes and set exercises is an exciting and fun experience with the nice side effect that just having fun can make you present. The disadvantages of a group warm up are: that individual improvisors are doing a warm up that is less optimal for them; the group is warming up at the individual's expense; and the whole group is priming ideas that will most likely come out during the performance. Experienced improvisors can learn to switch on the effects of group bonding, but without the exercises. However this usually still requires some degree of contact with the rest of the group in order to work.

When you consider the three aspects of IPS, different exercises contribute to each of these in various ways. As discussed previously, "Pass the Clap" contributes a lot to being present, it turns off thinking and requires you to pay attention in the moment. Adding complexity such as changing direction, crossing the circle and passing multiple claps increases this attention, but can also add to the stream of ideas, as the improvisors are having fun with the complexity or craziness of the passing.

Fun

While different exercises help with different aspects of IPS, there is an additional influence beyond the exercises themselves, and that's having fun. When people have fun, the main effect is that they become more present, but fun can also turn on the stream of ideas. This is why some exercises that seem to reinforce thinking, or at least don't on paper seem to contribute to IPS, do have some kind of effect on the players who are having fun. The act of having fun allows them to be more present, even if the side effect is having to think — the fun outweighs the thinking. But there are also exercises which can be both fun and not require thinking, so it's often better to find a set of warm up exercises that everyone finds fun, without the side effects. It's like two steps forward and one step back, better the exercise that is three steps forward and no steps back.

A warm up game I used to like was a variation of "Categories" we called "Lists". The players stand in a circle, one player names a list, and then the rest of the players go around the circle and say something that's on the list. For example, the first player might say "Things you find in a kitchen". Then going around the circle, each successive player might say "cutlery", "breakfast", "table", "fish bones", "sex", "poverty". Once everyone has offered a suggestion, the next person in the circle names a list and so on. Once everyone has named a list, then the reverse is played, someone names a thing, and everyone goes around and names a list it would be on, and so on until everyone has named a thing.

I liked this exercise because I thought it was opening my mind up to ideas, and preparing me to improvise. What it was actually doing was making me have fun, and the having fun is what relaxed me and made me more present, not the mechanics of the exercise. "Lists" makes you think ahead and devise the funniest answers as the focus gradually works its way around the circle. The players at the end of the circle have a lot of time to think up an answer, and because earlier players could potentially say the same thing, they either think of several, or an answer that's obscure enough that no one will think of it.

You could also argue that "Lists" helps you see things in an imaginary environment, such as in this example of a kitchen. But in reality it's an exercise in thinking and gag making. It's fun, but it will get you in your head. Sure, fun can lead to presence, but there are more efficient ways to become present that don't have as many negative effects. There are hundreds of exercises like this.

Exercises

Whether it be as training exercises, warm up exercises, or as performance pieces, every improvisor has played theatre games, even long-form improvisors.

Whether they originate from Neva Boyd or Viola Spolin as actor training exercises, or from various origins as short-form performance pieces, theatre games serve a number of purposes. In short-form circles they are often called "hoop games" because the improvisors are like performing seals jumping through hoops, or "games with a handle" because they are free form but with an odd fixed rule that must be held on to.

Whether used as training exercises or performance forms, theatre games have expanded within improvisation communities well beyond the ones described by knowledgeable practitioners like Spolin and Johnstone. They've expanded to the point where many games not only no longer require improvisational skills, but reinforce thinking ahead. Obviously this is fine if that's what you wish to do, but it's not improvising.

There are a lot of games that give players time to think ahead, in most cases probably not intentionally. But it was Viola Spolin who said that games have rules so the players can be creative about succeeding. Rhyming word games, rapping games, starting letter rounds and memory repetition games, most of them lead to thinking.

I've been in a number of shows over the years with a large cast, where directors used think ahead warm ups for the entire cast, and the results weren't great, especially when the cast included newer improvisors. One popular exercise involves players in a circle taking it in turns to sing or speak names of successive objects which begin with the letter A. When someone can't *think* of a word, they move to the letter B. With a large cast, you find up to a dozen or so people *thinking* ahead about which word to say when it's their turn.

I chose specifically not to include exercises in this book. There's countless books out there that already contain hundreds of theatre games and warm up exercises, without yet another to throw on the pile. Most things in this book can be turned into an exercise anyway, the same as every coaching, training or directing problem can be turned into an exercise, once you know how improvisation works.

Using dance marking

In theatrical improvisation as well as traditional theatre, we use show running techniques such as a top and tail, or a cue to cue, to mark scene transitions in rehearsal without having to improvise or act a scene. This is mainly used for technical rehearsals and not directly related to the scene content like dance marking is. However, it is used in improvisation for bedding in show forms such as *Harold* or *Theatresports*. If you consider that dance marking is the memorising and learning of dance choreography, then their use in theatrical improvisation is in fact quite similar.

These kinds of runs are very useful for learning the structure of new show forms. They may not make us a better scene improvisor, but they will make us better at understanding a specific show structure, and that in itself will make us more present and therefore less affected during actual scenes.

Rules and guidelines

There are core rules for theatrical improvisation, such as listening and responding, and they need to be adhered to, but guidelines are simply that, guidelines. When given a guideline in class, instead of taking the guideline on as a rule, ask your teacher why the guideline exists and what the reason is for having it as a guideline. Continue adhering to the guideline, because the teacher probably gave it for good reason, but it is also important to understand the underlying motive.

Internalising

Actual improvising will have the greatest effect on improving our play, but it is certainly not the only thing. Internalising improvisation includes not just the doing, but also the thinking about improvisation, and the more we learn about improvisation the better.

Information may include technical details such as how to improvise, how certain forms work, and the mechanics of stage performance, but also includes historical information and other stories and anecdotes on improvising. All of this contributes to our unconscious understanding of improvisation, and therefore improves our improvising ability, making us a better improvisor.

This information also includes the understanding of styles other than the one we use. In fact, understanding other styles can end up highlighting aspects of our own style that we may not have been particularly aware of that could use improvement. For example, an understanding of story is useful as a high level technique for longer long–form scenic improvisation which uses the Chicago method, and non–status transaction based relationship techniques can be useful in long–form which uses Johnstone's impro.

Internalising also requires time not learning. Studies show that after a learning period, down time is then required in order for the information learned to be stored in long term memory and internalised. Likewise, many hours of learning without a break can prevent additional learning, regardless if it is followed by a break.

So, take a break. Learn some stuff and then take a break. Go out with people who don't improvise, don't think about improvisation, and have a good time relaxing. Theatrical improvisation will always be there when you come back to it, and the experience outside of it will contribute enormously to not only your frame of mind, but also what appears in scenes.

Unlearning mimicry of priming and mirror neurons

Priming and mirror neurons are pretty powerful, but along with the benefits, come a number of negative side effects. Improvise some scenes, then analyse them to see if there was mimicry, and then actively work on not mimicking. This can be difficult when the benefits include group mind, but mimicry shouldn't take over a scene, otherwise that's close to just copying what a scene partner does.

Saccades and attention switching

We know that switching attention can cause the eyes to move their focus, and that doing so causes the information coming from the eyes to be ignored and averaged out for up to a fifth of second, then possibly another fifth to move back to the previous point of focus. But is this 400 milliseconds, almost half a second, enough time to miss visual information vital to an improvised scene?

Luckily enough, attention switching is improved when we are present and in the moment, so the priming of mental models during this process is already going to be pretty fast. Small eye movements are also going to have less of an impact than larger movements, so if you're focused on your scene partner's face for example, then the saccade is going to be much shorter. Likewise, if there is a greater distance between the players on stage, the saccade is going to be shorter because the one degree wide centre of the field of view will contain much more of the information needed for the scene. If the two players are right up close facing each other however, then the saccades will be larger and more frequent, but also the movements of the other player will be larger and more obvious, and potentially longer than the 400 milliseconds that have been averaged out. So, the impact may not be that great anyway.

Where saccades may have an impact is where a player turns fully away and then back again, such as when they are distracted by something in the audience or offstage, or they are in the middle position of three or more players on stage, or when they have a mimed action they are also involved in such as say cooking on a hotplate. The first movement away may have some delayed effect on cognitive processing, but later ones should not, as there will be an awareness of what is there once it is acknowledged the first time, along with the priming of it for fast attention switching. Once they've turned and looked at the fry pan on the hotplate the first time, it is easier to switch to and interact with it on subsequent occasions.

But this shouldn't be confused with general attention switching in the moment, and in fact the impact of saccades might not have any effect on improvisors at all. For example, if a phone goes off in the audience, there is a slight delay between the hearing of the ring, the analysis of it, the pulling up of the right mental models, and then the action that is taken. An unexpected event like a phone ringing is then usually ignored once the players realise what it is. Sometimes it might be integrated into the scene, depending on how in the moment the improvisors are, and the decision to do so is often due to priming of the mental models of answering a phone. Also keep in mind that saccades remember recent movements, so the eyes will move faster to points that have already been recently visited.

More research needs to be done, but it would seem that the negative impact of priming and pulling up mental models is greater than that caused by saccades, and in either case, being present most likely compensates for this anyway. And as far as saccades and switching are concerned, it's probably better to introduce mimed objects or out of periphery actions early, so they don't distract from being completely in the moment.

Cognitive loading

While cognitive loading — through divided attention — can increase mindfulness, it can also reduce the activities of other systems within the brain, such as our internal time keeping or short term working memory. So while divided attention is a great warm up exercise, it's not a great state to be in while learning skills and techniques.

In any class or workshop, exercises take up brain power. Old and familiar exercises do become internalised and take up less cognitive capacity, but then they begin to reduce in effectiveness. New exercises on the other hand, or exercises which involve scene work, take up conscious and unconscious brain capacity, not leaving much leftover for understanding the exercise and learning the skills that the exercise is supposed to be teaching. It makes sense that if we could dance mark the scenework, we'd have much more brain power available for learning.

Using video

The people who know the most about a scene we're in and how we're being affected are the audience. They see and hear everything because they have nothing else to do but watch and listen. And while audiences don't always see the subtleties or metapragmatics that we do as improvisors, they do read these signals unconsciously as they would any social situation on or off the stage — using mirror neurons and other systems and processes that we've looked at.

The next people who know the most about the scene, are our offstage troupe members. They're watching and listening, but also looking for opportunities for support and for whatever comes next for the show format. Next come our scene partners who are on stage with us. Their main task is to watch, listen and respond. And the person who knows the least about the scene and our effect on it, is us.

A coach or director will also have input on how we play, but depending on their role they will have their own priorities, and depending on the quality of their direction, may even accept some of our habits as just the way we play.

The best way to really see what we're doing in a scene, and to have our own input on what we should be working on, is by video recording our scenes. Often this is the only way as players we can fully recognise and understand a certain habit or trait we might have. This can be in a rehearsal or coaching situation, or on stage, as both have their uses.

Some improvisors feel uncomfortable watching themselves on video, but it's important to understand that video doesn't capture the vibe of the room and the audience's response to the immediacy of the improvised performance — a lot of which is what makes improvisation funny. Video is just an audiovisual representation of what happened in the scene, but is still useful for analysing our play and giving ourselves notes.

Learning to touch

As previously mentioned, touch is a part of life, and improvisors should be able to touch each other on stage in the moment as part of their character acting. For beginners, this means exercises in touching fellow players, so they can understand the various meanings that touches can have, and what it means for audiences when one improvisor touches another and it isn't reciprocated. Touching exercises also prepare improvisors for touching in the moment, so it can happen on stage exactly when it needs to, without anxiety or fear of being misunderstood as being intimate with their scene partner, the actor.

Not only does a group touching each other before a performance improve team bonding, but it also breaks down the barriers to social touching on stage. Players are more likely to touch each other in character, if they have already touched that person offstage. There's no longer a barrier that the actor must consider and then breach when the moment calls for touching a fellow player.

There are numerous exercises improvisors can use to learn character touching skills, so we won't cover them here. But on the pre-show side for both team bonding and breaching the touch barrier, don't underestimate the power of a group hugging each other or everyone touching or holding hands before going on to the stage.

Obviously when we talk about touch, we're also talking about having permission to touch. Some groups may not be comfortable touching each other or at least not in their early days, and so there should be complete agreement amongst everyone involved, that touching is OK and what the agreed limits are for the group. But acting by its nature requires touching, so to improve at improvisation, touching is inevitable.

Mixing styles

While explaining the differences between the Johnstone and Chicago methods to a friend many years ago, saying that with the Chicago method you don't think about story, he said "Everything has a story, how can you not think about story?!"

This is the biggest problem with understanding improvisation in recent times. Improvisors are trained to adhere to a set of guidelines for their particular school or method, and through the act of improvising, being present and reinforcing these ideas and internalising them, people are less inclined over time to believe anything which contradicts their improvisation world view. This is the same effect that cults have on people, and indoctrination is a powerful drug.

So, can the various styles of play be mixed? Can you learn and perform both Johnstone and Close's teachings at the same time, and can you integrate them into a single skill set? Can players who are trained in either style come together and perform just as well as two players from their own style? And what about the various schools within each of these models — should students be learning at more than one school at once?

It is certainly possible for players of differing styles to play together, but that doesn't guarantee that the play will be good. At higher levels of experience, players are able to adapt to the styles of different scene partners, but in most of the cases that I've seen, one of the players has adapted their play slightly to the model of their scene partner, often without realising that they've done so. Again, the better the improvisor, the more they are able to do this. It doesn't mean the styles are compatible, it means the improvisors have internalised so much of their own style that working with another style isn't overly difficult.

When a Johnstone and Chicago improvisor perform together and in their own styles, the result is an odd hybrid scene that seems out of place to an informed audience. To an uninformed audience watching a number of such scenes over time, the players will also seem to have certain different stylistic attributes.

The Johnstone improvisor will be making larger offers and advances in story, while the Chicago improvisor will be focusing on the current piece of business. As a result, the Johnstone improvisor will feel as though the scene is not progressing and will often try to advance the story more strongly to get it moving. The Chicago improvisor on the other hand will feel the scene being pulled away from them into more distinct story beats, and they'll try and pull their scene partner back from larger advances in order to deal with the specific detail of the now. Often these responses will be verbalised metapragmatically, for example "I'm leaving, just try to stop me", or "Stop changing the topic Mary. Get back to us. I'm in love with you!", or "Cut to when they shoot each other!", in an attempt to let their scene partner know what they think is wrong with the scene or their play.

When improvisors unknowingly pull techniques from other models into their own models, what often happens is that they will get stuck in a rut or a repeating cycle. A new technique will give them an initial boost purely because it is different to what they previously used and elicits new responses from their scene partners. Over time, the technique is then either overused or stands out against the rest of their model, and often ends up being contradicted by a later teacher or even themselves. This continual integration of incompatible techniques that aren't a part of the model they are learning, means that they're internalising the wrong way to improvise, which in turn de-emphasises techniques in the actual model they're trying to learn, causing them to undo correct techniques which they've previously learned. They're internalising *how not to improvise correctly*, and not internalising the knowledge they need to advance. I know many improvisors who have been caught in such a cycle for many years without realising it.[164]

Learning the Johnstone and Chicago models at the same time will greatly reduce the ability to learn how to improvise, or at least how to improvise well. Choose one, and master it first.

As for different schools within a model, the answer is more complex. UCB is a good example in the Chicago model, because it makes the game of the scene a rule and core principle. UCB trained players have internalised finding and playing the game, and it is integral to how they improvise. So when they then train at say *iO* or *Second City*, they must retrain themselves so game of the scene isn't the primary focus. So long as they're aware that there are two variations to the model, and where the boundaries are, then it is much easier.

Playing with better improvisors

When we play with better improvisors, we're falling into line with their processes, and we're experiencing how they respond to certain circumstances. We're internalising their better play and better scenes. When we play with less experienced players, we're internalising their less experienced play and their potential contradictions to our own internalised processes, meaning there's more chance of us being in our heads and not being present. This is especially a problem when playing with improvisors from other schools or methods.

---

[164] For example, it took me 3 years to undo all that I'd learned about improvisation and rebuild from scratch in a different model, and another 5 years to polish and round out the new style and fully internalise it so it's second nature. I could feel the negative effects of playing in my old style when playing with friends, so I stopped playing with friends. For me this was a controlled process, and still it took many years to pull off. If you're unaware that there are different models, then you could get stuck in a never ending loop.

Better improvisors do more scenes which are better. Their good scene success rate is higher. By playing with them, we're optimising the experience we're gaining, and experiencing scenes we would not have previously considered workable.

For example, let's assume a beginner's average percentage of good scenes was say 3 good scenes out of every 10, and that playing with a more experienced scene partner bumps that up to say 6 scenes out of 10. Then in order to get 6 good scenes out of scene partners at the same level as them, the beginner would need to play 20 scenes, twice the number they'd have to play with an experienced player. This doesn't guarantee they'll learn more or learn faster, but it gives them a better chance at doing so. Playing with better improvisors — in fact it's the same with most improvisation training — is like interest on an investment, in that small improvements over time can greatly increase the pay off and shorten the time it takes to get there.

Rituals

It is believed that theatre descended from rituals, and rituals were originally used to bring good luck upon people or their crops. So it is ironic that many actors use pre-show rituals to bring their performance good luck. A harmless routine you'd think.

The problem with rituals is that they show a lack of trust.

I've gone through a number of different rituals over the years, varying from what I ate or drank before a show through to silly things like running around the block just before going on stage. Rituals reinforce the idea that we personally have no control over success or failure, and it is the ritual that decided our fate more than anything else. The idea that a pre-show event that is unrelated to actually warming up, can have not only an effect, but a deciding effect on our performance, is crazy. If success is affected by whether we stood on our head while reciting poetry for example, then failure isn't about our improvisational ability, it's about how well we can headstand and recite poetry.

The effect of deflecting fear through rituals, reinforces the idea that failure exists in improvisation, that it's a bad thing, and we're not in control of it. This drives analytic focus, thinking, fear and being in our head.

If a show goes badly, then we either did the ritual wrong, or the ritual doesn't work. So we fret about the last good show we did and what rituals can be taken from it instead of the current ritual. Or we're convinced the ritual is OK but we didn't perform it correctly. Or maybe there's two rituals, and they need to be done in conjunction with each other, or we didn't correctly pick up exactly what the ritual was when we had that good show. And if the show goes well, then it must be the ritual that did it, or at least the ritual prevented the failure.

By now we're second guessing something that's completely beyond our control, and something we can't possibly find a solution for. It would be a much better use of both our time and brain power to just learn more about how to improvise and warm up, while acknowledging that there is no failure in improvisation, our performance is mostly outside our own control, and everything we do on stage is a learning experience.

Rituals don't work. There's no mysterious force in the universe that makes a show go well if we invoke it properly. Shows are good or bad based on skill level, audience, and the trust in ourselves enough to be comfortably confident on stage. We can't instantly fix a skill problem or a bad audience, but we can address our confidence on stage in a number of ways.

What if, just maybe, it was us trusting ourselves that made the show go well? What if that's the ritual, simple trusting ourselves?

The best way to fight fear, is to embrace it, and by that I mean doing what we fear most, until we trust ourselves that it's no longer something to be feared.

Most improvisors fear not being creative or not having an idea. In Sydney *Theatresports* there's a common team challenge where a team will come on stage and be challenged to do something by the captain of another team. The captain will simply say "we challenge you to do a scene... which starts in 5, 4, 3, 2, 1" and then the scene starts. Traditionally this strikes fear into the inexperienced, because how can you start a scene from nothing?

For intermediate level players, they'll usually pull out a stock "go to", something they always do when they have nothing, and start the scene that way. My main "go to" used to be frying a fish in a pan over a stove top.[165] Other improvisors I know use "go to"s such as putting up an umbrella, setting a table, wiping down a bar, getting a beer from a fridge, and starting the engine of a car — as if the only good scenes in a car are those which begin with the starting of the engine. Unfortunately "go to"s aren't improvising, it's acting out something that's already been prepared and rehearsed many times, it's playwriting, and that's not fair to the improvisors who are actually improvising.

As far as starting from nothing goes, these days an organic or soft initiation is pretty much a core skill and not such a big deal. But back then it was a scary prospect at the level I was at, and with the minimal training that was usually given to new improvisors. There are exercises to beat the fear of starting from nothing, but the best way I found was by going to rehearsal and simply beginning every single scene from nothing. Even in show formats where a harder or more detailed initiation was needed. Sure, I had mixed success at first, but as I got the hang of it, the fear of not having anything began to subside. This doesn't mean letting our scene partner do all the work though, it just means that we shouldn't start a scene with any preconceived ideas.

If you think about it, starting with nothing is improvisation at its most purest, and when used in conjunction with being present or in the moment, magical things can happen. If we're thinking about how to start a scene, as most improvisors do, then we're in our head, we're in analytic focus, we're processing our possible options, and we're not prepared for the answer to possibly be that we can't think of anything. Unless we're completely comfortable with having nothing to start a scene with, then we'll always have a fear of not being able to start scenes. On the other hand, if we have the ability to start from nothing, then there's nothing to fear, we'll always be able to find something when we think we have nothing.

---

[165] There are pros and cons to "go to"s obviously. One of the more questionable pros is that teachers who see us for the first time, don't know we're playwriting and think our mime or character skills are amazing. I was once in workshop where an improvisor played a stereotype of a Mexican from the old west era, perfect accent and everything. The note they received later was great character choice, and that they're really good at doing characters. The teacher didn't know the student, or that it was one of their stock characters they'd been using as a "go to" for years.

I'm not saying you should start every scene from nothing, but to do so in training so that it becomes internalised. Once internalised, this allows the unconscious to make more interesting decisions about how to start scenes which aren't from nothing.

Fear Conditioning

Improvisors can suffer from a degree of fear conditioning if they are not taught how to deal with fear from the outset of their improvisation training. While Johnstone's model has an inbuilt mechanism for dealing with fear, the Chicago model does not, and many Johnstone communities outside the main hubs don't seem to focus on fear either.

Without fear training, improvisors might begin strengthening a path to fear when improvising. When I first started improvising, I developed an ongoing fear of workshops, triggered partly by inexperience and a fierce want to succeed, but also from what Jimmy Carrane and Liz Allen refer to in their book *Improvising Better*, as playing to the committee, second guessing what I should do in a scene based on the fear that more experienced improvisors[166] will be judging me. Being fearless wasn't drilled into me at the beginning, so it took several years to do it once I began to better understand the nature of fear.

From studies of fear conditioning, we know that the initial time after conditioning is critical for laying down conditioning in memory, and that things like certain chemicals or sleep deprivation can reduce or prevent such conditioning. For improvisors this means mostly not ruminating over a bad show or the fear might be conditioned in. This is pretty common advice anyway, so is nothing particularly new.

---

[166] In our community, the longest performing improvisors are those who started between 1985 and the early 1990s, and who are still improvising at main stage level. They're often called "veterans" or "vets", quite often by themselves. While there are much better all-round players than many of these veterans, they're usually not called veterans. Veterans are veterans because they started early, not necessarily because they're the best. Improvisation theory has changed greatly over the years, yet many of the veteran players still play the way they always have, not embracing new techniques, methods and styles. Amusingly referred to as dinosaurs by some, they're typically still called veterans. This perceived "them and us" division has caused many improvisors to quit over the years and led almost directly to my fear of being judged in workshops. Only in the last 10 years, with the number of new stand out players increasing, along with the embracing of different methods, has this perception thankfully begun to wane.

One popular technique is to give yourself the rule of being able to be negative about a show for 24 hours, but then you have to forget about it and let it go. The problem with this is that any conditioning effect, if there is any, would have already had an effect after 24 hours. Studies show that small amounts of sleep deprivation can prevent conditioning, but large amounts may not. I find it difficult to sleep after a show anyway, and in such cases I do seem more dismissive of the show the next morning, as just being the nature of the beast. So maybe going to bed in the early hours after a show can be beneficial.

Considering that cortisol and other glucocorticoids can also prevent conditioning, eating sugary foods and trans fats after a show may also have a positive effect.

Going solo

When the world's greatest cricketer was young, he would hit golf balls against a wall with a round cricket stump, causing a faster and less predictable deflection of the ball off the stump than if using the flat faced bat actually used in cricket. This meant that Donald Bradman was able to hit all manner of shots that were not even possible in cricket, because his ability went beyond that required for the game. In tennis, reaction time at the net is enhanced by ball machines which fire balls at the player faster and more often than would occur in an actual game of tennis. This means that the time between ball returns in an actual game of tennis can allow the player more time for other thought processes as their reaction time improves. And top guitar soloists practise at speeds around 10% above what they perform on stage, so that their performances have additional qualities beyond speed, but yet they still have the reflexes they need to recover if unforeseen circumstances cause things to go out of control.

What all of these training regimes have in common, is the internalisation of a performance level at or above what is required for normal performance. This same approach can be used in improvisation by deepening engagement with scenes, internalising more theory, and increasing the agility of attention switching. But one of the best ways to work on all these aspects is by improvising solo.

When we improvise a two player scene, where each person is a single character, there are some improvisational skills that are used throughout the scene, and some that are only used for a small part of the scene. Initial character development, scene initiation metapragmatics, game of the scene discovery or negotiation — if that is part of our particular method — are all skills that are used almost incidentally or as building blocks before the real part of the scene begins. Learning these skills can also take a lot of time relative to how short a time they're used in scenes. So we end up needing a lot of scenes in order to flex those particular muscles.

What if instead of two players playing the scene, there was only one player playing both characters in the scene? Then we're possibly getting twice the stage time with those techniques. Not to mention the greater attention switching as we switch characters, and obviously being able to actively see both sides of character interaction throughout a scene as it occurs. This helps to internalise improvisation faster than if we only had one character to worry about.

The down side of playing solo however, is that the justification effects aren't as prominent. Much of the comedy in theatrical improvisation comes from the interplay between players, the support and other choices provided by other players, and the subsequent justification. When improvising alone, we are already on the same page, so we're not being influenced or "Yes Anded" by scene partners, and we aren't forced to justify their choices. Solo improvisations have a certain feel to them for this reason, as the players have developed skills for improvising scenes without the input of other players or being able to justify their offers or moves. But this can be a good thing, because it helps develop other techniques which aren't dependent upon playing with other people, or people who play differently.

While there are show formats for solo improvisation and well known improvisors who regularly perform solo, such as Andy Eninger and his *Sybil* format or Jill Bernard, this doesn't mean having to perform solo in front of an audience in order to improve. Solo improvisation as part of a regular training schedule, regardless of the quality or how funny it is, is going to greatly improve your improvisational ability. And who knows, you may even find an attachment to solo improvisation and want to take it to the level: public performance.

Solo exercises can be found on the Internet by searching Google, however Mick Napier's *Improvise: Scene from the Inside Out* also has some useful exercises. As has Viola Spolin's *Theater Games for the Lone Actor: A Handbook*, although they're mostly Spolin's stock acting exercises adapted for solo rehearsal. Rob Kozlowski's book *The Art of Chicago Improv: Shortcuts to Long-Form Improvisation* also contains a section on Andy Eninger and his *Sybil* format.

Playing multiple characters

Playing multiple characters in the same scene — where we switch between them in the middle of a scene — is another way to increase the internalisation of improvisation. By switching characters, especially from spoken line to spoken line, we're training ourselves to respond both faster and with more depth than we would playing a single character. When learning to play this way, the different characters will at first tend to merge into each other and the characters will often have very similar points of view or objectives. By learning to recognise this and to increase the differences between characters, improvisors find they can discover a wider of range of characters and can find them more quickly. It also improves the ability to sense changes between characters by our scene partners, which ultimately means much better listening skills.

Taking this a step further is the *Scram* format by Jill Bernard and Joe Bill, where they improvise up to 3 scenes at once while switching characters between each scene. So for example, one player might be speaking dialogue in scene 1, while at the same time the other player is miming an action in scene 2 and then responding to an implied line in their scene. The first player may then either switch to a scene 2 character to respond, stay with their scene 1 character, switch to scene 3, or switch to another character in scene 1. Again, this greatly improves skills that also apply when playing single characters, skills that would otherwise take many more years to learn if playing only single characters.

Festivals and guest teachers

Go to festivals, and train with guest teachers when they visit your town. It's that simple.

Festivals provide an intense almost 24/7 experience of watching, learning, performing and discussing improvisation. Not only does it provide us with an intense engagement with improvisation, but it also gives us the opportunity to compare the differences between different teachers, shows and performers, which all becomes internalised as well. It's the riding a bike principle. We won't be fully conscious of everything that is internalised until it suddenly comes out one day in our performance.

There is one major gotcha however, and that's with the method used by the organisers and guest teachers. Festivals usually focus on one particular method of improvisation, and spending a few days to a week doing workshops and watching shows in a method or style that you're not interested in, can be pretty frustrating[167], or even boring. As can training with a teacher who spends their time trying to figure out why nobody in their class understands their idea of the core principles.

In Europe and the Pacific, most festivals are almost 100% focused on Keith Johnstone's impro. Often, they'll invite a special guest Chicago method teacher as a marquee teacher for the festival, or they'll have a generic workshop such as intimacy or genre analysis for example, but the rest of the time the focus will usually be on Johnstone's methods. U.S. festivals however are usually focused purely on the Chicago method, and when European improvisors apply to give workshops or perform shows, they often don't realise that their style is different to the Chicago method, and they may end up derided or as an outsider.

So, absolutely go to improvisation festivals, and train with guest teachers when they visit you locally. But do your research and make sure you understand what will be taught. Look up the festival on the web and the workshop descriptions to see which model will be most prominent. And for individual teachers, check out their workshop descriptions and bio, and then research the groups they've worked with in the past.[168] Many teachers also like to hear from other improvisors, so don't rule out sending them an email

---

[167] I've been in workshops over the years by international guest teachers, where people were singled out for not having certain core improvisation skills that the teacher assumed they should have. In most cases, the teacher was either unclear about which method they used or was ignorant that there are different methods.

[168] A good example of this is the classic book by Carol Hazenfield, *Acting on Impulse*, which influenced me heavily when it was first published in 2002. Her ideas excitingly often conflicted with what I'd learned from Johnstone's work, and on the back cover were listed her many varied influences from the acting world. However, if you look inside to her acknowledgements, they are all about Keith Johnstone, and one of the larger groups that utilize his work, BATS, originally known as *Bay Area Theatresports*. To me it seemed like she'd developed a new method, but Hazenfield was actually just using acting techniques as her take on Johnstone's impro.

if you really want to find out what they do. Basically, do your homework and be prepared.

Training, jams, rehearsals and shows

There's a common belief that rehearsal is for work, and performance is for fun. Or more specifically, rehearsal is for thinking, performance is for being present. I could never understand why people would believe this, as it seems contradictory that you would practise thinking in order to not think. But this is effectively what needs to happen.

First off let's clarify what we mean by training, jams and rehearsals. These aren't exact terms used in improvisation, and they do have different definitions around the world, but let's give some definition to them now so we know what we're talking about.

Training is exactly that, it's the learning of improvisation skills, the general techniques that improvisors need to actually improvise. Training can also include learning new show formats, or even unrelated skills like stage combat or accents. Training is the learning of something new.

Rehearsals on the other hand are usually for devising, practising and polishing a show, which often means thinking about what to do next. Even with a director, performers will be consciously thinking about what they need to do. Depending on their level of experience, they may be thinking about improvisation skills as well as the show, or they may be experienced enough to be present in scenes but be thinking about the show. And as with dance marking, the focus is on the form or the techniques required for this particular show, and not so much on general improvisation skills.

Some show forms can be fairly complex, both structurally and in content, and during a performance we don't want to be thinking about this very much, so we rehearse the form in order to internalise it. The *Harold* is a great example of this, as a lot of training and rehearsal time is often spent on *Harold* specific skills.

Jams on the other hand, depend on where you live. In the U.S., the word jam is short for open jam or public jam, where random players or audience members can get up and improvise in front of an audience. In other countries — Australia at least — the word jam means the same as in other arts: to play together and generally practise without too much structure, usually in a private rehearsal space. In either case, jams are usually either learning or polishing improvisation skills, or for just having fun. If the point of the jam is to have fun, then the improvisors tend to be present throughout, and relatively little thinking is actually required.

So are rehearsals for thinking? Yes they are. Training and rehearsals are supposed to be about conscious thinking. They're about improvising, as well as consciously accepting instruction and guidance, thinking about it and practising it. This is important for internalising improvisation, and for rehearsal situations where the point is to receive and internalise technical knowledge.

What you need at any particular point will depend on you. Just don't forget to have fun on stage, otherwise why are you still improvising?

Continual learning

Because improvisation is a learned behaviour, and there are countless variations of method, style and form, it is impossible to learn and keep a high level of skill for every kind of improvisation. Even if two troupes perform the same show form and in the same method, then the differences between the players in each group will also reinforce or defocus certain techniques in relation to others. For example a highly physical *Harold* team will have very different skills to a highly verbal one.

Improvisation is a continual relearning process, because as we lay down new knowledge and muscle memory, we're also unlearning or rewriting the neural pathways for the skills we already have. As we focus on one skill, another one is affected in some way if no longer used or used in a different way. This is why all-rounder runners and swimmers for example, must eventually decide upon short or long distance or some other specialist style in which to concentrate their efforts. It is the overall balance and focus of particular skills in both the unconscious and conscious which makes the improvisor who they are.

If for example we were performing twice a week, say a weeknight *Harold* show and a weekend montage based on monologues, then the skills being used are different. Different show, different players, different skills. If we performed both for long enough, then we'd get used to performing at a high level in each, but it would be less likely that we'd be exceptional at each. If we were to then do a one-off hour long scenic long–form, then the skills required are going to be different again, and we'd need to do some rehearsals to relearn how to use those muscles. After a number of rehearsals and shows of the new format, we would then need some time to return to the high level of performance we had for the previous two shows. The more experience an improvisor has, the less effect these differences have, but still, no single improvisor is brilliant at everything.

Improvisation is a continual learning and relearning process. We're always learning about new methods and techniques, we're always learning how to apply them to new scenes and circumstances, and often we are relearning them after not having used them in a while. If we've stopped learning, we've stopped caring.

Fixed Attention (FA) and Open Monitoring (OM) meditation

There are a number of different methods for meditation, and many have been shown to have differing effects on the mind. Most are classified as either a focused attention style (FA) or an open monitoring style (OM), but within each there are still many variations.

The FA style is the most popular, where the practitioner focuses their attention on a single point of focus, perhaps a visual point in space, or a breath, or a part of the body. While focused, any other distractions are allowed to appear, be noticed, and are then are let go, with focus returning to the original point of focus. Aside from the other meditative benefits, this state also improves perceptual awareness and the ability to focus attention, all skills that we need for improvisation.

With the OM style, instead of a single point of focus, an open attentive state is used to openly monitor feelings and thoughts, without being pulled into them in detail. It is focused attention but without the focused attention. Studies have shown that the OM style improves our ability to notice and acknowledge a wide range of distractions, better regulates our response to emotion — something which can help improvisors with fear and judgement — and reduces attentional blink.

A study in 2012 also showed that the OM style of meditation improved divergent thinking — the ability to generate a number of different creative solutions to a problem, as opposed to convergent thinking where a single solution is devised via a set of logical problem solving steps. Divergent thinking is good for improvisation, and a common refrain in applied improvisation. So for improvisors, OM style meditation is certainly worth looking at.

Experiencing flow

Flow is when we perform in shows or scenes where it seems almost like an out of body experience, where we almost cease to exist, and we become improvisation personified.

Flow requires a skill challenge balance, which comes from the perception that what we're doing is difficult and requires a high level of skill. If flow is our desired outcome, then this should drive us to want more and more challenging experiences. Whether this is a part of the addictive properties of improvisation, is unclear, but it may also be a reason why a lot of improvisors move on to other things once they've reached a certain level of experience.

Teachers and coaches should make sure each student's perception of their ability and the challenges they face, match their actual levels of ability and challenge. This puts the student in the best position to experience flow, and flow in turn helps students rise to the next level of experience. Improvisation needs to be a positive experience at all levels, or else students may well quit out of frustration or boredom.

When it becomes difficult is when we don't have a current teacher or coach, and are unable to determine what the next challenge should be. One way to address this is to have a personal mentor, another player whose advice we respect, who is able to give feedback on our play and opportunities we should step up to. This mentor doesn't need to be better than us, just someone whose outside eye we respect. We're the last people who should be giving notes to ourselves, because we're the furthest down the line in respect to understanding the scenes we're in, and our own style of play. At times we can also be our harshest critic.

The top improvisors, the ones that are highly respected, don't just do the same thing all the time. They do different forms, different styles, play with different people, invent new techniques, and explore other avenues which will challenge them. Improvisors should always be challenging themselves at an optimum level, in order to receive more intrinsic rewards for their performance.

Method of Physical Actions

Stanislavsky's and Meyerhold's theories on psychophysical techniques seem not to have yet been adopted by mainstream theatrical improvisation. The idea that physical actions, gestures and movements can affect psychology and emotional state, would seem perfect for use in improvisation, yet I've not come across it outside the scripted acting world.

The scientific basis seems to be a combination of Ekman's facial micro-expressions, and mirror neurons, both of which convey to the audience a more believable palette of emotions and psychological states.

Modern improvisation already has a common use of this, with the idea that we should put emotion into physical actions. So, for example anger could be conveyed by endowing the action of washing dishes, by using fast, high energy, snapping movements. To endow with happiness, we could then use slower, flowing movements, that often overshoot where they would have to stop in order to actually wash dishes.

Viola Spolin also devised exercises and games for physical actions to invoke emotion or psychology, or to create characters with these traits. These are still used today in improvisation classes, even though it's often not entirely obvious that this is one of the possible outcomes.

Aside from these, the use of physical actions to specifically create psychology is mostly unknown in theatrical improvisation, and is certainly worth looking into in more detail in the future.

Question the guidelines

Guidelines help beginner improvisors improve, or help guide show forms. Instead of internalising guidelines, we should be internalising our understanding of them.

In the case of the guideline "Don't ask questions" for example, the origins and theory are more important than the guideline itself. And as improvisors we should be doing the same with every other guideline we come across. Question, understand then integrate.

Keep in mind that a lot of teachers aren't completely honest about why they give a guideline or exercise, or sometimes don't provide enough context. Often this is to do with not wanting to overload students with caveats and context they don't need at that point in their training. But sometimes it's because the teacher doesn't really know.

It's never a good idea to challenge a teacher in class. By all means ask questions, clarify, and give the teacher a chance to explain. But don't openly contradict them. They may be following a curriculum that they must follow. Or they may have good reason not to explain something. Or they just may not know or realise. In any case, making a teacher uncomfortable can sometimes make the other students in the class uncomfortable as well, and that's not fair to the students or the teacher. The best course of action I've found is to simply clarify what the teacher thinks, and verify it yourself outside of class, because not everyone believes the same things about how improvisation works.

Now whether that teacher should be teaching is another issue entirely. Some think the only teachers should be the ones who are exceptionally experienced and are brilliant teachers. Others believe that any training is good, and the experience of the teacher doesn't really matter in the big scheme of things. I think it also has a lot to do with the explosion of improvisation over the last 10 years. There's just not enough great teachers for the number of students wanting to learn improvisation.

Question exercises

Just like guidelines, improvisors should always question not just the point of exercises, but also the other effects they may cause.

For example, the "Lists" game described earlier emphasises thinking ahead and gagging, but mildly benefits presence by being fun. I'd say that's a bad warm up exercise, but maybe a fun party game.

I recently watched a mime exercise where students would pass a mimed object around a circle. It was useful in that students could see how the object was handled by students earlier in the circle, but they were in a holding pattern of expectation and potentially already thinking about how they would handle the object when it came to them.

Even the most obvious exercises can have aspects we don't always recognise. For example, the exercise "Crazy 8s" generates franticness and energy, in order to quickly induce presence. Players form a circle and count to 8 by holding up their right arm and shaking it 8 times while loudly counting each shake from one 1 to 8. Then the same happens again but with the left arm. Then the right leg, and then the left leg. At this point the exercise begins again but counting to 7 instead of 8. In order to build up energy, the group increases in speed as the counts continue, and it is important that each limb is passed through as quickly as possible to try and induce divided attention. In fact, you can feel the onset of divided attention, even though it's never fully reached.

But here's the thing. How fast is the exercise counting from 1 to 8 on each shake, compared to counting from 8 to 1 on each shake? Between 30-70% faster! Counting up is habitual, and increases speed and thus intensity and the need for more attention. Counting down isn't as habitual, because we don't do it as often, and there's usually some cognitive processing required beyond simply counting through our memory of ascending numbers. Counting up is how the exercise works, and yet I still see teachers counting down instead of up.

Exercises absolutely have their uses. But it is important to understand what other effects are happening with their use.

Let your unconscious do the work

If we go back to the significant written works in each method of improvisation, we'll find in almost all cases, references to being present and not thinking, often to the point of being a key chapter or the premise for the book. And yet the message doesn't always get through.

The unconscious is our improvising engine. It does most of the work, so that our conscious doesn't have to. Feed it, care for it, and respect it, and it will look after us well on stage and in life.

Conclusions

Improvisation teachers, books, blogs, podcasts, even entire improvisation communities, tend to contradict each other when discussing how to improvise. Often this is because we have different beliefs regarding what works for us personally, but more significantly because we come from different schools: Keith Johnstone; one of the Chicago schools; or some other model of how improvisation works.

When learning to improvise, adhering to one particular style is critically important, as it gives us insight into why we're being taught the things we are, allows our teachers to give accurate feedback on what we're doing, and our play improves because we're working with other improvisors who are training in the same model. And that's the point. The models are the way they are, because the players adhering to them have thrashed and pounded them into the working models that they are today.

Once we understand that there is a difference between methods, we're better able to answer the question of which school a teacher or book etc. is from, and from that we're able to figure out whether it's appropriate for the method we're learning.

Respect the models and their methods

As artists began to experiment with improvisation, they developed their own incompatible models of how improvisation worked, with sets of principles and guidelines which help the improvisor to — ironically enough — produce improvised theatre that's not so random, with high production quality and entertainment value.

They first discovered spontaneity, a state of mind based on being in the moment and letting the unconscious do much of the work. Then they discovered the importance of listening, acting and justifying, which brought order to the work. And finally, each discovered a different set of scene attributes which should be focused on in order to progress an improvised scene. Thus, theatrical improvisation was born. To this add the tenets of performance — emotion, acting and stagecraft — and it becomes theatre and is enjoyed by audiences.

We're now at a turning point in the development of improvisation. What happens next, and what happens to the unique models and variations that have developed all over the world?

Some improvisors still believe that improvisation is all just one big model, and that you can pick and choose the techniques that you wish to use from the big melting pot of improvisation methods and techniques, without it having any adverse effect. This is often the advice of experienced improvisors, who are better equipped to work with different methods without realising that they are. Others believe that while there are differing models, the basic principles and rules are the same, and while some techniques may need to be adapted to work in other models, it's not an onerous or complex task to do so.

And finally, there is a belief that regardless whether there are differing models, there has been too much argument over the years about which kind of improvisation is better, and so we should instead treat all improvisation as basically the same, merging everything together so we can all be friends again. This doesn't help preserve method diversity, it dilutes it. Merging models will force us down the same path as we're finding with languages and cultures — they begin to disappear or become diluted. Merging models and rejoicing in a single method of improvisation is not the solution to preventing different groups arguing over which is the best improvisation style. The solution to everyone getting along, is the recognition that there are different methods, they all have different approaches and uses, and they're all valid in their own unique way.

From mystique to science

> *Any sufficiently advanced technology is indistinguishable from magic.*[169]
>
> *– Arthur C. Clarke*

When we think about it, working together to discover scenes that are already there sounds like magic doesn't it? Creating wonderful art by simply responding and without thinking, is magical. If we read some of the earlier books on improvisation, such as *Truth In Comedy* by Charna Halpern, Del Close and Kim Johnson, or *Something Wonderful Right Away* by Jeffrey Sweet, there is an air of magic about improvisation.

In his 1925 book *The Theatre of Spontaneity,* Jacob Moreno writes:

> *There are players who are connected with one another by an invisible correspondence of feelings, who have a sort of heightened sensitivity for their mutual inner processes. One gesture is sufficient and often they do not have to look at one another, they are telepathic for one another.*

Truth in Comedy takes this further, and refers directly to ESP being real because it was experienced on stage, and that players were somehow linked up to a "universal intelligence" through improvisation. But obviously this can't be the reality, because magic in this sense doesn't exist — it's the domain of fairy tales and childhood dreams.

The magic we see when we improvise is part of the attraction and addiction to improvisation, and while only a few decades ago the magic could not be explained, we now do have the knowledge about how our brains work to

---

[169] Clarke was referring to technology specifically, and while in the case of improvisation it's not technology but an understanding of how the brain works, but for all intents, the quote is still relevant.

explain what is actually happening. We don't know everything yet, but we do know quite a lot.

In *Truth in Comedy*, it says:

> *On stage, one has a complete picture of what is going on, and also a clear sense of all potential moves. They are almost laid out in time. The pattern-making mechanism is kicked on, and yet, one's intellect does not desert him. [..] Somehow, the improviser is in the balanced right and left hemisphere state. He can almost see time as a dimension, as he can almost see his potential moves extend physically into the future. It's then very easy to decide which move to choose, and then go with it. Since everyone is on the same wavelength, each player sees what the other sees.*

With what we now know about improvisation, this quote now seems cute in its naivety. However, the sentiment is as true as ever — improvisation is a wonderful magical experience. And while we're finally beginning to understand the science behind it, it's much more fun to just go and experience the magic as *Truth in Comedy* describes it. Study it, practise it, and internalise it. But don't forget to enjoy the fun and magic of just going out and doing it.

Acknowledgements

This book took forever to complete, with about 5 years of thinking and then 7 years of writing and researching, all while improvisation, the science, and my health, were constantly changing. It is now 2018, and many of these ideas are now common knowledge — which would have been great if all those years ago I'd just stopped researching and started publishing. On the positive side, if not for the support of those around me, it would never have been completed at all.

Most importantly, a special thank you to my wife Louise, who wanted me to finish this book more than I did. She did all the great artwork, including the cover and chapter art, and spent countless hours reviewing the text and theory over the final months of this marathon project. Considering she had to quit improvisation 9 years ago, it would have been difficult to constantly reread the detail of what she was missing. Without her patience and support, this book would be at least twice as long, titled "Volume 1", and would still be unpublished.

And a special thank you to our daughter Molly — who has always known me as "still writing that book" — for her patience and support, and especially for entertaining herself over the final months when Mum and Dad were busy editing and drawing, and all she wanted to do was "go and do something exciting on the weekend".

Thank you also to my first-string reviewers Peter Lead and Tony Starr for checking my structure and theory. Having kept much of this information secret for almost 10 years, it was quite daunting to finally place it in the hands of people qualified to tear it to shreds.

Thank you also to the people who listened to the various ideas — big and small — that I was researching over the years, or who answered the questions I had, or who gave suggestions on the publishing and process side — some of whom possibly didn't even know I was writing a book at the time: Gunter Lösel, Bill Arnett, Jason Chin, Craig Cackowski, David Razowksy, Jimmy Carrane, Gary Schwartz, Will Hines, Amy Evenor — daughter of Lee Gallup Feldman, who I have unfortunately since lost contact with — Geoff Bartlett, Steve Kimmens, John Knowles, Peter Lead, Tony Starr, Thanassis Boulis, Suz Mawer and Cindy Tonkin.

This book is the result of all I have read and experienced in my years of studying and performing improvisation, and would not exist in its current form without input — good or bad — from everyone and everything I have encountered over all those years. It would thus be impossible to list everyone else who has contributed, but I will mention some of the key people.

Peter Bryant for agreeing to start a comedy radio show with me, which became the beginning of all this, Abe Killian and his blue M&Ms for preventing it from ending prematurely, and Leisha Forrest for my detour into *Theatresports*. Early podcasters, particularly Jason Chin and his *Green Room*, Andrew Hanson and his *Group Mind Podcast*, Elizabeth Quinn and Justin Zell with *Improvised New York*, and Marshall Stern and Nancy Howland Walker with *Zenprov*, then later Steven Perlstein[170] with *Improv Obsession Podcast* and Jimmy Carrane with *Improv Nerd*.

Jonathan Briden and I started collaborating on long-form when I was still learning to improvise, and we went on to spend many years exploring new long-form techniques and creating new show forms. While my minimal acting and improvisation skills would have annoyed many other experienced improvisors, Jon supported me while I learned the ropes, and I couldn't have continued to now without this early guidance. In our final years, we also worked with three great improvisors in each of our final three trios: Louise

---

[170] I agree with Perlstein when he says that we are currently in "The Golden Age of Improv", but we are perhaps now heading into "The Diamond Age of Improv".

McManus, Emily Beale and Peter Lead. I'm sure Jon would have continued this journey with me, had he not moved to Canada when he did.

Jason Chin was the first international teacher to visit Australia from Chicago, and he helped kickstart the Chicago method here. His death in 2014 was a big loss. I still think of him when I eat pie.

Peter Lead and I collaborated from 2010 to 2016, starting at a time when we were the only two people in Australia using the Chicago method. Peter is a joy to play with, he's completely fearless and grounded, doesn't mind a good pash with anyone who happens to be onstage, and sits, listens, questions and clarifies my theoretical ramblings for many hours at a time without a hint of disinterest.

Since 2015, I've been collaborating with Tony Starr on all manner of things, including some timely mixed method shows with Suz Mawer. He knows his stuff, doesn't stand for any bullshit, and continues to fight the good fight in Sydney improv. Tony was the final confirmation that I understand game of the scene.

David Razowsky was kind enough to take a detour to Sydney for me in 2014, and was the final tick box in confirming that I understand the intricacies of the Chicago model vs. Johnstone, and the Stanislavsky echoes in the Chicago model. Although his main memory of that trip is possibly the threat of death while changing a wheel on my car on the side of a freeway, and thus me possibly making my name for being the man who killed David Razowsky.

Cindy Tonkin has been consistently there for me over the years, from the day of my level 1 graduation show to now, although we've spent much of that time in different groups, and not performing together. She's been my closest confidant in our local community, and without that support I probably would have already quit improvisation. And to top it off, she was the one who brought Jason Chin to Australia.

John Knowles has supported my work from day one, and has unwittingly performed with me many times in my mixing methods experiments. He has an inspiring and varied back catalogue of work, and yet remains humble and supportive.

Thank you also to everyone who listened to my theories and then said that I was wrong. You made me do even more work to find the proofs that I should have included at the outset. I won't list your names. Maybe in the next edition?

And finally, everyone seems to quote Viola Spolin these days where she says "Everyone can act. Everyone can improvise." Thank you, Viola. Your principle has guided me for most of my years of improvising, and hopefully this book contributes to this ideal in some useful way.

Bibliography

The research for this book comes from many different sources, including teachers, fellow improvisors, books, podcasts, the web, and scholarly papers on improvisation, cognition and other related domains. To identify which sources contributed to which insights or even which ones were used in this book, would be impossible or require thousands of footnotes. Indeed, many Internet materials such as web text, videos and audio recordings cannot be referenced even by URL because they're always changing.

What follows is a list of the resources that are either referenced directly in the text, or which stand out as main influences — listed in order of author, with tags identifying the domains to which they relate.

JI = *Keith Johnstone's impro system*
CI = *Chicago method improv*
GI = *General improvisation*
M = *Miscellaneous topic*
CR = *Cognitive Research*
PA = *Performance Arts General*
A = *Acting Theory*
H = *Biography/Autobiography/History*

Books
Babbage, Frances. *Augusto Boal.* New York: Routledge, 2004. [H, GI, A]

Bakhtin, Mikhail Mikhailovich. *The Dialogic Imagination*. Austin, Texas: University of Texas Press, 1975, 1981, 2008. [CR]

Besser, Matt, Ian Roberts, and Matt Walsh. *The Upright Citizens Brigade Comedy Improvisation Manual*. New York: Comedy Council of Nicea, 2013. [CI]

Blair, Rhonda. *The Actor, Image, and Action: Acting and cognitive neuroscience*. New York: Routledge. [CR, A]

Blatner, Adam. *Foundations of Psychodrama, History, Theory, and Practice. Fourth Edition*. New York: Springer Publishing Company, Inc., 2000. [CR]

Boal, Augusto. *Games for Actors and Non–Actors*. London: Routledge, 1992. [M, GI]

Boal, Augusto. *Hamlet and the Baker's Son: My Life in Theatre and Politics*. New York: Routledge, 2001. [H]

Boal, Augusto. *Theatre of the Oppressed*. London: Pluto Press, 2000. [GI, M]

Caird, John. *Theatre Craft. A Directors Practical Companion from A to Z*. New York: Farrar, Straus and Giroux, 2010. [PA]

Callery, Dymphna. *Through the Body*. London: Nick Hern Books Limited, 2001. [PA]

Capra, Steve. *Theater Voices: Conversations on the Stage*. Lanham, Maryland: Scarecrow Press, Inc., 2004. [PA, H]

Carney, Ray. *Cassavetes on Cassavetes*. London: Faber and Faber Limited, 2001. [A]

Carrane, Jimmy, and Liz Allen. *Improvising Better, A Guide for the Working Improviser*. Portsmouth: Heinemann, 2006. [CI, GI]

Chabris, Christopher and Daniel Simons. *The Invisible Gorilla*. New York: Random House, 2010. [CR]

Clements, Paul. *The Improvised Play. The Work of Mike Leigh*. London: Methuen London, 1983. [GI, H]

Coleman, Janet. *The Compass – The Improvisational Theatre That Revolutionized American Comedy*. Chicago: University of Chicago Press, 1991. [CI, B]

Csikszentmihalyi, Mihaly. *Flow. The Psychology of Optimal Experience*. New York: HarperPerennial, 1990. [CR]

Cuddy, Amy. *Presence: Bringing Your Boldest Self to Your Biggest Challenges*. New York: Little, Brown and Company, 2015. [CR]

Davis, Martha, Elizabeth Robbins Eshelman, and Matthew McKay. *The Relaxation & Stress Reduction Workbook. Fifth Edition*. Oakland, CA: New Harbinger Publications, Inc., 2000. [M]

Drinko, Clayton D. *Theatrical Improvisation, Consciousness, and Cognition*. New York: Palgrave Macmillan, 2013. [CR, GI]

Dudeck, Theresa Robbins. *Keith Johnstone, A Critical Biography*. London: Bloomsbury Methuen Drama, 2013. [JI, H]

Elsam, Paul. *Acting Characters*. London: Methuen Drama Bloomsbury Publishing Plc, 2011. [PA]

Fox, Jonathan. *Beyond Theatre. A Playback Theatre Memoir*. New Paltz, USA: Tusitala Publishing, 2015. [H]

Frost, Anthony, and Ralph Yarrow. *Improvisation In Drama, Second Edition*. London: Palgrave Macmillan, 2007. [GI, H]

Gallup Feldman, Lee. *A Critical Analysis of Improvisational Theatre in the United States from 1955-1968*. University of Denver, Ph.D., 1969. [CI, H]

Gillette, William. *The Illusion of the First Time in Acting*. New York: Dramatic Museum of Columbia University, 1915. [A]

Gladwell, Malcolm. *Blink: The Power of Thinking Without Thinking*. London: Penguin Books, 2005. [CR]

Goffman, Erving. *Encounters: Two Studies in the Sociology of Interaction*. Middlesex, England: Penguin Books Ltd, 1972. [CR]

Goffman, Erving. *Forms of Talk*. Philadelphia: University of Pennsylvania Press, 1981. [CR]

Goffman, Erving. *Frame Analysis: An Essay on the Organization of Experience*. Boston: Northeastern University Press, 1974, 1986. [CR]

Goffman, Erving. *Strategic Interaction*. Philadelphia: University of Pennsylvania Press, 1970. [CR]

Grantham, Barry. *Playing Commedia: A Training Guide to Commedia Techniques*. London: Nick Hern Books, 2000. [A]

Hagen, Uta, and Haskel Frankel. *Respect for Acting*. New York: Macmillan, 1973. [A]

Halpern, Charna. *Art By Committee*. Colorado Springs: Meriwether Publishing Ltd., 2005. [CI]

Halpern, Charna, Del Close, and Kim Johnson. *Truth In Comedy*. Colorado Springs: Meriwether Publishing, 1995, 2001. [CI]

Hamilton, Clayton. *The Theory of The Theatre and Other Principles of Dramatic Criticism*. New York: Henry Holt and Company, 1910. [PA, A]

Hazenfield, Carol. *Acting on Impulse, The Art of Making Improv Theater*. Berkeley: Coventry Creek Press, 2002. [JI]

Hodgson, John and Ernest Richards. *Improvisation*. University Paperback, 1967. [GI]

Hurley, Matthew M., Daniel C. Dennett, Reginald B. Adams, Jr. *Inside Jokes, Using Humor to Reverse-Engineer the Mind*. London: The MIT Press. [CR]

Ilgner, Arno. *The Rock Warrior's Way – Mental Training for Climbers*. La Vergne: Desiderata Institute, 2003. [PA]

Jagodowski, T.J., David Pasquesi, Pam Victor. *Improvisation at the Speed of Life*. Chicago: Solo Roma Inc., 2015. [CI]

Johnson, Kim. *The Funniest One In The Room: The Lives and Legends of Del Close*. Chicago: Chicago Review Press, 2008. [CI, H]

Johnstone, Keith. *Book of the Moose.* Calgary: Loose Moose Theatre Company, 1990. [JI]

Johnstone, Keith. *Impro for Storytellers.* London: Faber and Faber Limited, 1999. [JI]

Johnstone, Keith. *Impro: Improvisation and the Theatre.* London: Methuen Drama, 1989. [JI]

Johnstone, Keith. *Impro: Improvisation and the Theatre.* New York: Routledge, 1992. [JI]

Johnstone, Keith. *Impro: Improvisation and the Theatre.* London: Faber and Faber Ltd, 1979. [JI]

Katritzky, M. A. *The Art of Commedia. A Study in the Commedia dell'Arte 1560-1620 with Special Reference to the Visual Records.* Amsterdam: Editions Rodopi B. V., 2005. [A, M]

Kirk, John W., Ralph Bellas, and Christina Kirk. *The Art of Directing.* Lexington: Xlibris, 2004. [A]

Kohl, Katrina and Ritchie Robertson, editors. *A History of Austrian Literature 1918-2000.* New York: Camden House, 2006. [B,H]

Kozlowski, Rob. *The Art of Chicago Improv, Shortcuts to Long–Form Improvisation.* Portsmouth: Heinemann, 2002. [CI, H]

Lecoq, Jacques, Jean–Gabriel Carasso, Jean–Claude Lallias. *The Moving Body (Le Corps poétique).* London: Methuen Drama, 2000. [A]

Leep, Jeanne. *Theatrical Improvisation. Short Form, Long Form and Sketch–Based Improv.* New York: Palgrave Macmillan, 2008. [GI]

Lösel, Gunter. *Das Spiel Mit Dem Chaos.* (English: *Playing With Chaos*). Germany, Bielefeld: transcript Verlag, 2013. [GI]

Lutterbie, John. *Toward a General Theory of Acting. Cognitive Science and Performance.* New York: Palgrave Macmillan, 2011. [CR, A GI]

Marineau, René F. *Jacob Levy Moreno, 1889-1974: Father of Psychodrama, Sociometry and Group Psychotherapy.* London: Routledge, 1989. [GI, H]

Mehling, Randi. *Marijuana (Drugs: The Straight Facts)*. Chelsea House Publishers, 2003. [M]

Merlin, Bella. *The Complete Stanislavsky Toolkit. Revised Edition*. London: Nick Hern Books, 2007. [A]

Moreno, J. L. *The Theatre of Spontaneity*. U.K.: North–West Psychodrama Association, 2010. [GI]

Moreno, J. L. *Impromptu*. U.K.: North–West Psychodrama Association, 2010. [GI]

Moreno, J.L. *Psychodrama. First Volume. Fourth Edition with New Introduction*. New York: Beacon House Inc., 1977, 1980. [GI]

Napier, Mick. *Behind the scenes: improvising long form*. Englewood, Colorado: Meriwether Publishing, 2015. [CI]

Napier, Mick. *Improvise: Scene from the Inside Out*. Portsmouth: Heinemann, 2004. [CI]

Newton, Robert G. *Acting Improvised*. London: Thomas Nelson and Sons Ltd, 1937, 1948. [GI]

O'Toole, John, Madonna Stinson, Tiina Moore. *Drama and Curriculum. A Giant at the Door*. Springer Science+Business Media B. V., 2009. [PA, A, GI]

Pashler, Harold E. *The Psychology of Attention*. Cambridge, Massachusetts: Massachusetts Institute of Technology, 1998. [CR]

Pierse, Lyn. *Improvisation: The Guide. Third Edition*. Australia: Improcorp Australia Pty Ltd and Ish Group, 2007. [JI]

Pierse, Lyn. *Theatresports Down Under. Second Edition*. Australia: Improcorp Australia Pty Ltd and Ish Group, 1997. [JI]

Pitches, Jonathan. *Science and the Stanislavsky Tradition of Acting*. London: Routledge, 2006. [CR, A]

Pollock, Walter Herries. *The Paradox of Acting*. Translated from Denis Diderot's *Paradoxe Sur Le Comédien*. London: Chatti & Windus, 1883. [A]

Porac, Clare. *Laterality – Exploring the Enigma of Left–Handedness.* London: Academic Press, 2016. [CR]

Roach, Joseph R. *The Player's Passion. Studies in the Science of Acting.* London: Associated University Presses, 1985. [A]

Sawyer, R. Keith. *Explaining Creativity. The Science of Human Innovation.* New York: Oxford University Press, 2006. [CR]

Sawyer, R. Keith. *Improvised Dialogues: Emergence and Creativity in Conversation.* Westport, Connecticut, Greenwood Publishing Group, Inc., 2003. [CR, CI]

Scheiffele, Eberhard. *The Theatre of Truth. Psychodrama, Spontaneity and Improvisation: The Theatrical Theories and Influences of Jacob Levy Moreno.* University of California, Berkley, 1995. [GI]

Schnitzler, Arthur, translation by J. M. Q. Davies. *Round Dance and Other Plays.* Oxford University Press, Oxford, 2004. [M, H]

Schutzman, Mady and Jan Cohen–Cruz, editors. *Playing Boal. Theatre, Therapy, Activism.* London: Routledge, 1994. [H, M]

Schwartz, Barry. *The Paradox of Choice: Why More Is Less.* Harper Collins, 2003. [CR]

Scruggs, Mary and Michael J. Gellman. *Process – An Improvisor's Journey.* Northwestern University Press, 2008. [CI]

Seham, Amy E. *Whose Improv Is It Anyway? Beyond Second City.* University Press of Mississippi, 2001. [CI]

Shaw, Patricia and Ralph Stacey. *Experiencing Risk, Spontaneity and Improvisation in Organizational Change.* New York: Routledge, 2006. [GI]

Smith, Hazel and Roger T. Dean. *Improvisation Hypermedia and the Arts Since 1945.* Oxon: Routledge, 2007. [GI, H]

Spolin, Viola. *Improvisation for the Theater.* Evanston, Illinois: Northwestern University Press, 1969, 1983. [GI, CI]

Spolin, Viola. *Theater Games for the Lone Actor. A Handbook.* Evanston, Illinois: Northwestern University Press, 2001. [GI, CI]

Spolin, Viola. *Theater Games for the Classroom A Teacher's Handbook.* Evanston, Illinois: Northwestern University Press, 1986. [GI, CI]

Sporns, Olaf. *Networks of the Brain.* Cambridge, Massachusetts: The MIT Press, 2011. [CR]

Stanislavsky, Konstantin, translation by Elizabeth Reynolds Hapgood. *An Actor Prepares.* New York: Routledge, 1936, 1989. [A]

Stanislavsky, Konstantin, translation by Jean Benedetti. *An Actor's Work (A Student's Diary).* Oxon: Routledge, 2008. [A]

Stanislavsky, Konstantin, translation by Jean Benedetti. *An Actor's Work on a Role.* Oxon: Routledge, 2010. [A]

Sweet, Jeffrey. *Something Wonderful Right Away.* New York: Limelight, 2003. [CI]

Tovstonogov, Georgi, translation by Bryan Bean. *The Profession of the Stage-Director.* Moscow: Progress Publishers, 1972.

van Gompel, Roger P. G., Martin H. Fischer, Wayne S. Murray, Robin L. Hill. *Eye Movements: A Window on Mind and Brain.* Oxford: Elsevier, 2007. [CR]

Wagner, Heather Lehr. *Alcohol (Drugs: The Straight Facts).* Chelsea House Publishers, 2003. [M]

Wagner, Heather Lehr. *Cocaine (Drugs: The Straight Facts).* Chelsea House Publishers, 2003. [M]

Wagner, Heather Lehr. *Nicotine (Drugs: The Straight Facts).* Chelsea House Publishers, 2003. [M]

Youngkin, Stephen D. *The Lost One: A Life of Peter Lorre.* University Press of Kentucky, 2005. [M]

Zaporah, Ruth. *Improvisation On the Edge: Notes from On and Off Stage.* Berkeley: North Atlantic Books, 2014. [GI]

Research papers and articles

It's common to find the full text of research papers — many of which are only a few pages long — hidden behind a pay wall[171], the cost of which severely restricts their study by amateur researchers. You can find most of these papers in the major science repositories by searching by title in *Google Scholar*, but often if you scroll down or look to the second page of results, the author or their employer may be giving away a free copy on their website.

Ambady, Nalini and Robert Rosenthal. *Half a Minute: Predicting Teacher Evaluations From Thin Slices of Nonverbal Behavior and Physical Attractiveness.*

Ambady, Nalini and Robert Rosenthal. *Thin Slices of Expressive Behavior as Predictors of Interpersonal Consequences: A Meta-Analysis.* (1992)

Axmacher, Nikolai, Sven Haupt Guillén Fernández, Christian E. Elger and Juergen Fell. *The Role of Sleep in Declarative Memory Consolidation — Direct Evidence by Intracranial EEG* (2007)

Baars, Bernard J. *Global workspace theory of consciousness: towards a cognitive neuroscience of human experience?* (2005)

Bargh, John A., Mark Chen and Lara Burrows. *Automaticity of Social Behavior: Direct Effects of Trait Construct and Stereotype Activation on Action.* (1996)

Bellini-Leite, Samuel and Alfredo Pereira Jr. *Is Global Workspace a Cartesian Theater? How the Neuro-Astroglial Interaction Model Solves Conceptual Issues* (2013)

Bishop, Scott R., Mark Lau, Shauna Shapiro, Linda Carlson, Nicole D. Andreson, James Carmody, Zindel V. Segal, Susan Abbey, Michael Speca, Drew Velting and Gerald Devins. *Mindfulness: A Proposed Operational Definition.* (2004)

Blanchard, Phyllis. *A Psycho–Analytic Study of Auguste Comte.* (1918)

Bloch, Susana. *ALBA EMOTING: A Psychophysiological Technique to Help Actors Create and Control Real Emotions.* (1993)

---

[171] It's not uncommon to find a six page research paper sell for up to US$40 or more.

Blum, David. *How Warren Beatty, Dustin Hoffman, and Elaine May made a farce in the desert for just $40 million.* New York Magazine, March 16, 1987 (1987)

Bower, Gordon H., John B. Black and Terrence J. Turner. *Scripts in Memory for Text.* (1979)

Brewer, Judson A., Patrick D. Worhunsky, Jeremy R. Gray, Yi-Yuan Tang, Jocen Weber and Hedy Kober. *Meditation experience is associated with differences in default mode network activity and connectivity.* (2011)

Brooks, Cassandra M. *Cultural Exchange: The Role of Stanislavsky and The Moscow Art Theatre's 1923 and 1924 American tours.* (2014)

Bryan, Janet, Michelle Tuckey, Suzanne J.L. Einöther, Ursula Garczarek, Adam Garrick, Eveline A. De Bruin. *Relationships between tea and other beverage consumption to work performance and mood.* (2011)

Cai, Wen-Hui, Jacqueline Blundell, Jie Han, Robert W. Greene and Craig M. Powell. *Postreactivation Glucocorticoids Impair Recall of Established Fear Memory.* (2006)

Carney, Dana R., Amy J.C. Cuddy and Andy J. Yap. *Power Posing: Brief Nonverbal Displays Affect Neuroendocrine Levels and Risk Tolerance.* (2010)

Carter, Curtis L. *Improvisation in Dance.* (2000)

Carter, Phil. *Towards a Definition for Spontaneity.* (1994)

Chadwick, Martin J., Raeesa S. Anjum, Dharshan Kumaran, Daniel L. Schacter, Hugo J. Spiers and Demis Hassabis. *Semantic representations in the temporal pole predict false memories.* (2016)

Colzato, Lorenza S., Ayca Ozturk and Benhard Hommel. *Meditate to create: the impact of focused-attention and open-monitoring training on convergent and divergent thinking.* (2012)

Conklin, Edmund S. *The Definition of Introversion, Extroversion and Allied Concepts.* (1923)

Crossan, Mary and Marc Sorrenti. *Making sense of improvisation. (Advances in Strategic Management, Volume 14)*. (1997)

Darwall, Stephen. *Empathy, Sympathy, Care*. (1997)

Davidson, Ian J. *The ambivert: A failed attempt at a normal personality*. (2017)

Desnon, Thomas F., Michelle L. Moulds and Jessica R Grisham. *The Effects of Analytical Rumination, Reappraisal, and Distraction on Anger Experience*. (2012)

Driskell, Charles B. *An Interview with Augusto Boal*. Latin American Theatre Review, Fall 1975. (1975)

Dzuback, Mary Ann. *Hutchins, Adler, and the University of Chicago: A Critical Juncture*. (1990)

Ekman, Paul. *Facial Expressions: New Findings, New Questions*. (1992)

Farb, Norman A. S., Zindel V. Segal, Helen Mayberg, Jim Bean, Deborah McKeon, Zainab Fatima, and Adam K. Anderson. *Attending to the present: mindfulness meditation reveals distinct neural modes of self-reference*. (2007)

Feldman, Lee Gallup. *A Brief History of Improvisational Theatre in the United States*. (1974)

Figley, Chase R., Judith S. A. Asem, Erica L. Levenbaum and Susan M. Courtney. *Effects of Body Mass Index and Body Fat Percent on Default Mode, Executive Control, and Salience Network Structure and Function*. (2016)

Fotis, Matt. *The Harold: A Revolutionary Form That Changed Improvisational Theatre & American Comedy*. (2012)

Fotis, Matthew N. *Improvisational Theatre: In The Vanguard of the Postmodern*. (2005)

Fox, Hannah. *The Beginnings: Reflecting on 25 years of Playback Theatre*. (2000)

Gallace, Alberto and Charles Spence. *The science of interpersonal touch: An overview.* (2010)

Gilliland, Kirby. *The Interactive Effect of Introversion–Extraversion with Caffeine Induced Arousal on Verbal Performance.* (1980)

Graves, Laurel A., Elizabeth A. Heller, Allan I. Pack and Ted Abel. *Sleep Deprivation Selectively Impairs Memory Consolidation for Contextual Fear Conditioning.* (2015)

Hertenstein, Matthew J., Dacher Keltner, Betsy App, Brittany A. Bulleit and Ariane R. Jaskolka. *Touch Communicates Distinct Emotions.* (2006)

Hertenstein, Matthew J., Rachel Holmes, Margaret McCullough and Dacher Keltner. *The Communication of Emotion via Touch.* (2009)

Hoermann, Hans–Juergen, Mona Mischke, Eva–Maria Elmenhorst and Sibylle Benderoth. *Differential Effects of Sleep Deprivation on Cognitive Performance.* (2016)

Ingvar, David H. *"Memory of the future": an essay on the temporal organization of conscious awareness.* (1985)

Jennings, J.R., T.H. Monk and M.W. van der Molen. *Sleep Deprivation Influences Some but Not All Processes of Supervisory Attention.* (2015)

Jones, Stanley E., and A. Elaine Yarbrough. *A naturalistic study of the meanings of touch* (1985)

Josipovic, Zoran, Ilan Dinstein, Jochen Weber and David J. Heeger. *Influence of meditation on anti-correlated networks in the brain.* (2012)

Josipovic, Zoran. *Neural correlates of nondual awareness in meditation.* (2013)

Juan, Chi–Hung, Stephanie M. Shorter-Jacobi and Jeffrey D. Schall. *Dissociation of spatial attention and saccade preparation.* (2004)

Kaul, Prashant, Jason Passafiume, R Craig Sargent, Bruce F O'Hara. *Meditation acutely improves psychomotor vigilance, and may decrease sleep need.* (2010)

Kendig, Michael D. *Cognitive and behavioural effects of sugar consumption in rodents. A review.* (2014)

Khemlani, Sangeet S., Anthony M. Harrison and J. Gregory Trafton. *Episodes, events, and models.* (2015)

Kipste, Egils. *The Directing Experience Handbook.* (2014)

Kirsh, David. *A Few Thoughts on Cognitive Overload.* (2000)

Kraus, Michael W., Cassy Huang and Dacher Keltner. *Tactile Communication, Cooperation, and Performance: An Ethological Study of the NBA.* (2010)

Kuhn, Gustav and John M. Findlay. *Misdirection, attention and awareness: Inattentional blindness reveals temporal relationship between eye movements and visual awareness.* (2010)

Levensen, Robert W., Paul Ekman and Wallace V. Friesen. *Voluntary Facial Action Generates Emotion–Specific Autonomic Nervous System Activity.* (1990)

Lindell, Annukka K. *Lateral thinkers are not so laterally minded: Hemispheric asymmetry, interaction, and creativity.* (2010)

Liu, Siyuan, Ho Ming Chow, Yisheng Xu, Michael G. Erkkinen, Katherine Swett, Michael W. Eagle, Daniel A. Rizik–Baer & Allen R. Braun. *Neural Correlates of Lyrical Improvisation: An fMRI Study of Freestyle Rap.* (2012)

Magliano, Joseph P. and Jeffrey M. Zacks. *The Impact of Continuity Editing in Narrative Film on Event Segmentation.* (2011)

Major, Brenda, Richard Heslin. *Perceptions of Cross–Sex and Same–Sex Nonreciprocal Tcouh: It Is Better To Give Than To Receive.* (1982)

Martin, Jeffrey J., and Keir Cutler. *An Exploratory Study of Flow and Motivation in Theater Actors.* (2002)

McIlwain, Doris, Alana Taylor, and Andrew Geeces. *Fullness of Feeling: reflection, rumination, depression and the specificity of autobiographical memories.* (2009)

McPeek, Robert M., Vera Maljkovic and Ken Nakayama. *Saccades require focal attention and are facilitated by a short-term memory system.* (1999)

Meineck, Peter. *The Neuroscience of the Tragic Mask.* (2010)

Memmert, Daniel. *The effects of eye movements, age, and expertise on inattentional blindness.* (2006)

Nehlig, Astrid, Jean–Luc Daval and Gérard Debry. *Caffeine and the central nervous system: mechanisms of action, biochemical, metabolic and psychostimulant effects.* (1992)

Nishida, Masaki, Matthew P. Walker. *Daytime Naps, Motor Memory Consolidation and Regionally Specific Sleep Spindles.* (2007)

Noy, Lior, Erez Dekel, and Uri Alon. *The mirror game as a paradigm for studying the dynamics of two people improvising motion together.* (2011)

Pashler, Harold. *Dual–Task Interference in Simple Tasks: Data and Theory.* (1994)

Radvansky, Gabriel A. and David E. Copeland. *Walking through doorways causes forgetting: Situation models and experienced space.* (2006)

Raffone, Antonino, Narayanan Srinivasan and Henk P. Barendregt. *Attention, consciousness and mindfulness in meditation.* (2014)

Raichle, Marcus E. *The Restless Brain.* (2011)
Brain Connectivity, Volume , Number 1, 2011

Raichle, Marcus E, Ann Mary MacLeod, Abraham Z. Snyder, William J. Powers, Debra A. Gusnard and Gordon L. Shulman. *A default mode of brain function.* (2010)

Raichle, Marcus E. and Abraham Z. Snyder. *A default mode of brain function: A brief history of an evolving idea.* (2007)

Ranehill, Eva, Anna Dreber, Magnus Johannesson, Susanne Leiberg, Sunhae Sul and Roberto A. Weber. *Assessing the Robustness of Power Posing: No Effect on Hormones and Risk Tolerance in a Large Sample of Men and Women.* (2014)

Roe, John. *An oral history of Loose Moose Theatre: 40 years of improv in front of and behind the scenes.* (2017)

Ruthruff, Eric, James C. Johnston, Mark Van Selst, Shelly Whitsell and Roger Remington. *Vanishing Dual-Task Interference After Practice: Has the Bottleneck Been Eliminated or Is It Merely Latent?* (2003)

Ruthruff, Eric, Mark Van Selst, James C. Johnston and Roger Remington. *How does practice reduce dual-task interference: Interference, automatization, or just stage-shortening?* (2004)

Sawyer, R. Keith. *Creative Teaching: Collaborative Discussion as Disciplined Improvisation.* (2004)

Sawyer, R. Keith. *Improvisation and Narrative.* (2002)

Sawyer, R. Keith. *Improvisation and the Creative Process: Dewey, Collingwood, and the Aesthetics of Spontaneity.* (2000)

Sawyer, R. Keith. *Improvisational Cultures: Collaborative Emergence and Creativity in Improvisation.* (2000)

Sawyer, R. Keith. *Improvised Lessons: Collaborative discussion in the constructivist classroom.* (2004)

Sawyer, R. Keith. *The Semiotics of Improvisation – The Pragmatics of Musical and Verbal Performance.* (1996)

Sawyer, Keith. *The Cognitive Neuroscience of Creativity: A Critical Review.* (2011)

Schank, Roger C. and Robert P. Abelson. *Scripts, Plans, and Knowledge.* (1975)

Schank, Roger C. and Robert P. Abelson. *Scripts, Plans, Goals, and Understanding: An Inquiry into Human Knowledge Structures.* (1977)

Schlenker, Barry R., Mark R. Leary. *Social Anxiety and Self-Presentation: A Conceptualization and Model.* (1982)

Sigman, Mariano and Stanislas Dehaene. *Brain Mechanisms of Serial and Parallel Processing during Dual-Task Performance.* (2008)

Sigman, Mariano and Stanislas Dehaene. *Dynamics of the Central Bottleneck: Dual–Task and Task Uncertainty.* (2006)

Simmons, Joseph P. and Uri Simonsohn. *Power Posing: P-Curving the Evidence.* (2016)

Slepian, Michael L., Simon N. Ferber, Joshua M. Gold and Abraham M. Rutchick. *The Cognitive Consequences of Formal Clothing.* (2015)

Smith, Andrew P. *Effects of caffeine on human behaviour.* (2002)

Smolko, Andrey. *The Active Analysis Method as an instrument of modern theatre.* (2009)

Stavrou, Nektarios A., Susan A. Jackson, Yannis Zervas, Konstantinos Karteroliotis. *Flow Experience and Athletes' Performance With Reference to the Orthogonal Model of Flow.* (2007)

Takashima, A., K. M. Petersson, F. Rutters, I. Tendolkar, O. Jensen, M. J. Zwarts, B. L. McNaughton and G. Fernández. *Declarative memory consolidation in humans: A prospective functional magnetic resonance imaging study* (2005)

Trousselard, Marion, Dominique Steiler, Christian Raphel1, Corinne Cian, Raffi Duymedjian, Damien Claverie, Frédéric Canini. *Validation of a French version of the Freiburg Mindfulness Inventory - short version: relationships between mindfulness and stress in an adult population.* (2010)

Vatansever, D., D.K. Menon, A.E. Manktelow, B.J. Sahakian and E.A. Stamatakis. *Default mode network connectivity during task execution.* (2015)

Viera, Maria. *The Work of John Cassavetes: Script, Performance Style, and Improvisation.* (1990)

Wallbott, Harald G. *Bodily expression of emotion.* (1997)

Watkins, Ed, and John D. Teasdale. *Adaptive and maladaptive self-focus in depression.* (2004)

Zacks, Jeffrey M., Nicole K. Speer, Khena M. Swallow, Todd S. Braver, and Jeremy R. Reynolds. *Event Perception: A Mind-Brain Perspective.* (2007)

Zelenski, John M., Maya S. Santoro and Deanna C. Whelan. *Would Introverts Be Better Off if They Acted More Like Extraverts? Exploring Emotional and Cognitive Consequences of Counterdispositional Behavior.* (2012)

Zhao, Min, Timothy M. Gersch, Brian S. Schnitzer, Barbara A. Dosher and Eileen Kowler. *Eye movements and attention: The role of presaccadic shifts of attention in perception, memory and the control of saccades.* (2012)

Other material

David Shepherd – A Lifetime of Improvisational Theatre. Documentary film directed by Mike Fly Fleischhaker. (2010)

Trust Us, This Is All Made Up. Documentary film directed by Alex Karpovsky. (2009)

Miscellaneous videos of improvised performances, from video sharing websites, purchased DVDs, and Richard Bennett's personal collection.

Extended Table of Contents

Many of the books on my bookshelves are covered in those little plastic sticky flags used for marking certain pages. Every so often I need a particular quote, reference or exercise, and finding these in books which usually have generic chapter titles is really difficult. Why don't they have an extended table of contents? Here's mine.

Preface	vii
Using this book	*x*
Improv isn't just improv	1
Method conflict and context	*4*
Impro or improv?	*5*
The modern era	9
The Chicago method	*11*
Keith Johnstone's impro system	*14*
Improvising in practice	*14*
Harold	*15*
Theatresports	*17*

Viola Spolin & Paul Sills	19
Jacob Levy Moreno	19
ComedySportz	20
Playback Theatre	20
The Upright Citizens Brigade (UCB)	21
The Internet	22
Movies and television	23
The future	23

The improvised mind 25

Sigmund Freud	26
Carl Jung	26
The Cartesian Theatre	27
Fame in the Brain	27
Global Workspace Theory	29
The inner game of everything	30
Muscle memory	32
Priming	33
Internalising the domain	35
Cognitive load	40
Analytic focus & experiential focus	41
Meditation and mindfulness	42
Exploring in the dark	45

What is improvisation? 47

Spontaneity	48
Presence	51
Fear of failure	53
Listening and action	57
Leveraging the unconscious	57
Justification	60
Agreement	62
Mirror neurons	63
Group mind	65
Intuition guiding action	74

1600s to 1920s 75

Commedia dell'arte	75

Music Hall, Vaudeville, Überbrettl	77
European movements of the early 1900s	78
Russian revolution in theatre	80
Jacob Levy Moreno	82
Living Newspaper	87

Spontaneity science 89

Dual Task Processing	90
Divided Attention	92
The Default Mode Network (DMN)	94
Memory of the future	95
Flow	96
Fear and anxiety	98
Conditioning	100
Fear conditioning	100

1930s to 1940s 103

Active Analysis	103
Viola Spolin	104
Method acting	106

Approaching scenes 109

Thinking	109
Choices	111
Rules, guidelines and principles	113
Discovering the scene	120
The Cone of Candidate Scenes	122

1950s to 1960s 125

Viola Spolin	125
David Shepherd	125
The Compass Players	126
The St Louis Rules / Kitchen Rules	128
Second City	130
Keith Johnstone	131

Scene progression 133

Offer and acceptance	137

Denial and blocking	*139*
The Keith Johnstone and Chicago models	*143*
Yes, and… and yes!	*145*
Scene attributes	*151*
The two main models	*156*
Evolution of styles	*159*
Show form differences	*162*
Cross training	*166*

1960s to 1970s 171

John Cassavetes	*171*
Mike Leigh	*174*
The Committee	*175*
Theatre of the Oppressed	*176*

Theatre, acting and empathy 179

Emotion	*179*
Theatre and empathy	*182*
Acting	*184*
Why is improvisation funny?	*185*
The rule of three	*199*

1970s 201

Contact Improvisation	*201*
Action Theater	*202*
Canadian Improv Games	*203*

How scenes work 205

Acting without text	*206*
Point of view	*209*
Metapragmatics	*211*
Game	*219*

General topics 227

Short–form and long–form?	*227*
Freedom to fail	*231*
Big and small audiences	*234*
Can anyone improvise?	*238*

Forms	*240*
Creativity	*240*
Personality types	*242*
Alcohol, drugs and stimulants	*243*
Sleep	*249*
BMI and obesity	*251*
Your perception is your perception	*251*
Clothing and connotative colours	*253*
The power pose	*255*
Side coaching	*256*
La Ronde	*259*
Foveal load	*262*
Blink and blindness	*264*
Scripts and event segmentation	*265*
Dance marking	*269*
Lateralisation of brain function	*270*
Touch	*271*
Becoming a better improvisor	275
Warming up	*275*
Using dance marking	*282*
Rules and guidelines	*283*
Internalising	*283*
Unlearning mimicry of priming and mirror neurons	*284*
Saccades and attention switching	*284*
Cognitive loading	*285*
Using video	*286*
Learning to touch	*286*
Mixing styles	*287*
Playing with better improvisors	*289*
Rituals	*290*
Fear Conditioning	*293*
Going solo	*294*
Playing multiple characters	*296*
Festivals and guest teachers	*296*
Training, jams, rehearsals and shows	*298*
Continual learning	*299*
Fixed Attention (FA) and Open Monitoring (OM) meditation	*300*

Experiencing flow	*301*
Method of Physical Actions	*302*
Question the guidelines	*302*
Question exercises	*303*
Let your unconscious do the work	*304*

Conclusions 305

Respect the models and their methods	*306*
From mystique to science	*307*

Acknowledgements 309

Bibliography 313

Books	*313*
Research papers and articles	*321*
Other material	*329*

Extended Table of Contents 331

www.ingramcontent.com/pod-product-compliance
Lightning Source LLC
Chambersburg PA
CBHW071855290426
44110CB00013B/1150